THE CONDITION OF THE
WORKING CLASS
IN BRITAIN

THE CONDITION OF THE WORKING CLASS IN BRITAIN

By
ALLEN HUTT

WITH AN INTRODUCTION BY
HARRY POLLITT

NEW YORK
INTERNATIONAL PUBLISHERS

PRINTED IN GREAT BRITAIN BY
THE   STANHOPE   PRESS   LTD.
ROCHESTER   :   :   KENT

CONTENTS

CHAPTER IV

CHAPTER V

CHAPTER VI

CHAPTER VII

CHAPTER VIII

CHAPTER IX

CHAPTER X

PREFACE

THE aim of this book is set forth in the Introduction which follows. I need only say here that my purpose has been the direct opposite of that defined by Mr. Fenner Brockway in his *Hungry England*. He declared: "My purpose has been to describe and not to diagnose." I have been throughout concerned to diagnose the ills of society in Britain to-day; for it is apparent that description alone is idle, if these frightful ills are to be cured. And cured they can be, but not by the methods of those who, like Mr. Brockway, reject alike the revolutionary understanding and the revolutionary methods of Marxism.

This book would not have been written if I had not had the assistance of the Labour Research Department. The Department's staff and voluntary workers gave unstinting aid in the preparation of material; and without the invaluable files and records of every kind that have been collected by the Department (the pioneer organisation of its kind in the world) in its twenty years of life, the completion of this considerable task in six months would have been impossible.

Detailed personal acknowledgment would extend this Preface to a chapter. I must content myself with expressing my warmest thanks in general terms—to the Labour Research Department; to its affiliated Trade Unions, Trades Councils, and Union branches; to the officials and active spirits of these bodies, who were eager to give me every possible help in the course of a number of tours of investigation through the industrial areas; and to the numerous rank-and-file workers, employed and unemployed, who spared no pains to enable me to get the fullest and most accurate picture of the condition of their class. I have also to thank many friends and comrades for their help in reading proofs, for advice and criticism.

From the standpoint of sources it may be of interest to note that the present study embodies the results of what I believe is the first extensive working of the rich mine of information buried in the annual reports of the local medical officers of health. The reports for 1930 and 1931 have been examined with particular care; the first are important because it was a "survey year," and the reports are much more detailed than usual; the second are the latest available, and since they were not issued, in accordance with custom, until the middle of the following year (1932), they embody general impressions up to that period.

Perhaps I may interpolate here two striking confirmations of certain of my contentions, which became known too late for incorporation in the text of the book. The first relates to the rising tide of revolt among the South Wales miners, discussed at the end of Chapter I, which has reached a new high-water mark in the unanimous decision of the delegate conference of the South Wales Miners' Federation on March 13 to strike in support of the miners in dispute at Bedwas colliery.

The second concerns the growth of impoverishment and the direct effect of the burden of high rents on health. This has received its most remarkable demonstration in the observations conducted during the past five years by Dr. M'Gonigle, the medical officer of health of Stockton-on-Tees.

Dr. M'Gonigle, in a paper read to the Royal Society of Medicine, has explained that during this period the death-rate of a number of families re-housed on a new Council estate rose by 8.47 per thousand, while the death-rate of families remaining in slum conditions fell by 2.9 per thousand:

> On analysing this surprising situation, he found that the transfer had involved an increase in rent from 9s. to 13s. 4¾d. weekly, and even with some sharing of houses the re-housed unemployed were left with only 36.7 per cent. of their income available for food. Their diet showed all-round deficiencies; fat, for example, was 34 per cent. short of normal needs. He could find no explanation of the poor health and increased mortality of this population except that the higher rents left them insufficient money to buy enough food. (*Week-end Review*, March 11th, 1933.)

I have thought it wise to document this book elaborately; but, for the convenience of readers, all references (which are merely bare indications of source) are collected together at the end. They are shown by superior figures, thus—[2]. The reader who is not immediately concerned to check the references will find his perusal more comfortable if he ignores these figures. Where sources require any discussion, or there is a subsidiary argument to develop, I have used footnotes.

                                                            G. A. H.

LONDON, *March, 1933.*

INTRODUCTION

IN 1845 there was published in Germany a book written by Frederick Engels, entitled *The Condition of the Working Class in England in 1844*. It was the most authentic analysis of the conditions of the working class that had been written up to that time and constituted a damning indictment of the poverty and misery of the working class in this country at that stage of capitalist development.

Engels' book has become an international classic. Thousands of active workers have drawn from it their hatred of the capitalist system and a clear understanding of the causes which produced the misery depicted by Engels. The supreme merit of his book is that it so clearly and simply foretold the inevitable development of capitalism and in particular the vital problems which would face the British working class as the capacity to produce increased and powerful rivals grew up to challenge the monopoly of British capitalism.

It is pertinent to recall that challenging paragraph in which Engels so clearly presented the situation to the workers, a situation which to-day has become a matter of life and death for the workers: "Should English manufacture be thus vanquished, the majority of the proletariat must become for ever superfluous, and has no other choice than to starve or rebel."

There have been many doubters of the correctness of Engels' analysis, particularly among those who have for years led the Labour movement of this country. But in their writings both Engels and Marx constantly showed that the development of the capitalist system would be accompanied by ever deeper economic crises, resulting in the growing impoverishment of the mass of the working class. This was not merely doubted, but in the official Labour movement theories were developed that revolution was not necessary in Britain—that mass starvation was a figment of the imagination of Communist doctrinaires.

Ceaseless propaganda has been carried on by various schools of capitalist economists and politicians to the effect that capitalism is an ever-expanding, progressive system of society, in which the workers will be able to achieve ever-rising standards of life. But it was left to the leaders of the Labour movement actually to base their entire political line on this assumption. They, above

ix

all, have been tireless in declaring to the British working class that
Marxism is a foreign doctrine which does not take into account
the special situation of Britain; that, for Britain, the forcible
overthrow of capitalism is unnecessary; that, on the contrary,
everything can be achieved by peaceful parliamentary means;
that the growth of education and the propaganda of sane,
constructive Socialist ideas will inevitably lead to the building up
of a Labour movement capable of forming a Labour Government
which, in the course of time, can legislate peacefully and gradually
in such a way that capitalism will be unconsciously transformed
into Socialism. But the ugly reality behind all this was expressed
in the classic words of Mr. Herbert Morrison in a "victory"
speech at Hendon after the General Election of 1929:

> I want every business man and every business manager to realise that
> the Labour Government is not their enemy, but that every minister
> in this Government wants to take him by the hand, treat him as a man
> and brother, and help to make his commercial or industrial enterprise
> more successful than it has been in the past (*Daily Herald*, July 1st,
> 1929).

It is above all significant to recall that it was Ramsay Mac-
Donald, now the Prime Minister of the "National" Government,
who became the theoretician of the reformists. For him the class
struggle was only a descriptive phrase, as for example where he
stated: "The existence of a class struggle is of no importance to
Socialism unless it rouses intellectual and moral antagonism. . . .
The motive force of Socialism is therefore not the struggle, but
the condemnation of the struggle by the creative imaginative
intelligence and by the moral sense. . . . The Socialist, therefore,
cannot consistently address himself to class sentiment or class
prejudice. . . . The appeal to class interest is an appeal to the
existing order, whether the class addressed is the rich or the
poor" (*The Socialist Movement*, pp. 148-149).

To-day, as the head of the most brutal and ruthless anti-
working-class Government, he carries reformism to its logical
conclusion, and shows to the working class where the denial of
Marxism leads.

The theory of the mass impoverishment of the working class
was also scoffed at. The most roseate visions were conjured up of
ever upward development, of ever higher standards of life and
all that this implies. To-day all these false theories have been
unmasked in the light of bitter experience, but not before they
have had the most terrible consequences for the working class,
whose ranks have been disorganised and split. The revolutionary
fight against capitalism has been held back as the direct result

of the leadership of those who have denied the teachings of Marx and Engels, and have attempted to corrupt the working class by theories of a special type of "British" Socialism.

In Allen Hutt's present book we get an indictment even more damning than that which Engels penned in 1844. For since that time gigantic new forces of production have been developed, great inventions perfected, so that we can say that all the natural obstacles on land, sea and air have been conquered. But because of the capitalist basis of society, the real problems that have always confronted the working class—the problems of bread, work and peace—are more acute to-day than ever before. In point of fact, the situation is now worse than it was in 1844 as far as the mass of the working class is concerned, when we take into account the great technical developments and scientific conquests.

The growth of large-scale industry, the tremendous increase in productive capacity, the springing up of new formidable capitalist competitors like America, the impossibility of finding new markets, the contraction of existing markets, have all led to the position where to-day in every capitalist country in the world, whatever its form of government or fiscal system, attempts are being made to drive the working class into the abyss of starvation and Fascism. In this way the capitalists try to solve the crisis at the expense of the workers, who fiercely fight back to retain their existing standards and build up their revolutionary power for the overthrow of capitalism.

In order to cover up the exposure of the capitalist system, which both support in their varying ways, the capitalists and the Labour leaders are ceaselessly engaged in attempting to show that while to-day there is a certain amount of lamentable hardship, due to the temporary circumstances of the economic crisis which has suddenly struck the world, on the whole the condition of the working class, and especially that of the British working class, is better than ever it was before.

To this end we are constantly regaled with stories of Post Office deposits, large attendances at the cinemas, the great vogue of wireless, and so forth. This sort of argument is peddled round to cover up the bankruptcy of capitalism and the treachery of those Labour leaders whose false theories are entirely responsible for the position of the working class to-day. Closely allied to this type of propaganda is the impudent attempt on the part of the capitalist Press to work up indignation about disgraceful housing conditions. It is now fashionable for star feature writers to write up bad housing conditions as if some new discovery were being made. The social conscience is expected to be shocked by facts

that have always been known to the ruling class, and to the
Labour movement, without a finger being lifted to get at the root
causes. Every medical officer of health has been writing in vain
for years about the bad housing conditions. When new housing
schemes have been carried out the rents are absolutely beyond
the limits of existing wages. The workers who have left slum
areas and gone to the new housing estates have had less food and
clothing than before because the high rents have taken a larger
part of their wages.

Now, all these bold statements that there is "no limit to what
we shall do to build new houses" represent but a further phase
in distracting attention from the other evils of working-class life,
accentuated by the capitalist crisis, and a further endeavour to
deceive the workers.

The stark reality is that in 1933, for the mass of the population,
Britain is a hungry Britain, badly fed, clothed and housed.
Allen Hutt proves this from the actual facts and figures pro-
vided by life itself and the reports of capitalism's own agents.

In the brief period since the end of the war the working class
has been through political experiences which are leading to a
clearer understanding of the issues that Engels so sharply outlined in 1844. We have had the Lloyd George Coalition Government, two Tory Governments, two Labour Governments, and
now a "National" Government with unprecedented power and
majority. A revolution has taken place in the fiscal policy of the
country. Free Trade has been abandoned and a system of high
protective tariffs adopted.

In this connection it is interesting to recall how Engels, writing
in the 'eighties of the problems British capitalism would be faced
with as its competitors became more formidable, in spite of its
basis of Free Trade, said:

> But the manufacturing monopoly of England is the pivot of the
> present social system of England. Even while that monopoly lasted,
> the markets could not keep pace with the increasing productivity of
> English manufacturers; the decennial crises were the consequence.
> And new markets are getting scarcer every day; so much so that even
> the negroes of the Congo are now to be forced into the civilisation
> attendant upon Manchester calicoes, Staffordshire pottery and
> Birmingham hardware. How will it be when Continental, and
> especially American, goods flow in ever-increasing quantities—when
> the predominating share, still held by British manufacturers, will
> become reduced from year to year ? Answer, Free Trade, thou
> universal panacea.

A fundamental change took place in financial policy when
Britain was forced off the Gold Standard. And during and

alongside all these changes ever-increasing attacks have been made on the standards of the working class. Where has it all led to? To prospects of better times later on? No. On the contrary, to prospects of ever-deepening capitalist crisis, the sharpening of the class struggle at home and the fierce intensification of the antagonisms of the rival imperialist powers, so that as these lines are being written mankind is already beneath the shadow of the world war which has commenced in China and South America.

The question, therefore, inevitably arises: Are the conditions depicted in this book the result of capitalism? They are. And so long as the existing system remains there is no way out of this situation. They are not the result of some "economic blizzard" which will pass away. They are the result of the fact that a robber class owns the land, rivers, railways, minerals, banks, mines, mills and factories; that this ownership is only for private gain; that the happiness and contentment of the mass of the population is not the aim of private ownership; that when commodities have to meet other commodities in competition everything that stands in the way of profitable transactions is brutally attacked and swept aside; that there is nothing too low, too mean, too desperate, for this robber class to resort to in order to safeguard their rent, interest and profit; that sentiment, right and morality have no place in capitalist policy, and that as the crisis of capitalism intensifies, so do the attacks of the capitalists upon every standard of the working class at home and upon their foreign competitors.

Such a situation can only be overcome by the forcible destruction of the system which gives this robber class the power of life and death over the working class. To hide this fundamental fact from the workers is to commit a terrible crime against them. During the period of rising capitalism false illusions are thus created about the future, and in the period of acute crisis, such as the present, the capitalists are objectively helped to attack the working class by declarations that "It's a time for common sacrifice," or "You can't take more out of industry than there is in it," or "It's no use fighting the capitalists during a crisis." It is the latter theories which the official Labour leaders have so assiduously propagated and carried into practice, until to-day there is a growing recognition of the fact that the workers' fight is a fight on two fronts, against the capitalists and against the Labour leaders.

In regard to the present crisis, many and varied have been the explanations and conjectures. Any and every cause has been sought except the real cause. Two years ago *The Times* summed up in these words the situation then existing in America: "There are voices crying out to know how a country can produce so much food that people starve, and so many manufactured goods that people go without." The unspeakable Churchill, who now demands still fiercer repression of the workers at home and in India, stated in his Romanes lecture in 1930:

> The root problem of modern world economics was the strange discordance between the consuming and the producing power. Who would have thought that cheap and abundant supplies of all the basic commodities should find the science and civilisation of the world unable to utilise them? Had all our triumph of research and organisation bequeathed us only a new punishment—the curse of plenty?

Others protest that the crisis is caused through the wicked bankers, that it is the fault of too many inventions, the dislocation of markets through high tariff barriers, the low price levels that obtain. There is too much machinery, say others, let us go in for "technocracy"; and so they all go on. They do not see that here is the greatest contradiction of capitalism—between social production and the private appropriation of the product. And what lies behind their fine words? Savage wage cuts, the infamous Means Test, speeding-up, more workshop accidents, rotten housing conditions, an increasing number of suicides, increased infant mortality, a higher death rate of mothers in childbirth.

In all our industrial centres death and disease lay their clammy hands on whole areas and menace millions of decent working men, women and children. And as if to mock them, those who decry Communism as "destructive" and "violent" bemoan the fact that nothing is being done to stop new inventions. Shipyards, engineering shops, textile mills and pits are bought up in order to have their machinery deliberately destroyed to limit competition. Millions of tons of food are destroyed. Wheat is burnt in locomotive fireboxes, cotton crops are ploughed into the soil—all this madness and anarchy to try and find a way out of the crisis that will ensure the continuance of capitalism, the system that has brought about the conditions exposed in this book.

At this very moment Neville Chamberlain, probably the most ruthless member of the "National" Government, calmly informs the country that we are in for another ten years of mass unemployment; a statement which made his own class gasp, as witness this comment of the *Observer*, on February 19th last:

> The grim announcement which Mr. Chamberlain, as Chancellor of the Exchequer, felt compelled to make on Thursday that the only sure cure for unemployment is the revival of trade, and that but little relief is to be expected for ten years, visibly staggered the House of Com-

mons. Members gasped at each other with consternation. It was so wholly unexpected. Members had met, as they supposed, to hear the much-talked-of plans of the Government for a determined frontal attack on the solid mass of unemployment, only to have this disheartening prospect held out to them. Ten years, in the circumstances, seemed an interminable time. There has hardly been a scene like it since the announcement, during the South African War, of the defeat and capture of Lord Methuen by the Boers.

It is significant that this book is being published at the time when the revolutionary working class movement is commemorating the fiftieth anniversary of the death of Karl Marx, the founder of scientific Socialism, whose whole line has been so deliberately distorted by the reformists of every capitalist country. It was Marx who so clearly laid bare the cause of capitalist crises when he wrote: "The last cause of all real crises always remains the poverty and restricted consumption of the masses as compared to the tendency to develop the productive forces in such a way that only the absolute power of consumption of the entire society would be their limit" (*Capital*, Vol. III, p. 568).

It is true, as the capitalist and reformist leaders agree, that there have been crises before, and following them things have got better (how much better for the workers is glaringly shown in this book). But what is also true (and this decisive factor is missed) is that each crisis is deeper than the previous one. When it has been solved it has laid the basis for a succeeding crisis, until a point has been reached in the present economic crisis, occurring as it does within the general crisis of capitalism, where the end of partial capitalist stabilisation has been reached. As the events in the Dutch navy, in Rumania, Germany and China show, we are moving to a new round of *wars and proletarian revolutions*, in which the capitalists and the working class are both striving to find a solution of the crisis, each in their own class interests.

The value of a book such as this is that, by the facts and conditions it depicts, it uproots and entirely destroys the pernicious theory which has enabled the reformists to retard the struggle of the working class—that a workers' revolution is not necessary in Britain, that "there is an easy way out if you will vote for us." To support the "easy way out" theory, it has been their policy to depict conditions as always being on the upgrade, or to declare that the present crisis is only temporary, and soon things will be on the upgrade again.

Allen Hutt has taken the lid off Britain. He has revealed the real Britain, where, in spite of all the triumphs of science and invention, of the conquest of great natural difficulties and obstacles, our industrial centres, where the whole wealth and power of British imperialism have been built up, are centres of mass poverty, disease, and death.

The other aspect of the problem he presents is that of the working class finding its way forward, struggling against capitalism and reformism, building up in unemployed and strike struggles the power and leadership that can go forward to the revolutionary overthrow of capitalism, the establishment of the workers' dictatorship, and the building of Socialism, which will, as Marx put it, "develop the productive forces in such a way that only the absolute power of consumption of the entire society would be their limit."

Can it be done? Can the idle land, pits, shipyards, textile mills, blast furnaces, engineering shops be got going again on the basis of Socialist production and under workers' control? They can, and the proof is before our eyes. It is already being done in the Soviet Union. It would have been possible in 1914 to have written a book on the conditions of the working class in Tsarist Russia that would have seared the conscience of all who read it. It is impossible to write such a book in 1933, so far as the Soviet Union is concerned. Why? Because the workers' revolution and dictatorship have enabled a new Russia to be built. Once the political power of the old ruling class was destroyed, the land and large scale industries confiscated, then, and only then, was it possible for a planned economy to be organised.

To-day a backward agrarian country has been transformed into a land of Socialist industry and collective farming. Even the enemies of the Soviet Union are compelled to speak about the breathless advance, the conquest of unemployment, the new basic industries, factories, collective farms, the new life and culture, all carried through with enormous self-sacrifice and the conquering of almost incredible difficulties.

This is in the young Soviet Union. What we have in Britain is told in Allen Hutt's graphic language with unchallengeable facts, and arguments. It is the enemies of Communism in Britain who in this book are shown to be responsible for conditions the exposure of which will win new thousands for Communism in Britain.

It is to be hoped, therefore, that just as Engels' exposure of the conditions of the British working class in 1844 played an invaluable part in educating and creating an army of working-class fighters, so the present book will carry this work forward, enriched by all the experiences since that time, and particularly since the end of the war. It will be of value not if it merely makes some sentimental reader feel uneasy at the state of Britain to-day, but only if it makes them want to fight the Britain of to-day, if it makes them understand that the book is as much an indictment of reformist theory and practice as it is of capitalist rule and power. Then it will lead to the strengthening of the revolutionary forces, who to-day in factory, street and trade union, are slowly building up the fighting front of the working class to beat back the attempts to worsen their conditions in order that the capitalists may find a way out of the crisis.

In the building of this front the revolutionary forces are developing the leadership and power that can, by its effective protection of the everyday interests of the workers, deepen their class-consciousness, widen their revolutionary political outlook, until, as the objective situation reaches a point where it can no longer be tolerated, mass action can be taken that will lead to the forcible overthrow of capitalism. The establishment of the workers' dictatorship, the freeing of the colonial countries, and then, in fraternity and unity, the conscious building up of Socialism by the exchange of our common resources, will bring a tremendous increase in the standards of millions of workers at home and in a Socialist India, Ireland, Africa, etc. In this way there would be unlimited scope for the expansion of the Socialist productive forces, the welcoming of new inventions, the wiping out of the death-traps where millions are now compelled to live. On the basis of Socialist planned economy every idle pit, factory and shipyard in the country, could be set going.

It is the task of this book to hasten this process so that by 1934 a new page of working-class history shall have been written.

HARRY POLLITT.

CHAPTER I

THE SOUTH WALES COALFIELD TO-DAY

A HUNDRED years and more ago the valley-beds and mountain-sides of South Wales and Monmouthshire cradled the newborn capitalist heavy industries—coal mining and the manufacture of metals. The ironmasters who had driven levels and worked outcrops to obtain coal as a necessary adjunct to the smelting of the ore began to sink deep pits and work the coal for its own sake; the development of the steam engine and the discovery of the steam coal seams of the Aberdare, Rhondda and Monmouthshire Western Valleys combined to provide the technical basis for a constantly expanding capitalist coal mining industry. South Wales rapidly became a heavily industrialised area concerned mainly in the mining of coal; and the South Wales coal-owner was now primarily interested in producing coal for export, and not in the development of other industry to which the pits would act as fuel suppliers.

Immense fortunes were made out of the coal industry. Nature had been prodigal of her gifts in the Welsh seams; coal was there in unlimited quantity and of infinite variety. It was the highest quality coal in the world. As the nineteenth century wore on coal capitalism grew and grew in South Wales; it was a wild and feverish growth, a frenzied competitive race for more and still more profit. Family concerns were turned into companies; capital, scenting rapid and prodigious returns, poured in; the landowning aristocracy, my lords of Bute, Tredegar, Dunraven, and the Talbot family (among others), levied fabulous tribute to the tune of hundreds of thousands of pounds sterling a year by way of mineral leases, royalties and wayleaves; at the ports there grew up a host of middlemen battening on the industry—factors, shippers, exporters, brokers.

But coal-capital could naturally only fructify as a result of the social relationships it established; on the one hand were the coal-owners and their fellow-exploiters waxing rich; on the other hand was the growing army of the miners—the working-men who had nothing to sell but their power to toil in the pit, their ability to handle a pick or haul the coal along the narrow, dark galleries to the shaft. The labour-force of the Welshmen was vastly augmented by a constant immigration from the impoverished agricultural labourers of the nearby West of England, especially Somerset, Gloucestershire, Hereford and Devon, and from Irish peasants driven by hunger from the land.

From the very beginning of capitalism in the South Wales coalfield the class struggle was exceptionally bitter. The bestial exploitation of the early days found its answer in the terrorist secret society of the "Scotch Cattle" and the armed insurrection of the Monmouthshire men in 1839. The long strike of 1875 was followed by the enforcement of the sliding-scale swindle, which was terminated only after the equally long strike of 1898. In 1910-11 came the fiercely-fought and historic Cambrian Combine strike, when the Rhondda was under military occupation. South Wales was a storm centre of the national struggles of 1912, 1921 and 1926. And even a bare chronicle of the legion of pit and district strikes would require a substantial volume.

The Welsh mining valleys have always been a battle-field; but the casualties have not been confined to wages and conditions of work. The onward march of coal capitalism was marked by the corpses of thousands and tens of thousands of miners crushed by falls of roof, burnt, mangled, asphyxiated in devastating explosions. In South Wales the seams are exceptionally fiery and gaseous; and the drive for coal at all costs found its most hideous reflection in the fact that near one-half of the worst disasters recorded in British coalfields between the eighteen-fifties and the outbreak of the war took place in South Wales. The tale of disaster runs from Monmouthshire in the east to the Afan valley in the west; from Mardy, Ferndale, Wattstown, Penygraig, Tonypandy in the Rhondda valleys to the north, to the bituminous workings of the South Crop, where, on the lonely seashore near Taibach the grass-grown ruins of the long disused Morfa pit still remind the passer-by of the four terrible explosions which blasted that one pit during its working life. In 1913, the peak year of the coal industry's expansion, came the crowning horror of the Universal colliery at Senghenydd, when the worst explosion known in British mining history massacred 427 miners.

The culmination of the long process of profit-making in the coal industry was reached during the imperialist war and the brief post-war "replacement" boom of 1919-20. In the five years of the war the sums appropriated as profits and royalties from the British coal industry greatly exceeded the total pre-war capital of the industry. In 1918 profits alone had increased 200 per cent. over the mean level for the five pre-war years (which were boom years), while wages had only been doubled—an increase which lagged behind the steep rise in the cost of living. In these tremendous gains the coalowners of South Wales notably shared. Let us take note of two of the outstanding Welsh colliery concerns, which are of especial interest because they are "pure" coal-owning concerns and not heavy industry groupings. For example, the Powell Duffryn Steam Coal Company Limited, with a pre-war capital of less than £700,000, disclosed net profits of some £5,250,000 in the fifteen years to 1918. The company distributed bonus shares free to its shareholders during this period to the tune of £1,100,000; the profit-hunter who, in 1903, had invested £1,000 in Powell Duffryn shares would have turned over his capital nearly four times in the succeeding fifteen years, and would, with the bonus he had received, have been able in addition to sell his holding for five and a half times its initial cost. A similar picture is afforded by Ocean Coal and Wilsons Limited; this concern, with a very heavy capitalisation before the war, was able during the eight years ending 1917 to pay dividends totalling more than 100 per cent. on its capital, and to give a free bonus of £1,000,000, which by the end of the period had more than trebled in market value.[1]

Such were the great and glorious days of "prosperity" in the South Wales coalfield. The immense gains of the coalowners far exceeded the concessions the miners were able to force by their powerful organisation and militant action. The state of the industry was chaotic, anarchic, unplanned; there was a multiplicity of undertakings, of infinite variation in technical resource and equipment, caring nothing for rational organisation so long as they could get coal and dispose of it at the constantly soaring prices that prevailed. Then, in 1921, came the crash; and for over a decade now the coal industry in South Wales has endured a prolonged depression. There was a brief "boom" in 1923-4, due solely to the occupation of the Ruhr, and ceasing when that ceased; again, in 1929, there was a temporary, and small, improvement in demand as a result of the abnormally cold winter. But since then the smashing blows of the world crisis have brought the Welsh coal industry to the lowest depths it has ever known.

MONOPOLY AND MASS IMPOVERISHMENT

The central social fact in South Wales to-day is the development of monopoly on the one hand, and on the other the terrible and growing impoverishment of the toilers of the valleys. I say the central *fact*, because here are no two separate things: capital-

ism can only reproduce its own, capitalist social relationships—
and in an ever sharper contradiction. The biggest drive towards
monopoly in the Welsh coal industry has come in the past decade
of depression and crisis. And now half a dozen great combines
control three quarters of the total output of South Wales (excluding anthracite, which is practically all in the hands of the Amalgamated Anthracite combine, itself financially linked with its steam
coal counterparts). These are giant monopolies, whose normal
annual outputs range from three to a dozen million tons apiece.
The three biggest are Welsh Associated Collieries, Powell Duffryn
and the Ocean Coal Company—the last two are already familiar.
Then come the Ebbw Vale and Tredegar groups, and Cory
Brothers.

To journey in South Wales is not to journey from one county
or one valley to the next, but to travel from territory to territory
of one or other of these combines. Let us imagine that we are
making an aerial survey of the country. How do these monopoly
territories lie, and who are their rulers? In the centre of the
coalfield are the two Rhondda valleys. Here Welsh Associated
is an especial power, as befits a concern based on the notorious
Cambrian Combine founded by the late D. A. Thomas (Lord
Rhondda); there is a solid block of W.A.C. pits at the lower end
of the Rhondda Fawr, and over the mountain ridge to the east,
in the adjoining Rhondda Fach, an unbroken line of pits from
Tylorstown up to Mardy at the head of the valley, where the
combine recently acquired the famous collieries of the bankrupt
Lockets Merthyr concern for a song. North-westward lie some
score of pits in and about Aberdare, Mountain Ash and Merthyr
Tydfil, stretching from the bleak uplands of Hirwain right down
to where the valleys of the Cynon and the Taff meet at Abercy-
non. To the westward the Llynfi valley, from Maesteg up to
Caerau, presents another solid line of Welsh Associated pits
(the noted North's Navigation collieries); there is an intermediate
enclave at Gilfach Goch and a northern outpost in the Duffryn
Rhondda colliery at Cymmer, just over the mountain from
Caerau, in the upper reaches of the Afan valley. Further westward still, on the borders of the anthracite field, we note pits at
Clydach-on-Tawe, in the Swansea valley, Pontardulais, midway
between Swansea and Llanelly, and at Llanelly itself.

Near sixty pits come within the orbit of the Welsh Associated
Collieries, which was only formed in 1930 as a rearrangement
of the colliery interests of the mammoth iron and steel combine of
Guest, Keen and Nettlefolds (now partially fused with Baldwins,
its opposite number in iron and steel), and of the personal

colliery concerns of Sir D. R. Llewellyn, leading spirit of Guest, Keen, and foremost advocate in 1926 of a longer working day as the means of "saving" the coal industry. Apart from its heavy industry interlocking, Welsh Associated Collieries have their own worldwide selling agency in the big allied exporting firm of Gueret, Llewellyn and Merrett. And the lords of this monopoly are very different from the "captains of industry" of an earlier generation. They are gentlemen whose part is the far easier and more parasitic one of financial scheming; and their remoteness from the task of industrial organisation and management is seen in the way in which they diffuse their remarkable capacities over the boards of anything up to twenty-five companies (including railways, banks, insurance houses, as well as coal, iron and steel) with, say, a dozen chairmanships thrown in.

Of such, for example, is Sir John Field Beale, who resides very far indeed from the Rhondda in the opulent tranquillity of Porchester Terrace, Bayswater; or Lord Camrose, chieftain of the Berry clan, millionaire newspaper proprietor among his many other lines, and inhabitant of that select Mayfair neighbourhood, Seamore Place; or Sir D. R. Llewellyn himself, who plays the squire at The Court, St. Fagans, in the quiet and lovely countryside of the Vale of Glamorgan; or Mr. Wentworth Smith, who directs North's Navigation pits from that placid parasitical backwater, Palmeira Square, Hove. And the miners who toil to keep these lords and fine gentlemen in rotten luxury and ease, or who have been flung out of work by them, where do they live? Perhaps, like the Rhondda miner whose case is described later on, in basement rooms which are damp and ill-ventilated; perhaps, like the Monmouthshire miners described by the county medical officer, "compelled to sleep in the same bedroom" as their adolescent children, and living in houses which "have none of the advantages which tend to promote a healthy life," many being "in a condition only fit for demolition."*

The organisation of Welsh Associated was an attempt to answer the challenge of the Powell Duffryn Steam Coal Company, which, especially in the past six years, has been expanding rapidly. Financed by the international banking and finance house of J. Henry Schroeder and Co. (which is linked with the Bank of England), Powell Duffryn has bought up big colliery concerns, that were in the hands of the banks, at very low prices. It has amalgamated its selling concerns into Stephenson Clarke and Associated Companies Limited, perhaps the biggest coal factoring concern in the world. It has a number of foreign

* See pp. 14 and 40 below.

subsidiaries, and controls one of the biggest Durham colliery concerns, the Harton Coal Company.

Powell Duffryn territory runs roughly in a half-circle, stretching southward . along the Monmouthshire-Glamorgan border from Rhymney down the valley through the Bargoed and Gelligaer areas by Ystrad Mynach to Llanbradach; then south-westward, by way of Abertridwr and Senghenydd, to Nantgarw, a bare half dozen miles from Cardiff; from here the valley of the Taff is followed, through Llantwit-Fardre to Pontypridd, at the mouth of the Rhondda valleys. Thus far the territory is "solid" P.D. Its further branches march with the territory of Welsh Associated; to the north, where it stretches, via Cilfynydd and Treharris, to Mountain Ash, and the lower portions of the Aberdare region; in the centre, where it runs through Trehafod to Ynishir at the bottom of the Rhondda Fach; to the west, along the southern limit of the coalfield, to Llantrisant.

The rulers of Powell Duffryn are of the same type as their Welsh Associated rivals. Their leader is Evan Williams, who has for many years been the president of the Mining Association; the commander-in-chief of the coalowners in their national battles against the miners. The others are the usual absentee coupon-clippers. There is Sir Stephenson H. Kent, for instance, the squire of Chapelwood Manor, in the heart of Ashdown Forest, the most beautiful (and most landlord-ridden) part of the Sussex Weald; or Mr. C. B. O. Clarke, who abides in the old-world charm and quiet of the ancient town of Steyning, set in the midst of the Sussex downs; or Lt.-Col. Sir F. K. McLean, who prefers the ease of a riverside existence at that exclusive preserve of the wealthy, Henley-on-Thames; or Sir Leonard Brassey, Bt., whose modest home is in Upper Grosvenor Street, turning off Park Lane.

Powell Duffryn and its thirty-odd pits has a directoral link with the third of the Big Three, the Ocean Coal Company. Acquisition of important Rhondda concerns such as the old United National collieries has confirmed the Ocean in its position as the dominant concern in the upper half of the Rhondda Fawr; here is the heart of its territory, from Pentre up through Treorchy to Treherbert. Westward it reaches an arm over the mountains to Abergwynfi, Blaengarw and Nantymoel, at the head of the Afan, Garw and Ogmore valleys respectively. Eastward it thrusts, through Wattstown in the Rhondda Fach, across to Ynysybwl (in the little valley of the Clydach, between the Rhondda and the Cynon), and thence on to Treharris, with a last lone outpost further east still at Ynysddu in Monmouthshire.

The Ocean's territory largely coincides with that of the lesser concern of Cory Brothers, who have pits in the Rhondda (from Ystrad up to Treherbert) and in the Ogmore valley (at Nantymoel and Ogmore Vale), with a far western outpost at Resolven, in the Vale of Neath, and a north-eastern outpost at Penrhiwceiber, near Mountain Ash.

There remain the two large combines which dominate the coal industry in Monmouthshire; the Ebbw Vale Steel, Iron and Coal Company Limited and the Tredegar Iron and Coal Company Limited, with their associated concerns. Tredegar's territory runs right down the Sirhowy valley, from Tredegar at the head, through Hollybush and Oakdale to Ynysddu; it is exceptionally compact, and its pits, though few, are large. Its head is the octogenarian Lord Aberconway, who is also one of the largest Yorkshire coalowners (an old associate of the Markham family), and the chairman of the Metropolitan Railway; in the intervals of rushing from one board meeting to another my Lord and his son and fellow-director, the Hon. H. D. McLaren, find a humble lodging in, respectively, Belgrave Square and South Street, Mayfair.

To the east of the Tredegar territory lies the land of Ebbw Vale. It occupies the two parallel valleys of the Ebbw Fawr and the Ebbw Fach, with the latter's tributary, the Tillery; and after the junction of the two valleys the main valley of the Ebbw as far south as Abercarn and Cwmcarn. Dotted up and down the dozen miles from north to south in this narrow valley system are the score of the Ebbw Vale group's pits, which count among them the largest undertakings in South Wales. From the iron and steel-working town of Ebbw Vale, at the head of the Ebbw Fawr, the line of big collieries runs through Cwm (where the Marine No. 1 Colliery was the scene of the disaster in 1927 which called forth severe strictures from the Chief Inspector of Mines) down to Crumlin; a short distance up the Ebbw Fach is the important centre of Abertillery, covering a whole group of collieries, from the Arrael Griffin pits at Six Bells to the south, to the Cwmtillery and Rose Heyworth pits to the north—and so up the valley to derelict Blaina. Then there are the group of Ebbw Vale-controlled pits in the Rhondda— the Fernhill collieries at Treherbert, in the heart of the Ocean and Cory country.

This is a summary survey of the present-day monopoly "geography" of the South Wales coalfield, of the huge capital concentrations of the past decade. Let us now turn to the other side of the medal.

"And Wealth Accumulates while Men Decay"

The South Wales coalfield to-day is a land of unemployment and under-employment on a scale that it is hard to describe. The figures are grim enough. At the peak of employment in 1923-4 there were 250,000 workers in the collieries; in the autumn of 1932 there were 135,000—and most of these on short time. While the total of insured mineworkers has dropped to something over 200,000, to one in every three of these coal capitalism has no work to give.

The grimmest picture is afforded by the towns and areas along the northern limit of the coalfield; these are the oldest coal-working areas, and the former centres of the iron and steel industry. They have not been suddenly struck by the present crisis, but have been derelict for a decade and more. Merthyr Tydfil, Dowlais, Brynmawr, Rhymney, Nantyglo and Blaina, Blaenavon—these were centres whence generations of such families as the Guests and the Crawshays, whence such concerns as the Rhymney Iron Company extracted their millions; they are now graveyards—of living men and women. This line of towns along the northern fringe was the birthplace of capitalism in South Wales. And a century and a half afterwards the result is to be seen in unparalleled social deterioration, in the worst housing conditions in Wales, in atrocious impoverishment and misery.

In Brynmawr there are some 2,000 unemployed out of a total population of just over 7,000. Half the families in the town have an income of under 30s. a week. Of the lads between fourteen and eighteen, practically none have ever worked at all. Out of the 1,700 houses approximately 500 have no separate lavatory accommodation. The infantile mortality rate, which for the ten years up to 1929 averaged 78.3, was 88 in 1931, when for England and Wales as a whole it stood at an average of 66. These figures alone are a terrible indictment; and the position they reveal has led to Brynmawr being taken up by members of the Society of Friends as a centre for charitable "salvation." Much publicity has been secured for this effort at tinkering with the devastating results of capitalist decay by organising local boot, tweed and furniture manufacture on a tiny (but "commercial") scale. Much might be said about the methods employed in Brynmawr by "gentlemen of considerable experience in business management on a very large scale" to establish this manufacture "upon a profit-making basis"; the only comment needed here is that of an authority favourable to the Brynmawr and similar "experiments"; namely, that "what has been attempted has not touched the fringe of the unemployment problem, even in the localities concerned."[2] For the Quaker schemes at Brynmawr do not employ more than a score or so of unemployed workers.

A little distance southward from Brynmawr lie Nantyglo and Blaina. Here over 80 per cent. of the insured population are unemployed. It was a bright autumn afternoon when I walked up the main street of Blaina; but there was no brightness in these drab, gloomy and silent streets. Decay is in the air. The bearing and manner of the workers testifies to their enforced low standard of life. There are families in Nantyglo "living" on three halfpence a meal and three such "meals" a day. Right along the street the eye is caught, in house window after house window, by sad little hand-written notices—"Boot Repairing Done Here," and the like. This is a town whose inhabitants are striving to scrape a shilling or two together almost literally by taking in each other's washing. There are not a few houses in Blaina which were built a hundred or more years ago; tiny cottages, with no parlour of course, and no ceilings—the boards of the upper floor simply laid over the joists and painted underneath. There are also council houses; and so great is the poverty that rent arrears alone on these houses amount to £19,000. Up to 1921 there were five collieries working in and around Blaina; in that year they were all closed down and the Ebbw Vale combine sunk a new pit in the centre, the Beynon Pit, complete with the most modern electrical equipment, to work all this coal. To-day even at the Beynon Pit there are only a hundred or so men who from time to time get a fortnight's work. Up on the mountain-side above Blaina is a house coal level of the Bargoed Coal Company, employing some 250 men (mostly not from Blaina); and that is all there is left of mining in this area.

What has been said of Blaina is equally true of the other derelict areas at the head of the Monmouthshire valleys. Two years ago the medical officer of Blaenavon reported in these terms:

No new houses are being erected, and the difficulties become more acute each year. Overcrowding, not only in the older type houses, but in the new Council houses, is becoming rampant. It is not uncommon to find in the case of a mother giving birth, that the child has to be delivered by the nurse or doctor in an only bedroom, which is of necessity the sleeping place of sometimes three, four and often more children of varying ages. Most houses were built between sixty and seventy years ago, and are in a more or less dilapidated condition. They run in long rows or terraces, are invariably mean and unattractive, and some are so badly arranged and exist in such environments that nothing short of demolition is desirable. About 104 houses are in such condition as to be unfit for human habitation, and in respect of which closing orders have been served. This, however, becomes more or less a farce, unless they be made operative, which cannot be done until more houses are provided at economic rentals.[3]

The same officer, Dr. Reynolds, comments strongly in his latest report on the continuance of scandalous overcrowding, and instances a number of houses with an average of 10.6 persons living in each, or five persons per bedroom. Vivid light is thrown on other unhealthy conditions by his report that of four unfiltered samples taken from local water supplies all were found to be polluted, and that "of the six slaughter-houses in the town, none conform to anything like a satisfactory hygienic standard."[4]

But viler than all these things is the blow that declining capitalism has struck at the children of the working-class in these derelict areas. A most exhaustive investigation was carried out in 1931 by the assistant medical officers in Monmouthshire on the state of nutrition of school children in that county. An exacting standard of malnutrition was adopted, which excluded all but the most pronounced cases; and the result was that in each of the three derelict Monmouthshire areas, Rhymney, Nantyglo and Blaina, and Blaenavon, general malnutrition was revealed. Detailed graphs of height and weight were plotted for each age-group of children, separating the sexes, and covering each of the ten areas into which the county was divided for the purpose of this investigation. And in the three areas named every graph touched its lowest point, being far below the standard of children in the one rural area investigated. The Monmouthshire workers' children, it is concluded, have "felt the effects of prolonged poverty," and "(1) They get insufficient good food; (2) They get insufficient rest; (3) They have insufficient warm clothing and sound footwear."[5]

Let us move westward from the stricken Monmouthshire areas to Merthyr Tydfil and Dowlais. The same picture faces us. The iron and steel works at Dowlais were the most famous in South Wales; but when the Guest, Keen and Nettlefolds combine fused its iron and steel interests with those of Baldwins a couple of years ago to form the British (Guest, Keen, Baldwins) Iron and Steel Company, these historic works, which had long been working far below capacity, were finally abandoned. Many other works and pits have been derelict for many years. And in 1929 the medical officer of health in Merthyr was reporting that there was no advance in housing; that there were in the town

no fewer than 834 houses which required entire rebuilding to
make them habitable; and that 118 cellar-dwellings, many of
which had previously been closed, were now each occupied by a
separate family, owing to lack of suitable accommodation.
Instances were also given where "houses that had been closed
but not demolished, were broken into and occupied by families
who were unable to get housing accommodation. The sanitary
circumstances of these houses were deplorable."[6] And in Dowlais
the district sanitary inspector, Mr. Jenkins, stated that:

> The small number of notices served in his district to reduce over-
> crowding does not represent the extent of the "family" overcrowding.
> . . . Owing to the scarcity of suitable accommodation for a large
> number of families, consisting of young people with two or three
> children, who now share dwelling-houses by occupying the kitchen
> cellars, or form one of the families in a large inconvenient house under
> decidedly unfavourable conditions, only verbal pressure and frequent
> visits can be brought to bear, and he is frequently met with the retort
> "we cannot find better accommodation or we would soon get out."[7]

Here is a typical case of a Dowlais family living under "decidedly
unfavourable conditions"; the husband was a steel worker, but
for many years has been denied the privilege of toiling to swell the
profits of the Guest, Keen combine; with his wife and two
children he lives in one-half of a house, which costs him seven
shillings a week in rent. The house has not been repaired for
fourteen years. Its windows do not shut tight, and it is damp.
The lavatory is thirty yards away from the house, at the top
of the adjacent yard. There is one water-tap for both families.
This family's income is the father's unemployment benefit of
27s. 3d.; after paying rent they have roughly a pound left to
live on. Coal costs them half-a-crown a week; and the remaining
17s. 6d. they are at liberty to "live" on. This is their normal
daily menu: BREAKFAST: toast, margarine, tea. DINNER: a few
pennyworth of meat and potatoes, an onion, bread and tea.
SUPPER: same as breakfast.

Fresh milk is unknown in this family, who consume four tins
of a cheap brand of skimmed condensed milk a week. It is not
surprising that the eldest child was found to be suffering from
malnutrition and was developing tubercular glands.

Here is another Dowlais family, this time a large one. Father,
mother and eight children (of whom the eldest is twelve and a
half years of age) live in three rooms and occupy a landing which
they use as an additional "room." For this they pay also seven
shillings. The total income, for ten people, including extra
relief for two of the children, is 46s. 3d. Their staple food is bread;
and, for the whole family, they only spend two shillings a week

on meat and 1s 3d. on fresh vegetables, and buy four pints of fresh milk, the remainder being tinned. They pay 3s. 5d. a week in insurance premiums, which they have been paying for many years and which (though they realise the outrageous swindle of it) they are loth to cease paying, since it will mean losing all that they have paid in so far.

The children of this family all suffer from sores, due to malnutrition; but seven of them share two beds. Only one boy, who is especially delicate, has a bed to himself, at the express instructions of the doctor. These children play in the yard just outside the house, where are the lavatories serving the houses in the row. The mother, when asked why she didn't send them out on the mountain slopes to play in the fresh air and the sunshine, replied that she was afraid that they would return with too large an appetite. Could there be a more damning exposure of the conditions in the derelict areas of South Wales, of the privation and want to which the rich monopolists condemn little children as well as grown men and women, than this simple, tragic answer?

"Cwm Rhondda"

Turn now from the derelict areas of the northern fringe to the steam coal valleys of the centre and east of the coalfield. Greatest of all are the two Rhondda valleys, whose big development dates back no earlier than the seventies and eighties of last century. Taking the Rhondda and the steam coal valleys of the Port Talbot hinterland together (the Afan, Maesteg, Garw, Ogmore and Gilfach valleys), the average numbers of miners employed during the years 1927-31 were little more than half those employed in the peak year of 1923. The world crisis has made the situation even more acute; in the summer of 1931 the numbers employed were only 38 per cent. of the numbers employed in 1923. The position to-day is still worse. Even making allowance for the reduction in the number of insured mineworkers in these areas since 1923 (rather more than 20 per cent.), it is doubtful whether at the most 50 per cent. of the Rhondda miners are still employed. Of the nature and uncertainty of that employment we shall have occasion to speak later; here it will be enough to notice how unevenly employment is spread throughout these valleys. At the lower end of the Rhondda Fawr, around Tonypandy, the Welsh Associated pits last autumn were working very irregularly, and 8,000 men are signing on at the Labour Exchange; where a colliery formerly employed 2,000 men, working all seams, it now employs 500 men working one seam only; or out of a group of several pits only one will be working. On the other hand, at the upper end of the valley, around Treherbert and Treorchy, the Ocean and Cory pits were working with a fairly full complement of men and much more regularly. In the Rhondda Fach, which, as we have seen earlier, is 100 per cent. Welsh Associated from Tylorstown up to the valley head at Mardy, sinking operations have for some time been in progress at the Mardy No. 4 pit, while a pit at Ferndale has been closed down, and one seam permanently abandoned; meantime over 2,000 miners in Mardy remain idle, as they have done for years, and only 300 have been working in one of the four Mardy pits.

The two Rhondda valleys together constitute far and away the biggest urban district in South Wales. From Porth, where the valleys meet, the mining townships straggle and sprawl along the main roads, and clamber up and down the bare mountain-sides, running into one another with hardly ever a break right the way to the valley heads at Blaenrhondda and Mardy respectively. It is possible to make a jolting and jerking journey on antiquated and uncomfortable tramcars right up both valleys; the urban prospect en route is one that does not substantially vary, except that the Rhondda Fawr is urbanised on a larger scale than the Rhondda Fach, and its ugliness is therefore quantitatively more depressing. Everywhere there are the same long rows of drab stone-built houses, slate-roofed, built straight on to the pavement so as to save space, each identical the one with the other—so that they look as if they had been manufactured from some common mixture in a gigantic machine whence they had emerged in an endless stream, been cut off into the lengths required, and flung down casually to stick where, and as best, they might. Subsidence has brought the earth up against the backs of many houses. Their walls are cracked. Windows and doors will not shut tight to keep out wind and weather. Where there are not houses there is a colliery; and alike in the valley-bed and on the very top of the mountains the dark-grey slack-tips heave their ugly mass upwards.

Capitalist development has made of the Rhondda the reverse of a beauty spot; but, ugliness apart, it is the fact that housing conditions in the Rhondda were frequently better than in the older industrial areas in South Wales, or than in big cities like London, Manchester or Glasgow. Unemployment and growing poverty has put this advantage to naught by compelling families to share one house in order to save on the rent. Dr. Jenkins, the Rhondda medical officer, reports:

Although a considerable reduction in the population of the Rhondda is estimated to have occurred during recent years, there still remains evidence of overcrowding. A large number of houses, which were originally designed for the accommodation of one family, are occupied by two or even more families, and in spite of the fact that there is a considerable number of empty premises in the district, occupiers have been driven by financial considerations to sublet portions of their houses to other families who are similarly circumstanced. Life under such conditions produces the evil effects of overcrowding which becomes aggravated as the families increase in size and as the individual members reach adolescence. [8]

This is a case of an unemployed Rhondda miner who, with his wife and young baby, shared a house. They occupied the ground floor; that is to say, since the row of houses was built on a slope, it was the ground floor at the back, but on the front it was a basement, some six feet below street level, with a very narrow well in front of the windows. Winter rainstorms, and a blocked drain in this narrow well (which the landlord did not trouble to repair) made one of the two front rooms so damp as to be uninhabitable. The other front room, though damp and ill-ventilated, was used as the bedroom; the main back room, only twelve feet square and the largest room in the house, had the range and was used as the living-room. When this family was visited last summer the father had only just completed his first year of unemployment; he felt his idleness acutely, and was still desperately hoping for a job to turn up. The wife's pale, sunken cheeks and unnaturally large eyes told the tale of ill-health due to want; and the baby, despite the pint and a half of milk a day allowed it from the welfare clinic, looked very worn. The family income was 25s. 3d. from the Labour Exchange; they were £1 in arrears with their rent; and their dietary was bread, butter and cheese for breakfast, boiled potatoes and a little meat now and again for dinner, bread and butter for tea, with the latter drink accompanying every "meal." Their only variation was to have ham and tomatoes for dinner on Sunday.

It is not such a far cry from the Rhondda to the Western valleys of Monmouthshire; and, indeed, the position in wide areas there is even worse than it is in the Rhondda. I am referring, of course, to areas south of the derelict spots, which have already been discussed. Last October, in Abertillery, the biggest mining centre of these parts, there was not one of its half-dozen pits working. The Cwmtillery colliery, which had hitherto always worked regularly, closed at the end of September for an indefinite period, and 1,600 miners were thrown idle. Other pits, like the big Arrael Griffin pits at Six Bells, had been idle for a year and more. In 1921 there were nearly 10,000 miners living in the Abertillery urban district; to-day there will not be more than two-thirds that number—and that two-thirds on the street practically to a man. Poverty in Abertillery is resulting in the same overcrowding that characterises the Rhondda; the new council houses are sublet—for what unemployed man can afford 12s. 3d. in rent? It is common to find, for example, a family living in two rooms sublet in a council house; the living-room serves also as kitchen and scullery, with a bowl on an up-ended sugar-box for washing-up; the bedroom is common to father, mother, and children. The dietary is of the meagre order noted in the derelict areas: bread is the staple food, washed down with tea, and fresh milk is rarely seen.

One is not surprised that the infantile mortality rate in Abertillery has leapt upwards by nearly twenty points from 1930 to 1931, increasing from 54.3 to 73. And a most moving aspect of the ever-growing poverty is indicated in the latest report of the school medical officer, Dr. Baillie Smith, where he speaks of the number of children found with "very poor and deficient" clothing and footgear. He says:

> In most of these cases the little children had practically no boots at all, so bad was the condition of their footgear. The large number of children attending school in canvas shoes was especially noted. This is to be accounted for by the very trying economic conditions existing in your area. There was a considerable falling off in the condition of the boots and clothing, especially underclothing, of girls and boys as compared with previous years. On enquiring into the absences of children from school, one finds the reason given is that the children had not got boots in such a state of repair as to enable them to attend school, especially in inclement weather. The school attendance officer's monthly reports also bring out the fact very vividly. [9]

Social conditions are acute also even in those parts of the Western valleys where there are still pits working. In Ebbw Vale itself, hard hit by the closing down of the iron and steel works in 1929, the medical officer of health reported in that year that "there are still a number of houses in occupation which have been condemned as unfit for human habitation, and a further number of very poor standard." [10] And last September the Health and Housing Committee of the Ebbw Vale Urban District Council received a report from the medical officer in almost identical terms. A member of the committee remarked that there were 400 or 500 people who had their names down for houses. This characteristic little dialogue ensued:

> He did not know whether any good purpose would be served by drawing the attention of the Ministry to the matter. It was amazing

c

to think how many people were living in such houses. The Chairman
said the Council had discussed a scheme under the 1930 Housing
Act, but owing to their financial obligations nothing was done.[11]

Strong comment was made on the alarming fact, also revealed
in the medical officer's report, that practically 300 children out
of the 5,000 at Ebbw Vale were physically unfit and required
to be placed in open-air schools; the obvious connection between
this and the bad housing conditions was stressed.

In the Abercarn area, lower down the Ebbw valley, the pits
have worked more regularly; the Cwmcarn collieries, for instance,
only began to lose shifts last October. But the medical officer
of the Abercarn Urban District Council reports that for some
time the people's savings have been exhausted and there is now
"considerable poverty"; the general standard of house repair has
gravely declined, "and there was overcrowding at Cwmcarn,
due principally to the economic conditions, for many people
were compelled to sublet."[12]

The Western valleys are the territory of the huge Ebbw Vale
combine, as we have seen earlier. And the condition of the
workers in these valleys is an instance of the working out of monopoly capitalism in truly barbarous poverty and wretchedness for
the masses. Faced with a shrinking demand, a concern like the
Ebbw Vale combine can and will unhesitatingly close down all
its pits in one area (like Abertillery), and concentrate on working
the pits in others (say, in Ebbw Vale, Cwm and Abercarn) where
circumstances make the margin of profit greater. So the Ebbw
Vale chairman, Sir John Beynon, can tell the last annual general
meeting of his shareholders that "considering everything, the
results achieved by the Ebbw Vale Company were satisfactory."
Blaina is derelict. Abertillery is closed down. Families are
forced to crowd into small houses only meant for one of their
number. Condemned houses are still inhabited. Little children
are trudging to school practically barefoot. Humble savings
have been dissipated. Truly "satisfactory results" for Sir John
and his crew! And more satisfactory still when their capitalist
reflection is seen in the £100,231 profit recorded by the Ebbw
Vale Company in the last financial year. Certainly, bank and
debenture interest absorbed all this bar £16,738; the share and
8 per cent. note holders have not been satisfied; but the big
debenture holders have got their solid 6 per cent. safely. An overwhelming majority of these idle persons has now agreed to a
scheme to slash the Company's bloated capital from £3,700,000
to £425,000, by cancelling 15s. in the £1 on preference, and 19s.
in the £1 on ordinary, shares. In this way they trust that results

will satisfy them even more; incidentally, they give a good example of the unreality of capital, of the fact that capital is only a "fetish", as Marx said, is only the expression of a social relationship, a relationship between classes. In times of boom capital can be written up by a stroke of the pen (the issue of bonus shares); in times of crisis it can be as easily written down. In either case it is nothing but the outward and visible expression of the existing relationship between the capitalists and the working class; it is nothing but the scrap of paper which entitles the great monopolists to get something for nothing, to extract profit from the exploitation of the working class because they, the capitalists, are the ruling class in society.

We have seen something of what this social relationship means in terms of mass poverty and social deterioration in the derelict areas, and in the steam coal valleys of the Rhondda and Monmouthshire. With this picture in mind it will be fitting to listen once more to Sir John Beynon telling his applauding shareholders: "I think we have agreed for years that the social expenses of this country are too high."[13] In other words, let misery increase, let children have grossly inadequate boots and clothing, let malnutrition spread—as long as "results are satisfactory." There is the authentic and ruthless creed of the coal monopolist of to-day.

Some Social Effects of Unemployment

One broad effect of the prolonged depression in South Wales is visible in the emigration of nearly a quarter of a million persons from the region in the ten years up to 1931. In the principal urban districts of the steam coal valleys the census figures show a net decrease of population between 1921 and 1931, averaging some 12 per cent.; and in the Monmouthshire valleys the decrease ranges as high as 18 and nearly 20 per cent.[14] Up to 1921 these populations were constantly increasing; and the emigration that then took place was mainly the movement of women and girls seeking employment in London and the big cities of England. After 1926 the Government introduced the Industrial Transference scheme, which was intended to stimulate and regulate the migration of unemployed workers from the Welsh valleys. The ultimate effect of the scheme was negligible; of those transferred some 40 per cent. subsequently returned to South Wales, either because the work to which they were sent came to an end, or the conditions were too bad. Altogether it is estimated that the numbers transferred who have found what is modestly called "some measure of employment" elsewhere do not exceed 30,000. A certain number of these found work in the newer coalfields, such as Notts and Derby or Kent; but the majority obtained work as builders' labourers or navvies, and were in fact employed on unemployment relief work of various kinds. Even if the transference scheme had been enormously extended, and had violently uprooted the whole of the "surplus" population of South Wales, setting them to work building roads, houses and other amenities in various other parts of the country, it would merely have meant that large areas in South Wales would have relapsed to waste and ruin. And the position to-day is that while the migrant from South Wales might have hoped to find work before the onset of the world crisis, he has no more hope to-day in London or the south of England than he has in his home valley.

It might have been supposed that the migration of young men from the Welsh valleys would in some degree offset the migration of girls and women; but the economic pressure has been so great that the migration of miners' daughters in search of work as domestic servants, as waitresses and hotel maids, as shop assistants, and so forth, has increased at such a rate that in many areas the proportion of females to males in the population has declined, despite the male migration.[15] In many a Welsh miner's home to-day it is common to find that the daughter is "in service" in London, or working as a barmaid or waitress in some far away city. Her work will be arduous, uncertain and probably uncongenial; and if she loses her job then, after a bitter struggle, she may be driven into prostitution.

There has not only been a movement out of South Wales of girls and lads in search of labour; in South Wales itself the unemployment and depression in the basic industries has led to an increase in the number of workers employed in the distributive trades, which develop parasitically as the heavy industries decline, and to a general increase in female and juvenile labour. Between 1923 and 1930 the number of insured workers in the distributive trades in South Wales increased by 46 per cent.; a brief table illustrates some significant aspects of this development:

PERCENTAGE INCREASES IN NUMBERS INSURED IN DISTRIBUTIVE TRADES IN
SOUTH WALES BETWEEN 1923 AND 1930

Men: 58 (26)	Women: 26 (47)
Boys: 85 (60)	Girls : 40 (92)

The figures in brackets represent increases in hotel and restaurant service in the Cardiff-Barry area, the "metropolitan" area of South Wales. It appears clearly from this table that the main new entrants into the distributive trades have been juveniles; and the fact is that these are unorganised, low wage, "blind alley" trades; that the wages earned by the youngsters who enter them are insufficient to maintain them independently, but serve to eke out the family income, consisting probably only of what the father draws in unemployment benefit. As for the growth of female labour, it may be noted that while the number of insured males in South Wales fell by 7 per cent. between 1923 and 1930, the number of insured females rose by 13 per cent. The recent *Industrial Survey of South Wales* comments:

> In the industrial depression which has overtaken the region parents have become more anxious that their daughters should earn wages, and employers have a strong incentive to substitute female for the more expensive male labour.[1]

In the same eight-year period the number of insured boys in all industries in South Wales declined by 4 per cent., while the number of insured girls increased by 34 per cent.

It is evident that during the past two years unemployment has more and more severely hit the distributive trades in South Wales; and they do not now serve as an outlet for the boy and girl labour of the valleys as they did in the manner indicated in the figures cited above. Walk to-day through the main street of such diverse towns as Barry, the seaport and holiday resort, or Tonypandy, typical Rhondda mining township, and count the number of shops standing empty; it is instructive. In Tonypandy, which is a small place, I counted twenty-three. And wherever you go in South Wales it is the same.

What of the mass of the unemployed miners themselves? Many have not worked for five, six and more years. "Since 1926," a man will tell you, "the only thing I've had is ten weeks on the roads." The date and the figure may differ; but the formula is universal. The roads throughout South Wales have been transformed in a decade; new wide main roads and by-passes have been made, old dangerous corners straightened out, great highways flung across the mountains linking up the Rhondda valleys with the Vale of Neath and Aberdare to the north and the Port Talbot hinterland to the west. If it is possible to make new roads is it not possible to construct new houses, to build a new life for the working people? The answer is "Yes"; but capitalism cannot give that answer. It is not possible to travel along these magnificent roads without constantly reflecting that these fine, smooth ways are monuments to capitalist decline; for they were all constructed by the labour of unemployed miners taken on by the local authorities in batches of so

many for a certain period, to be followed by another batch, and
so on until the job was completed. Thirteen weeks has been a
typical period of employment, and the rate of pay £2 15s. a
week. That these schemes have not been able to absorb, even
temporarily, more than a mere fraction of the unemployed is
shown by the statement that for every vacancy on a big Monmouthshire road scheme there were twenty applicants.[17] During
the past year the regime of "economy" has further meant the
general refusal of the Government grants which alone make
public works schemes possible; and there is practically nothing
of the kind now in progress in the whole of South Wales.

Ironically enough, one of the main preoccupations of the
unemployed miner is to get coal. Without coal he and his family
cannot live; very many houses have electricity for lighting (and
outrageously dear electricity too—7½d. or 9d. a unit, compared
with the 3d. a unit of an average London municipal supply,
though the Welsh power-stations have their fuel on their door-
steps), but for all cooking and heating they have to rely on a
big range, which needs a lot of coal to keep it going. Coal can be
bought, of course, at 1s. 3d. a hundredweight; but for the majority
such expense is out of the question. One way out is to steal coal;
and coal-stealing is the commonest "crime" in South Wales to-
day, the daily fare of every police court and every local newspaper. Coal may be stolen from full wagons in the railway
sidings, from colliery tips, or from outcrops on company property.
In a recent typical case in the Rhymney valley a miner was
charged with stealing coal from an outcrop, though it was
admitted that the company (the Powell Duffryn combine) would
never work this coal; they had nevertheless refused permission
for unemployed men to work the coal; and the miner was duly
ordered to pay 15s. costs. In the Rhondda a lad and his uncle
went into an old disused level to get coal; as they emerged they
were sighted and chased by a policeman; the lad got away, but
the older man was caught and fined £2, a heavy sum for an
unemployed miner, with a family to keep, to find.

While outcrop working is tolerated in some parts it is generally
treated as an offence alike by the coal owners and the police.
The owners' agents frequently try to stop it by blasting down
the primitive workings; they make some parade of humane feelings
to justify their action, and claim that these workings, without
proper timbering and so on, are very dangerous. They certainly
are, and accidents are prevalent—witness the tragic killing of
three men by falls in a Caerau outcrop in August 1931; but
since the humane gentlemen do everything in their power to

prevent the unemployed miners obtaining coal safely, their protestations are unconvincing.

The commonest method of getting coal, however, is from the tips—either from the colliery tips now in use (this is permitted in some places) or from the old disused tips. In the Rhondda the present tips are frequently right on the top of the mountains, 1,200 to 1,400 feet up; after the long climb to the tip the two score or so of unemployed coal-hunters will wait until the train of trams slowly ascends the track up the mountain-side. There follow two general scrambles: first, to pick any visible pieces of coal off the trams as they come to a standstill, and then among the slack as it is tipped. Men may spend eight hours on the tip and only fill a hundredweight sack—harder and more thankless graft than a day in the pit; it is a day's fighting and scrambling for 1s. 3d. Then the coal, so bitterly won, has to be laboriously shouldered for the dreary trudge over the mountain-top and down the steep side to the township in the valley below. It will keep the home fires burning for perhaps three days.

A more bitter sight still is to see men searching for coal on the old tips. These are usually at the valley bottom, or low down the mountain-slopes. Walk along the valley road and watch those figures dotted up and down the sides of that ancient tip. They are digging, and turning over each shovelful with a scrutiny as careful as if they were alluvial gold-miners examining the precious mud. Two or three shovelfuls will pass without yielding a lump of coal the size of an egg; and each lump found is certainly treasured as if it were a gold nugget.

In the streets of a Welsh mining township nowadays you may meet many men in their pit clothes who have not been to the colliery for years; they greet you: "I'm just going up to the tip." Capitalism can no longer give these miners work in the pit; but they cannot escape from coal; where they once toiled at the rich seams and won their tons upon tons for the profit of the coal magnates, they now have no option but to scrape at their own leavings for a meagre sackful to keep some warmth on their hearths and a fire beneath their scantily provided pot.

THE CONDITIONS OF LABOUR IN THE PITS

The output of coal in South Wales in 1932 was approximately 20,000,000 tons below the 1913 level. We have already noted the enormous reduction in the number of miners employed, and the extent of under-employment, the universal short time. It is common for a colliery to work three days or less a week, while only employing a fraction of its "normal" complement of men. The operation of the quota system of output regulation under the Labour Government's Coal Mines Act of 1930 has assisted the concentration of production in the hands of the great monopolies and in fewer pits. Quotas can be bought and sold and the pit whose quota has been thus transferred will be closed down while the purchaser can add the quota to that of his other pit or pits.

The miners who are still "fortunate" enough to be employed work harder, and for lower wages, than ever before. Monopoly has developed in the South Wales coal industry as an accompaniment, not only of growing unemployment and the impoverishment of the unemployed masses, but of the impoverishment and increased exploitation of the men in the pits. Visit a few mining townships in, for example, what is now the territory of the Powell Duffryn combine; men will tell, with a wry face, of "how the P.D. came" to their area, as if it were a pestilence or a barbarian invasion. The initials of this huge concern are bitterly translated always as "Poverty and 'Dole' ". The grim jibe is justified, not only for Powell Duffryn, but for each one of the Big Six, whose expansion and territories we have earlier surveyed.

Some idea of the increased exploitation of the miners is seen in the rise in the annual output per head of all persons employed in the South Wales coal industry from 238 tons in 1927 to 280 tons in 1929; and this process has gone still further since that date, for "even within the last two years improvements have been such that the output of 1929 could be produced in 1932 with substantially fewer than the 159,933 workers who were 'in employment' in that year."[18] This increase in output per head is by no means mainly due to the introduction of coal-cutting machinery, which proceeds slowly in South Wales, though the percentage of coal cut by machinery more than doubled in the eight years ending in 1929; but the introduction of such machinery, as also face conveyors, mechanical haulage and so forth, enables sheer speed-up to be applied more effectively and the labour of each individual to be greatly intensified.

In one anthracite colliery the introduction of conveyors displaced fifty colliers; and in a typical Rhondda pit the introduction of three conveyors in one district gave that district a far higher output than other districts, though considerably less than half the number of men were employed than in any one of the districts without conveyors. The miners' lodge secretary at the collieries of which this pit is part writes:[19]

These machines have greatly increased our difficulties, such as the amount of overtime the men are forced to work, the speeding-up and the increase in the number of accidents. The conveyors have also displaced a number of skilled colliers. Now there are about 6 or 7 men emplóyed with 10 to 12 boys, where under the old method a man and a boy used to work in each place.

These collieries are owned by the biggest combine, Welsh Associated; they reveal vividly the general process. One pit was closed down last September, throwing near 500 men out, and in another pit some 200 men were stopped who were working in what was once the principal and richest seam in those parts: the men were told that this seam was closed down permanently because it was "too costly to work." The lodge secretary comments:

The cheapest seams these days are the thin seams where coal-cutters and conveyors are installed. We are rapidly approaching the time when mostly all the old method of heading and stall work will be abandoned in favour of machinery with a few men in charge of a number of boys. To illustrate this I will give you the actual gross output of coal in the different districts of —— Pit for one week in July:

Districts		No. of Colliers	Gross Tonnage		Average weekly output per collier	
OLD METHOD OF WORKING (HEADING AND STALL)						
			tons	cwts.	tons	cwts.
Five feet seam	..	47	596 —	7.5	12 —	13.76
Gellideg "	..	127	856 —	9.5	6 —	14.87
Bute "	..	88	1,063 —	6.5	12 —	1.65
Six feet "	..	19	186 —	14	9 —	16.52
NEW METHOD (COAL-CUTTERS AND CONVEYORS)						
Yard Seam	..	61	1,454 —	13.5	23 —	16.93
TOTAL	.. ..	342	4,157 —	11	12 —	8.99

Thus machinery enables output per collier to be doubled (and not by lightening labour); while, as the table shows, little more than one-sixth of the total number of colliers in this pit produce one-third of its gross tonnage. It is an impressive instance of the way in which technical improvement, under declining capitalism, means increased misery and exploitation; whereas it should mean, and under the workers' rule does mean, precisely the reverse.

Not only is there a ruthless speed-up, but wages are very low; favourable price-lists that had been won by years of struggle have been swept away (at Mardy, for instance), unfavourable price-lists have been enforced (such as the substitution of a rate per yard worked forward in the seam, instead of per ton filled, with no allowance of any kind for timbering or other deadwork), and the proportion of men on the minimum wage is far greater than it ever was before. A full six shifts on the minimum wage mean that a man will not take home, after stoppages, more than 42*s*. to 43*s*; and the inroads made into this miserable sum by short time can be imagined. Of course, if a man works three days or less in a week he can draw unemployment benefit for the remainder; but it is common for the pit to work short time in such a way that many of the lost days do not link up to qualify for benefit. A man who works four days in one week, for example, will be debarred from drawing benefit for the remaining two; if he is on the minimum he will earn less than 30*s*., after stoppages, to keep himself and his family for a week. And it is quite a usual thing for colliery managements to refuse even to make men's wages up to the minimum, although this is a legal obligation. In Aberdare there is a colliery known locally as "Half Price Pit," where to ask for the minimum wage is to invite immediate dismissal. The Rhondda lodge secretary already quoted illustrates these processes in his colliery:

> Low wages are a subject of general complaint. This is connected with the short time that is being worked at the collieries. We have already lost 61 days since January 1st, 1932 [he was writing in July; by October they had lost 103 days] and 28 days of this total did not link up for unemployment benefit. If a man fights for his rights under the Minimum Wage Act the management soon find some excuse, such as "inefficiency," etc., to give him fourteen days' notice.

The general conditions of safety in the pits are steadily deteriorating, despite all the official "safety first" ballyhoo. Our Rhondda authority tells a tale that is typical:

> Men doing repair work, such as repairers and their labourers, have been dispensed with. You will find districts in the pit where they used to employ *six* parties of repairers and about five or six labourers; now they employ *one* party with a couple of labourers. It is obviously impossible for two repairers to do the work that twelve did formerly; so the state of repair and the safety conditions of the collieries may be imagined. In order to try and alter this state of affairs we send Workmen's Examiners down occasionally, but our financial position is such that we cannot afford to keep this up.

The steam coal pits of South Wales have always been the most dangerous, from the point of view of liability to explosions; this is due, not only to the gassy nature of the seams, but to the exceptional volume of coal dust produced. This factor of danger can be checked by a number of simple technical measures, including the provision of proper dust-proof trams. Year after year the mines inspectors have stressed this fact; and still, in his report for 1931, Sir Henry Walker, the Chief Inspector of Mines, is constrained to remark that "in the main" the South Wales trams "do not comply with the spirit of the law." He comments that:

It is significant that in that part of the South Wales coalfield in which the most devastating coal dust explosions in this country have occurred the trams are in the most neglected condition.[20]

At the Llwynypia colliery, in the Rhondda, eleven men (including two of the rescue party) were killed in an explosion of fire damp last year. As often happens, the majority of the victims did not die from the burns they received; they were asphyxiated by carbon monoxide gas, the deadly "after-damp." Rescuers told terrible stories of the burned and bruised bodies of the dead, huddled up in the workings, some in a crawling position, caught and killed by the after-damp that they knew was coming and had desperately made a final effort to escape. One of the victims had been unemployed for a considerable time; it was his first shift back at work. The explosion took place in a conveyor run. It was stated that the bolts on the conveyor had worked loose, and excess dust was being deposited. There was a big fault in the seam, the presence of gas was known, and much small coal had accumulated in the waste, a potent factor in the generation of gas.

Roof conditions in the Welsh coal seams are such that plentiful and careful timbering is essential to avoid falls; but falls of roof and side continue to be the main cause of fatal accidents. The latest reports of the two mines inspectors whose divisions cover the South Wales coalfield show that the greater number of these fatal accidents occur within a narrow radius of the end of the heading driven up to the coal face; this is the spot where the roof is normally weakest and where the most rigid support is needed —and not provided. If we take a five-year comparison, the fatalities due to falls of roof and side in the Cardiff and Forest of Dean division show an increase relative to output; the figure for 1931 was 75 deaths, a reduction of just over 6 per cent. on the figure for 1927—but in this same period output fell by well over 20 per cent. With tight-packing of the waste behind the coal face (which used to be the rule at many of the biggest Welsh pits) the likelihood of falls would be greatly reduced, while the accumulation of gas and the initiation of gob fires would be prevented. These observations are made by Mr. Macleod Carey, the Cardiff and Forest of Dean divisional inspector, in his report for 1931; he adds, in connection with the support of the roof on main haulage roads, that "steel arched roadways can be made as safe as railway tunnels." Sir Henry Walker quotes this observation, and says:

If this be true, and I have no reason to doubt it, as steel arches were first introduced into the South Wales coalfield by the late Mr. W. W. Hood of the Glamorgan Collieries in 1890 or thereabouts, it is curious that any other form of support for roads is in use in that coalfield at the present day.[21]

"Curious" it certainly is, from the technical standpoint; the reverse of curious, considered as a natural accompaniment of capitalism in the coal industry.

But when the mines inspectors have done with their admirable technical expositions, what does it all amount to? What is the reality behind the "safety first" conferences, at which fine speeches and reports are made, the assembled colliery managers and officials applaud, and go their ways? That question was answered for me in the course of a recent underground tour of a Welsh colliery owned by one of the big combines. The old and experienced fireman who was my guide felt deeply on this very point; and what he said was very simple, namely, that while colliers were only paid for the coal that they won, and not a penny for timbering, there would be no lessening in accidents from falls. Pay men for timbering, and you won't get falls. Pay men a low "all-in" rate per ton, and they will naturally use all their time getting coal in order to earn more wages; they have themselves and their wives and families to keep, and so they just take the risk. At this particular colliery the colliers get 2s. 9d. a ton for coal; time spent on timbering is unpaid "deadwork."

Underground haulage accidents are also very frequent. Some remarks by Mr. Macleod Carey in his report for 1931 give an illuminating survey of the negligent fashion in which underground haulage is treated under the rule of the big monopolies. He writes:

> The practice in this coalfield is to drive the main roadways in one seam and to follow the undulations of that seam even when disturbances of considerable displacement intervene. . . . The accepted system of piecemeal repairs tends to aggravate rather than mitigate the evils. . . . The resultant roadways are a series of undulations and bends. It is not uncommon to have to cross a haulage rope thirty to forty times in a distance of 1,500 to 2,000 yards. . . . Uniform gradients would result in much less wear and tear on haulage plant. Overrunning of ropes with consequent breakages and derailments would be avoided; plucking and bumping through swamps would not occur; dangers of "rising shackles" would be reduced and dangerously rising ropes would be eliminated. All these are frequent causes of vexatious and costly delays and accidents; and all could be easily avoided.
> Generally, road-laying receives nothing like the attention it deserves. The frequency with which derailments occur affords ample evidence of this. Roads tend too often to become mere tracks, are costly in

maintenance and are the frequent cause of accidents. Defective tracks have been estimated to be responsible for nearly 12 per cent. of the total of haulage accidents. Multiplicity of "gadgets" is neither practicable nor desirable. A few well chosen, judiciously placed safety appliances, maintained in perfect working order and regularly operated, give greater security than the indiscriminate use of complicated appliances which are pe functorily maintained and which, in time, tend to become mere "eyewash."

So, as Sir Henry Walker comments on this passage of Mr. Carey's, it is clear "that the most elementary matters in connection with the making of haulage roads are very frequently neglected." Bad roadways are an important element in the hampering of ventilation; and the South Wales inspectors comment on the defective ventilation practice shown in over-lengthy and neglected airways, leakages from the intake to the return airway, and numerous other technical shortcomings. It is also pointed out that firemen have sometimes districts that are too large for effective supervision.[22]

A good picture of conditions in the pit which result in fatal accidents was given at an inquest a few months ago on a miner named Watts, killed by a runaway horse in Blaensychan Colliery, Monmouthshire. The following is quoted, without comment, from the report in the local newspaper:

Ernest Wilfred James, a haulier, said that he was driving a horse with two trams of coal, when he heard the noise of a horse running loose behind him. There was a crash, and when he went back he saw the leg of the runaway horse tight against his full tram. The front tram, to which the runaway was attached, was off the rails. Watts was crushed between the tram and the side. The accident took place forty yards from where he saw Watts working. At the point he passed Watts there were three or four feet spare. At the point of the accident there was about eight inches. The Coroner: Are they supposed to have manholes? Mr. T. Bassett (Inspector of Mines): Yes. Every twenty-five yards. The Coroner: Are there no manholes? James: No. The under-manager of the colliery, Mr. James Davies, stated that in most places on the road there was ample room. The Coroner: But if the journey ran wild there would still be danger. Godfrey Clark, haulier, said he was in charge of the horse which bolted. The horse was high-tempered. Clark said that the day following the accident the horse bolted again at the same spot. The Coroner: Don't you think the horse ought to be brought out? Mr. James Davies replied that the horse had been moved to another place. Trevor Hart, over-man, said there were no manholes at the point because of the extraordinary width of the road. It was an old double parting. The Coroner: There is no special refuge?—Only between the timbers.—You think that is sufficient?—Yes. The Coroner said that the Act did not mention width, but stated that manholes must be provided. Whatever the width of the road it does not take the place of a manhole.[23]

Miners toil to-day in South Wales in the face of increased danger and for miserable wages; and yet even such a simple aid to work and safety (to say nothing of a protection against the disabling and frightful nystagmus) as really efficient illumination is denied them by the lords of the combines. It is true that electric safety lamps are in general use; but these are the low candle-power type, and the high candle-power 4-volt lamp is employed in very few collieries. But even the use of electric lamps is frequently little help to the collier at the face; because of the danger of gas a flame safety lamp (giving a very poor light) is used there, and the collier's helper uses the electric lamp. The many devices for improving illumination, such as fixed electric lighting on main roadways and at double partings, pneumatic-electric flood-lights on conveyor-runs, and so on, are little used. The Swansea divisional mines inspector, Mr. Ashley, sets forth the position clearly in his latest report:

> Fixed electric lighting could be used more frequently than it is at pit bottoms and main double partings. . . . There are also several types of heavy semi-portable electric safety lamps in use at double partings, which might be used for face lighting. . . . The number of cap lamps in use has increased slightly; they could with advantage be supplied to all haulage hands. . . . Lighting underground would be considerably improved, where the conditions are dry, by the use of limewash. All pit bottoms, main junctions, double partings and roads supported by steel arches should be limewashed. At two mines where steel props are used in a number of stalls on longwall faces, all the props are limewashed, and the illumination of the face is thereby greatly improved. Limewash is used only to a very small extent on the roads in this division. A great deal more should be done in this respect; it not only greatly improves illumination, but also tends to avoid accumulations of coal dust. [24]

How does the standard of living of the employed miners compare with that of their unemployed brothers? From what has been said above it will be evident that in the steam coal valleys a miner working constant short time may be very little better off than an unemployed man. Let us, however, take the case of a miner in the anthracite coalfield, where output has actually increased in 1932 as compared with 1931, where the percentage of unemployment is relatively small, and where full time is worked. An anthracite collier, on piece rates, will earn from 10s. to 12s. a shift, sometimes more; his weekly wage runs from £3 to £4 a week. Housing and general living conditions, especially in the Amman valley, are the best in the South Wales coalfield. The anthracite is the one area where union organisation continues to be really strong; there is a traditional and powerful militancy general among the men; many pit strikes have taken place during 1932. The anthracite miners at the same time constitute a solid "national minority," at any rate in the cultural sense. Welsh and not English is the universal language of daily life. I recollect very vividly being invited to attend a meeting of the Gwaun-cae-Gurwen miners' lodge committee (this colliery, with its near 2,000 men employed in three pits, is the largest in the anthracite field); out of politeness to their guest the committee ceased conducting their proceedings in Welsh, and spoke in English; none the less, as the business went on they couldn't help relapsing here and there into Welsh.

Do not imagine that the anthracite miners are not engaged in a constant struggle to maintain their relatively good conditions. The number of pit strikes shows that. Monopoly developed to its full height in the anthracite earlier than elsewhere in the coal-field; and to-day the Amalgamated Anthracite Collieries Limited (the creation of the late Lord Melchett) has as nearly a complete monopoly as is to be found anywhere. Monopoly has meant the closing down of many pits and, as the anthracite miners expressively say, the "smothering" of small independent companies outside the Amalgamated. Mechanisation is being pushed ahead, and the usual process of speed-up and drive, of scamped repairing, of the cutting of costs by reducing the number of non-face workers (rippers, repairers, etc.) to face workers, is in full swing.

Here are two actual budgets of anthracite miners, one employed, the other unemployed. Both men live at Glyn-Neath, at the head of the Vale of Neath, on the border-line of the anthracite and steam coal areas. They are both married, and have each one child. The unemployed man has 25s. 3d. unemployment benefit; the employed man earns not more than £3, from which his average stoppages are something over 6s. The first difference between the two appears in their housing accommodation; rents are high at Glyn-Neath; and the unemployed man pays 9s. for two rooms, while his employed comrade pays 12s. 6d. for a four-roomed house. The dietary of the unemployed man and his family follows the lines that we have observed in the derelict areas; bread, butter, potatoes, bacon, tea, with minute quantities of meat, fresh milk (only one pint a week), vegetables, cheese and lard. There is nothing left for coal (which he picks from the tip), for clothes or for any of the minor necessities of life. The employed miner, with the same sized family, has 60 per cent. more bread, 30 per cent. more butter, twice as much milk, meat and vegetables, three times as much potatoes, six times as much cheese, twice as much lard, and in addition has fish, eggs, fruit, currants, rice, jam—which are unknown on the unemployed family's table. Small sums can be put by for clothes and foot-wear, coal is bought cheap from the colliery, and there is a little left over for such items as newspapers, a modest allowance of tobacco and such like small amenities.

On the straitness of the unemployed man's budget further comment is hardly necessary; what should be stressed here is that the employed miner is only able to spend on vital foodstuffs sums that by any proper standard are derisory. Thus the family considered above only spend 3s. a week on meat, 1s. on vege-tables (apart from potatoes), 1s. on fruit and 6d. on fresh milk (two pints). And the anthracite miners are the aristocrats of the Welsh mining valleys!

Among the big coalfields South Wales has been especially backward in the installation of pit-head baths; only a handful of these baths exist in the coalfield, mainly in Monmouthshire. So the Welsh miner, like his father and his grandfather, is con-demned to trudge home or crowd into the "workmen's car" on the tramway, covered in coal-dust, wearing his wet and filthy pit-clothes. When he arrives home he most likely has not got a bathroom, and has to wash in a tub in front of the kitchen fire. Next morning his pit clothes are stiff and uncomfortable after drying. The extra labour for the miner's wife that this barbarous business entails has often been the subject of bitter comment; especially if more than one man in the house is working in the pit, and on different shifts. I only wish to add that I saw some very fine, new pit-head baths in South Wales. They were at collieries in Abertillery—every one of which was closed down.

One fact directly connected with the conditions in the pits remains to be considered; and that is the long distances travelled by many men to and from the pit. This is a new development for South Wales, and is a product of the depression in the steam coal valleys. Men will travel from the upper end of the Rhondda or from Aberdare over to the anthracite pits at the head of the Vale of Neath; or they will journey across from Brynmawr to Ebbw Vale, or right down from the derelict upper end of the Western valleys of Monmouthshire across and up the Sirhowy valley to Tredegar. Journeys like this not only mean rail fares up to 6s. a week out of a meagre wage. They turn the miner's life into a dreary and unrelieved cycle of work, bed, work, as effectively as if he were working the terrible hours underground of a century ago. If you happen to stay in the Western valleys, at Abertillery for instance, and you wake at four a.m., you will hear the train going down the valley bearing miners to work at far distant pits; they will not return until the evening, to bath, eat and sleep ready to rise again in the small hours and once more entrain.

MONOPOLY IN METAL

The area of the South Wales coalfield is one of the most important metallurgical centres in the country; within a radius of some fifteen miles of Swansea there are to be found steel works with a capacity of one-seventh of the total steel output of Britain, and also the major part of the country's tinplate industry. Apart from this western area, which stretches from Port Talbot on the east to Llanelly on the west, there is a secondary steel and tin-plate area in the Monmouthshire valleys, leading down to Newport and Cardiff. As monopoly dominates the coalfield, so it dominates the metallurgical industries; and the growth of monopoly has been accompanied by the abandonment of the historic iron and steel working centres on the northern fringe of the coalfield. In our survey of the derelict areas we have noticed the closing down of the famous Dowlais steel works and what it has meant to the steel workers thrown out; the same process has operated at Tredegar, Ebbw Vale, and Blaenavon. Briefly, it may be said that the iron and steel industry, alike in the west and the east, is now concentrated at, or near, the coast; the surplus thousands of workers in the old inland centres have been left to rot.

One of the biggest steps in monopoly development was registered as late as 1930, when the heavy steel interests of the two great coal, iron, steel, by-product and miscellaneous metal manufacturing combines of Guest, Keen and Nettlefolds, and Baldwins, were combined in the British (Guest, Keen, Baldwins) Iron and Steel Company Limited. This new £5½ million concern formed a link, so far as South Wales went, between the huge Guest, Keen coal combine (Welsh Associated Collieries) and their sheet metal works (through the subsidiary firm of Lysaghts), and the light steel and tinplate interests of Baldwins. Altogether the link-up embraced some eighty firms, with an aggregate capital of nearly £60 million, a steel capacity of 3,000,000 tons, and a coal capacity of about 12,000,000 tons. The operations of the new combine are now concentrated in the big modern open-hearth steel works at Port Talbot, which obtains its pig-iron from the neighbouring (and associated) Margam Iron works, and its coal from the Cribbwr Fawr collieries, another associated concern, a few miles to the east along the southern limit of the coalfield.

D

There is a clear demarcation between heavy steel plants like the Port Talbot works, producing steel sections, slabs, plates, rails and so forth, and the steel works which concentrate exclusively on the manufacture of "tin bars," the mild but tough steel bar which forms the raw material of the tinplate industry. There are thirteen steel works of the latter type in the western area; they are owned by seven firms who in their turn operate some 80 per cent. of the tinplate and sheet works. Combination has thus reached a high level in steel and tinplate; outstanding is the Richard Thomas combine, owning five steel works and twenty-five tinplate and sheet works with an installation of 181 mills, plus a number of colliery companies. The Llanelly Steel Company own one steel works, 13 tinplate and sheet works (77 mills); Baldwins own two steel works, 8 tinplate works (56 mills); the Briton Ferry Steel Company own two steel works, 10 tinplate and sheet works (55 mills) and are linked with colliery concerns; while of slightly smaller range are Gilbertsons, at Pontardawe, the Upper Forest works, at Morriston, and the Bynea works, at Loughor.

Monopoly in the steel and tinplate industries has gone hand in hand with rationalisation in all its forms; mechanisation, speeding-up the work, and general short-time are features. The development of mechanisation was marked in the steel industry twenty years ago. Now magnetic cranes and chargers, powerful gantries and rollers, handle everything from the scrap and other material through the whole process of manufacture to the dispatch of the finished steel article. In the old days five smelters attended a 30-ton furnace; to-day three smelters attend an 80-ton furnace; all the mechanical aids have not lightened labour, for, as any Welsh smelter will tell you, the pace is much faster and the technical standards more exacting, while the raw material used is inferior. Instead of clean steel scrap any old junk is piled into the furnaces, to the extent of 70 per cent. of the charge.

In the Port Talbot works at the present time modern sloping linings have been installed in the furnaces; this saves both time and cost on furnace repair, and is both a measure of economy and an aid to the speeding-up of production. This will be an immense consolation to the smelters; they have for a long time past lost one week in four, and when I was in Port Talbot last October only three of the six furnaces were in, and the smelters were losing still more time than this. It should be noted that the smelters are not only the highest-paid workers in the steel industry, but they are usually fortunate in having some degree of work even when other departments of the works, such as the rolling and sheet mills, are closed down for long periods. The position of the labourers, who only earn 45*s.* for a *full* week, and of the semi-skilled machine-minders, gantry-hands, etc. (who work so irregularly that they are reputed to be lucky to make 30*s.* a week) is far worse.

A typical story of the policy of monopoly comes also from the Port Talbot works. When the Guest, Keen, Baldwins combine was formed their first move was to try to enforce on the Port Talbot men the North of England scale (steel workers are paid on tonnage rates adjusted according to a sliding scale). Hitherto the considerably higher South Wales Siemens steel scale, which covers the "tin-bar" works, had operated at Port Talbot; the combine's claim was that since Port Talbot was a heavy steel works it should be governed by a heavy steel, and not a "tin-bar" scale. This wage-cutting move was successfully resisted, but it is none the less characteristic.

This attitude of the combine to its workers contrasts with its solicitude for its managers and officials. The process of rationalisation means wholesale short-time and the concentration of production in the most modern and profitable works; the Guest, Keen works at East Moors, Cardiff, for instance, have been closed down; but the under-managers, sample-passers and other officials are being brought to Port Talbot to be carried on the overheads there. The already spacious building of the combine's general offices at Port Talbot, between the railway station and the works, has had a large new extension built in recent months to house these gentlemen.

Steel and tinplate workers are unemployed and under-employed to the extent of nearly half their total number; the January figures were 44.9 per cent. in steel and 40.7 per cent. in tinplate. But a considerable proportion of these high percentages are accounted for by organised short-time working; of the steel figure 20.1 per cent. are "temporary stoppages," and of the tinplate figure 26.7 per cent. This chronic under-employment shows very clearly how monopoly capitalism is a brake on the development of the productive forces; the productive capacity of the "tin-bar" steel works to-day is 30 per cent. more than before the war, but they never work near capacity; in tinplates output in 1929 was 7 per cent. higher than the peak pre-war production, but the industry was not employing more than 70 per cent. of its productive capacity.

In the summer of 1932 decline had proceeded so far that the tinplate industry in the west was only working to 45-50 per cent.

of capacity, and in the east to 60 per cent.; the long schemed-for
tariff on iron and steel imports aided the steel industry not one
jot—in the Monmouthshire valleys only one steel works, Panteg,
was working regularly, the big works at Pontymister, by Risca,
only working intermittently. And last October "tin-bar" steel
works were only working two days a week.

It will be noticed that in tinplate the percentage of those
"temporarily stopped" is particularly high; this is due to the
systematic sharing of work and the operation of the employers'
pooling scheme. The tinplate pool was first introduced to
replace a rough-and-ready output restriction scheme by which
every tinplate works was required to close down for at least
three weeks in every quarter. Under the pool each firm was
allocated a quota, with heavy penalties for producing in excess
of the quota, and compensation for producing less than the
quota. The big steel-cum-tinplate combines formed the core
of the pooling scheme; and while demand kept up, as in 1929-
30, the pool was able to maintain a high monopoly price. The
price of tinplate per box (a "box" weighs rather less than a
hundredweight) was actually slightly raised from 1928 to 1929.
And, at the same time, firms which found it more convenient
to close down their works in whole or in part were amply com-
pensated for doing so. But when demand fell the pool got into
difficulties; the attempt to maintain the high monopoly price
on a rapidly contracting market, when tinplate firms outside the
pool were selling at prices up to 30 per cent. a box less, broke
down; firms left the pool as they saw their orders taken from
them by independent price-cutters; and, amid a general revival
of the traditional "tooth and claw" tinplate price-cutting
competition, the pool collapsed. The workers, who had had
more unemployment and short-time as a result of the pool, now
had their wages cut by the operation of the sliding scale, reflecting the low level to which the renewed orgy of competition had
reduced tinplate prices. Latterly the pooling scheme has been
revived.

The manufacture of steel and tinplate are alike dangerous and
exhausting trades. The work, as one Llanelly millman said to
me, is "very aggravating." It certainly is, whether it is the
labour of the steel smelter, pouring with sweat as he tends the
white-hot furnace, dazzling with the glare of the molten steel—
or the toil of the girl plate-opener, opening bundles of sharp-
edged tin plates or "pickling" them in an acid bath. The heat,
the noise, the pace and the constant risk of serious accident make a
modern Welsh steel or tinplate works a place where a six-hour

shift, not the present eight, would be ample—and at wages far above the present level.

When they leave the furnace or the mill to what kind of homes do these steel and tinplate workers go? An indication of the answer is afforded by the statement that such centres as Port Talbot, Swansea and Llanelly are among the early areas of capitalist development in South Wales; and housing conditions therefore approximate to those in Merthyr, Dowlais and the other derelict old areas on the northern fringe. Swansea may be taken as the largest and most typical centre. In all South Wales I know few more depressing sights than the industrial area of Swansea, running up the Swansea valley from the city proper through the suburbs (the neat and prim name is misleading) of Landore, Morriston and Llansamlet. Steel and tinplate works of the Richard Thomas combine, of Baldwins, and of the Upper Forest concern are scattered here and there, bristling with .chimney stacks; and at the same time the valley bed is a chaos of derelict and abandoned spelter, copper and other metal works and their hill-high slag tips. The Morfa Copper works at Landore (owned by the Imperial Chemical Industries mammoth) is all that is left of the once-thriving and world-famous Swansea copper industry; but the ruins of that industry are everywhere. Battered remains of what were once busy works litter the area; one crumbling wreck proclaims to an indifferent world, in ancient letters that once were white on its stack and roof, that it is "TO LET."

In and among this decaying and dilapidated wreckage of industries from which the Mond, Baldwin and other families extracted great fortunes, run the squalid and gloomy working-class streets. If you approach Swansea from the east along the main road, coming through Llansamlet, turning left at Morriston and continuing straight down through Landore, you pass along a main street of shabby and poor shops, obviously old structures, interspersed with small houses of equal age and gloom; to your left and right, down and up the hill respectively, stretch streets of similar houses. It is not surprising to learn from Dr. Evans, the Swansea medical officer of health, that 35 per cent. of the pre-war working-class houses in the town are fifty to a hundred years old, while 15 per cent. are aged seventy-five to a hundred years and over.[25] The same authority pronounces all the pre-war types of working-class house in Swansea "unsatisfactory in one respect or another"; he particularly notes the existence of dark back kitchens and he observes that where there are gardens these are mostly uncultivated. Summing up the state of housing, he says that "the prevailing defects are decrepitude, dis-repair, lack of damp-proof courses, smallness of rooms, low bedrooms, small windows, narrow staircases and lack of amenities." Large numbers of the applicants for Swansea corporation houses were living in seriously overcrowded conditions, many in rooms. On this Dr. Evans comments:

> The houses that are sublet for this purpose are without separate family amenities, there is no separate and proper accommodation for cooking, for storage of food, for washing, or separate closet accommodation—*and yet*—it was estimated that half the applicants for Corporation houses would be unable to pay the rent of a post-war Corporation house. [26]

Under these conditions it is no surprise that the infantile mortality rate in Swansea in 1930 ranged in the working-class wards far above the city's average of 63; thus in the Landore ward the rate was 86, in Llansamlet 82, and in Morriston 83. These rates are in strong contrast with the rate of 47 in the holiday neighbourhood of Oystermouth, or 44 in the middle-class suburb of Sketty, high up to the westward of Town Hill, well away from the industrial area. [27]

If steel workers have been able to get into the better conditions of Council houses, they now find the burden more than they can bear. Here is an instructive report of a deputation from the Council Tenants' Association in Panteg, a Monmouthshire steel town, which recently besought the local Council to reduce their rents:

> The deputation said there had been a general reduction in wages, and one member of the deputation declared that some of the conditions in which the people were trying to live in Panteg were "heart-rending." Mr. S. Wilkie (Chairman of the Tenants' Association) said that as work was so bad and wages down so much, they had decided to approach the Council. There were in Panteg 250 workless people, 600 on short time, 50 unable to get benefit and 50 uninsurable, making a total of 950. Mr. George Woodley reminded the deputation that the Council had to borrow money when the houses were built. Mr. Wilkie: Our case is bread and butter or arrears or lower rents. [28]

After being thus bluntly told that the interest of the loan capitalists had to come first, the Panteg steel workers could hardly have been surprised to learn that a reduction which was granted a year previously was the limit to which the Council could go. From which, no doubt, they will draw their own conclusions.

THE TRANSPORT SYSTEM

Anyone who has had occasion to travel from place to place in South Wales will be acutely aware of the importance of transport in a country of such pronounced geographical peculiarities. These peculiarities governed the industrial and social development; industry and population concentrated along the valley beds, running roughly in a north to south direction and separated by mountain ridges. The development of the lines of communication followed the same general direction. Capitalism was not interested in a general opening-up of the country, but in getting the coal from pit to port and in ensuring that labour could move easily from outside up the valleys. West to east communication was only developed at one or two points (for instance, the Rhondda and Swansea Bay railway) and the valleys remained largely isolated from one another until the last decade. We have seen how the availability of a large, skilled labour force, in the shape of unemployed miners, enabled the whole road system of South Wales to be reconstructed, and new trunk roads built across the mountains, during recent years.

The new roads, coupled with the development of bus services, have revolutionised daily life in the valleys (when you can afford to pay the fare).* Some idea of this development is given in the fact that between 1923 and 1930 the number of tram and bus workers in Wales increased by over 73 per cent., and the number of other road transport workers increased by nearly 96 per cent.; in both cases the increase was far in excess of the average increase in the numbers of these workers in the whole of Britain over this period.[29]

Monopoly has developed in passenger road transport in South Wales no less than in the basic industries. The largest concern is the Western Welsh Omnibus Company Limited, controlled jointly by the Great Western Railway and a group who started in a small way in 1920 and by the absorption of Monmouthshire bus companies had established themselves in a leading position when the railway company stepped in. Western Welsh has a fleet of 300 vehicles, and its routes cover the whole of South Wales; it works in co-operation with the two other large concerns, the South Wales Transport Company (160 vehicles) and the Red and White Services (250 vehicles), the latter controlling some fifteen smaller companies. The expansion which has gone on in recent years can be seen from the figures of Western Welsh;

* The growth of monopoly in passenger road transport in South Wales has resulted in the level of fares being kept particularly high. These arbitrarily maintained monopoly fares are a serious hardship for workers who wish to travel. Anyone who journeys much by bus in South Wales, and then (say) in Lancashire, where even the inter-urban traffic is largely in the hands of municipal bus and tram undertakings, will be struck by the wide difference in fares for similar distances.

between 1928 and 1931 this concern nearly quadrupled the
number of passengers it carried and the total mileage run, and
increased its receipts nearly three and a half times; but its staff
increased less than three times, which is some indication of
growing intensification of labour.

Reliable information as to the wages and conditions of workers
for these bus companies is not easily available. It is generally
known, of course, that they are bad; and it is said that, in many
of the smaller local concerns, men have to pay a premium to
secure employment at preposterous wages and work all hours.
It is certainly noticeable that conductors on the local buses are
usually young fellows (sometimes girls), and in the conditions
of unemployment prevailing in the mining valleys it may be
conceived how acute is the competition to secure these jobs, and
how low the wages are consequently driven. In this connection
it may be worth noting that, even on Corporation transport
services in South Wales, conditions are poor. On the Newport
tram and bus services, for instance, drivers only earn £2 14s. 1d.
(after stoppages), conductors from 30s. to £2 13s. (less stoppages);
recently the management wished the men to "share work" and
stand off in turn, which the men claimed would mean a wage-
cut of 3s. a week.[30]

While the Great Western Railway is able to skim the cream off
the road passenger traffic, through its control of Western Welsh
omnibuses, it has been carrying through a ruthless drive against
the railwaymen in South Wales. The long depression in the
coalfields has naturally meant a heavy reduction in the main
freight carried in the area; and the number of insured railwaymen unemployed in South Wales rose by more than three times
between 1923 and 1930. All over the area to-day you may read
railway posters announcing the closing of this or that branch line
for passenger traffic or the closing of this or that station. Men are
constantly being de-graded and transferred. Last August 330
engine-drivers were pensioned off before their retiring age—
long-service men who at the most would receive little more than
30s. a week, and at the least less than £1. The de-grading
process, and the system of transfer, was well illustrated by a
delegate to the South Wales and Monmouthshire District
Council of the National Union of Railwaymen; he said:

> I have had fifteen different shifts to different parts of South Wales.
> In some cases I have been able to travel night and morning from and
> to my home, but in other cases I have had to get lodgings and keep
> two homes going. During this period I have been reduced in grade,
> resulting in a loss of 15s. a week in wages.[31]

The Great Western Railway has not only the rail monopoly of South Wales (apart from one or two London, Midland and Scottish branch lines); it is also the owner of the principal docks, which are, of course, mainly coal-exporting docks. The effect of the decline in exports on dock-workers' wages can be seen from the statement by a union official that Cardiff coal-trimmers (who pool their earnings and share out from the pool) were, last summer and autumn, only averaging 10s. to £1 in weekly wages.[32]

To visit a South Wales coal dock nowadays is an illuminating experience. One day last autumn I made a complete circuit of the modern and well laid out coal staiths at Newport; of the twenty giant tips only one had a vessel under it. My experience was not unique by any means: for shortly after Armistice Day a local authority wrote: "There could have been no more suitable day than last Friday for the 'two minutes' silence.' Not a coal tip was working—surely a state of affairs which has not before happened at Newport Docks upon a normal working day! Furthermore, only one small coaster was loaded on Friday night and Saturday morning respectively."[33]

Housing and Health: "The Most Sensitive Index of Social Welfare"

We have now surveyed the growing mass of poverty in the Welsh valleys, the wretchedness and social stultification of the derelict areas, and the way in which overcrowding, arising directly from the need to economise on rent, has nullified the comparatively tolerable housing conditions that existed in some of the newer mining areas. It remains to make here a general summary of housing and health conditions, with special reference to the steep downward movement that has been the result of the world crisis.

With regard to housing in South Wales such an authority as Mr. E. A. Charles, the secretary of the Welsh Housing and Development Association, wrote in 1930 that "the conditions were bad twenty years ago; to-day they are far worse. Areas that in the earlier period were described as slums, in many instances have been worsened by the hand of time"; and two years later he declared that "in the districts where the need for better housing is greatest but little has been done to meet such needs."[34] In 1931 there were only 3,008 houses built in the whole of Wales and Monmouthshire, a steady decline from the figure of 10,851 in 1927.

Dr. Rocyn Jones, the Monmouthshire medical officer of health, gives a summary of housing conditions in his county which might well apply to the whole of South Wales. After observing that "there are no special difficulties in providing suitable building sites" he remarks in his latest report:

> In the thickly populated areas of the County the housing question cannot be regarded as settled . . . there is still a shortage of houses for the working classes. In some of the areas serious overcrowding is still prevalent, and this becomes more acute each year. . . . It is evident that this state of affairs is not conducive to good health or decent morals. At many of the older houses, where the accommodation is limited, it is quite common to find two families living in the same house. Parents and children, some of whom have reached puberty, are compelled to sleep in the same bedroom, whilst it is not uncommon for members of both sexes of advanced ages to use a common sleeping-room. These houses have, in addition, none of the advantages that tend to promote a healthy life, as most of the household washing, cooking, etc., have to be carried out in the one living room, which is often the only room on the ground floor. Many of these older type of houses are in a condition only fit for demolition, but it is unfortunate that most of these houses are to be found in the areas where the industrial depression has been most keenly felt and the tenants, in most cases, are not in a position to avail themselves of better housing accommodation, even when provided. The houses erected by the Local Authority under the Housing Acts, have been designed for occupation by one family only, and are not in any way suitable for dual occupation. It is regretted that a number of these houses are now occupied by more than one family . . . as there is the danger that the houses so occupied will soon become little more than slum property.[35]

The nature of the overcrowding shows that the problem is not at all only one of house shortage; inability to pay high rents is the cause of the co-existence of overcrowding and vacant houses, while in Newport Dr. Howard Jones points out that overcrowding is due to "high rents and small incomes of a considerable proportion of the wage-earners, due chiefly to lack of employment."[36] It was recently stated in a debate on Newport Town Council that "people in Newport were going without food and clothes to try to pay the rent"; and a councillor said that "he knew of a house in Canal-parade which for the last fifty years had been let at 9s. a week. It had been recently bought, and a rent of 15s. a week was now being charged. In some instances £1 or 30s. was being charged for two or three rooms."[37]

Newport affords an excellent instance of the relationship between housing and general social conditions, and health; the following table sets out certain statistics for 1931 for two Newport wards, the one working-class (Tredegar) and the other "residential" (Maindee). They need no comment:

Ward	Persons per house	Density of population per acre	MORTALITY RATES Infantile	Infectious diseases	T.B. (lungs)
TREDEGAR	6.36	90.14	106.1	3.370	1.545
MAINDEE	4.14	27.46	63.2	2.000	0.933

Between 1930 and 1931 the tuberculosis death-rate in the Tredegar ward shows a nearly four-fold increase, while in Maindee it shows a decrease. And we may remark here the rise in the maternal mortality rate in Newport, which in 1931 stood at the extremely high figure of 7.25, compared with a previous five-yearly average of 4.81; the medical officer of health observes that "deplorable conditions of overcrowding still exist in a considerable number of houses in which births occur."[38]

It would be possible to adduce much further evidence on the lines of the Newport example given above to show the wide discrepancy between working-class and middle-class areas in regard to the infantile mortality rate, that "most sensitive index we possess of social welfare and of sanitary administration, especially under urban conditions." For instance, in Glamorgan the rate in 1931 was seventy-seven for the whole County; but for the urban districts it was eighty, while for residential districts such as Cardiff Rural and Porthcawl it was as low as forty-four and fifteen respectively. The significant new fact, however, is the general rise in the infantile mortality rate over the latest two recorded years, which shows in graphic form the effect on health of the crisis and the accompanying driving down of the workers' standards. This is demonstrated in the tables below, compiled from the reports of the local medical officers of health:

INFANTILE MORTALITY RATES

County Boroughs	1930	1931	Glamorgan	1930	1931
Cardiff	72	77	County	69	77
Newport	55	79	Urban Districts	70	80
Swansea	63	69	Monmouth		
Merthyr Tydfil	91	105	County	65	72
Carmarthen			Urban Districts	65	76
County	73	78			
Urban Districts	55	66			

INFANTILE MORTALITY RATES IN INDIVIDUAL MINING AND METALLURGICAL
CENTRES

Urban Districts (Glam.)		1930	1931	Urban Districts (Mon.)		1930	1931
Gelligaer..	..	63	104	Rhymney	..	66	100
Neath ..	..	53	90	Tredegar	..	64	95
Aberdare	..	69	87	Ebbw Vale	..	80	92
Caerphilly	..	72	85	Blaenavon	..	67	90
Bridgend..	..	21	82	Bedwellty	..	79	83
Port Talbot	..	68	81	Abertillery	..	57	70
Glyncorrwg	..	58	79	Nantyglo & Blaina		57	64
Pontypridd	..	67	75	Risca ..	..	37	59
Mountain Ash	..	70	73	Urban Districts (Carmarthen)			
Maesteg	..	65	68	Llanelly ..	..	47	74
Rural Districts (Glam.)				Ammanford	..	19	43
Llantrisant & Llant-				Breconshire			
wit Fardre	..	63	86	Brynmawr Urban		83	88
Pontardawe	..	64	72	Ystradgynlais Rural		82	88

It is significant to notice that the Newport rate not only shows a
big increase over 1930, but also over the two previous five-yearly
periods, in which it averaged respectively seventy-five and sixty-
five. With the one exception of diarrhœal diseases all other causes
of infant death in Newport show an increase in 1931 over the
average of the five-yearly period 1926-30. The category of
"wasting diseases and prematurity," for example (a sure index
of under-nourishment and lowered tone of the mothers) has risen
in rate from twenty-three to thirty-four.[39]

The grave effects of prolonged trade depression on the health
of the working class have been noted by Dr. Picken, the Cardiff
medical officer of health; in this connection he was already
writing in 1930 that "in recent years there has been a definite
rise in the prevalence of diphtheria and scarlet fever." Dr.
Evans, in his report as school medical officer for Swansea, stresses
also the rising diphtheria incidence; he had 300 cases in 1931,
compared with an annual average of 229 in the five-year period
1926-30. Dr. Picken further points to "the greater proportion of
children found at routine school medical inspections to be suffering from some physical disease or defect [the incidence in Cardiff
rose from an average of 14 per cent. in the five years 1925-29
to 19 per cent. in 1931], and to the increase in disease and
abnormality among expectant, parturient and nursing mothers."
He gives the view that this "may be the first signs of the influence
on health of these bad times," and opines that the public health

services "could do little more than apply an ineffective brake to the downward progress of the health of the people if it once started along the road of poverty."[40] Our survey has shown that there is no "if" about the road of poverty, and the long distance the workers of South Wales have travelled along it.

Not only is the proportion of school children found requiring treatment for various diseases and defects high, and rising (it is as much as 29 per cent. in Swansea), but the health arrangements at the schools leave much to be desired. Dr. Colston Williams, in his report for 1931 as Glamorgan school medical officer, states that "the oldest schools are hygienically unsatisfactory . . . no amount of patchings can ever make good. . . . In very few schools are there adequate arrangements for drying clothes and boots"; there are no arrangements for complete privacy in conducting medical inspections; there is no open-air education in the full sense of the term, though hundreds of children would benefit by it (the Monmouthshire school medical officer plainly states that it is financial considerations that check the much needed development of open-air schools in that County); the closing of one colliery at Maesteg, which entailed the cessation of water supply to a swimming bath, debarred children from ten schools from continuing their swimming; lack of suitable pitches and facilities for work in wet weather seriously hamper organised games.[41] And the results of all this? Typical is the table given by the late Dr. Burpitt in his report for 1931 as Newport school medical officer; from this we see that at age fourteen boys at the High School were on the average nearly two inches higher and over five pounds heavier than their mates of the same age at the elementary schools; at the same age girls at the Municipal Secondary School were over four inches higher and no less than twenty-one pounds heavier than girls at the elementary schools.[42]

It is from Newport, too, that we may take a final and revealing comment. Dr. Andrewina Laird, who is in charge of maternity and child welfare, reports that:

It has been noted lately that the mothers are much worse shod and clothed than formerly, and I am afraid in a number of cases the level of cleanliness is not so high as in late years. Continued out-of-work conditions no doubt have contributed to this, and the mothers have become disheartened and more careless. During the year several of the new cases of rickets have been breast-fed babies, probably due to a deficiency in the diet of the expectant mother. Many of the older mothers are showing less good physique and nourishment. With the lower wages and "dole" incomes the mother denies herself to give adequate nourishment to the husband and children.[43]

And a grimmer revelation is made by Dr. Mary Scott, one of the assistant medical officers in Monmouthshire, who says:

> The disease of rickets seems to be on the increase and shows itself in milder forms even where the child's diet has been correct. *It would almost seem that the prolonged industrial depression in these parts is having its effect in some way on the mothers, and the possibility is that the disease has started in the child before birth.* Where there is wrong feeding and over-crowding the disease in toddlers manifests itself in gross deformities.**
> [My italics.]

Dr. Scott's area covers Pengam, one of the centres of the Powell Duffryn combine; such is the fate to which the rule of the lords of "Poverty and Dole" condemns the mothers and little children of the working class.

How the Working Class is Reacting

What is the mood and outlook of the workers in the valleys to-day; how is the relationship between the two opposing class forces expressing itself in terms of political development? Throughout our survey we have sought to show the inter-connection of monopoly, the centralisation of capital in ever-fewer hands, and the never-ending sweep of mass impoverishment; and we may sum up with Marx's famous passage at the end of the first volume of *Capital*:

> Hand in hand with this centralisation, or this expropriation of many capitalists by few, develop, on an ever-extending scale, the co-operative form of the labour-process, the conscious technical application of science . . . the transformation of the instruments of labour into instruments of labour only usable in common, the economising of all means of production by their use as the means of production of combined, socialised labour, the entanglement of all peoples in the net of the world-market, and with this, the international character of the capitalistic regime. Along with the constantly diminishing number of the magnates of capital, who usurp and monopolise all advantages of this process of transformation, grows the mass of misery, oppression, slavery, degradation, exploitation; but with this, too, grows the revolt of the working-class, a class . . . disciplined, united, organised by the very mechanism of the process of capitalist production itself. The monopoly of capital becomes a fetter upon the mode of production, which has sprung up and flourished along with, and under it. Centralisation of the means of production and socialisation of labour at last reach a point where they become incompatible with their capitalist integument. This integument is burst asunder. The knell of capitalist private property sounds. The expropriators are expropriated.

One of the obstacles confronting the revolt of the workers in South Wales is precisely that degradation of which Marx spoke as an accompaniment of the growth of impoverishment under monopoly. A member of a recent deputation to the Tredegar Urban District Council on behalf of the local unemployed made an appeal for the single men: he said "they were in a difficult position and conditions were becoming intolerable . . . Some of these men had never done any work at all. Their outlook was absolutely stunted, and they were rapidly deteriorating in all senses."[45] Engels tells how capitalism, in its early and expanding days a century and more ago, kept "the education and morals of the mining population . . . on an excessively low plane"; and now capitalism in decay is responsible for the crime of spreading demoralisation among its victims, as an essential part of its whole effort to maintain its power.

That demoralisation takes many forms, and varies in degree. In those townships where all the pits are closed down, where perhaps the majority of the miners have been without work for years on end, a feeling is engendered that there will never be work any more. There seems to be no prospect for the future. Men will tell you that "the mining industry's finished here"; they say it with an air of finality and not meaning that mining is only "finished" under the present system of social relationships. This outlook is one that is widely fostered by the spokesmen of reformism, and it inevitably encourages moods of hopelessness among certain sections of the workers. Most notably in the derelict areas the pulse of social and cultural life is slowed. Apart from the fight for coal on the tip there seems little to do but play billiards or cards (sometimes for very tiny stakes) or put a few pence on a horse, or once a week spend threepence on the cinema and escape into a world of fantasy.

It is necessary to spend some time in the townships of the Welsh valleys to realise what the mental torture of prolonged unemployment means to active men. The boredom of life becomes insupportable. While the Llewellyns, the Evan Williams, the Beynons, the Aberconways and their like have been building their huge monopolies, the human victims of this process of capital concentration, and of capitalist decline and crisis, are flung on the scrap heap in their scores of thousands to rot. No one can contemplate this spectacle in South Wales to-day without being consumed by a fierce hatred for the social order and its ruling class, which commits such crimes against humanity; for the workers who are suffering in this way are those who were the cream of the working-class in South Wales—the most advanced, most militant, most conscious workers.

The essence of this process of demoralisation lies in its distraction of attention from the class struggle, from the economic and political·fight of the workers. From this point of view the efforts made by the churches, the Quakers, the "social service" ladies and gentlemen and other charity-mongers in South Wales, avowedly to combat demoralisation, are in fact affording it the widest encouragement. To Brynmawr reference has been earlier made; but all over South Wales there are similar efforts, which particularly disorganise and hold back the unemployed lads. Such are the opening of church halls as gymnasia, the building of playing fields by voluntary labour, and so forth. The point has been put bluntly in connection with the provision of wireless receiving sets through the National Council of Social Service for the unemployed in the institutes. This, it is said, gives the men "recreation and new mental stimulus," and leads them *"to take an interest in subjects outside the daily routine of life"* (my italics)— to elevate their eyes, in other words, to the mirage of "pie in the sky" so that they can "forget" their empty bellies here below.

Monopoly capitalism, as it is seen in operation in South Wales, is not only a brake on the development of the forces of production. It is also a brake on the development of culture; indeed, it is driving culture downhill, is stultifying the cultural and intellectual growth of a whole working population. This appears the more strikingly in contrast with the extremely high cultural level which the workers in South Wales, and notably the miners, have won for themselves through generations of effort. One example must suffice—the Workmen's Halls and Institutes which are to be found in every mining township. These institutions (to which the coalowners have to contribute under the welfare scheme—when the pits are working) have halls for cinemas and dances, games rooms, reading rooms, lecture rooms and libraries. These libraries and reading rooms have been in fact the public libraries of the valleys; and many of them in the past have built up collections of books which in their scope, especially as regards subjects like history, political economy, and social and political questions in general, have been far above normal public library standard. But to-day these Institutes have a desperate struggle to keep their doors open and to save themselves from drowning in a sea of debt. The purchase of new books is an impossibility. Subscriptions to newspapers and periodicals have to be cut down ruthlessly. To-day you may go into Institutes in the Rhondda, for example, and find that they have not been able to buy any new books for several years; while in the reading room only a handful of the newspaper and periodical stands, out of perhaps two·score or more, now have publications upon them. At the same time it is not possible for the Institutes to maintain their buildings in the spick and span state that is needful for such social and cultural centres. New Institutes are naturally fresh-painted and bright (like the spacious new establishments at Gwaun-cae-Gurwen and Pyle), but old Institutes desperately need a thorough spring-clean and several new coats of paint to banish the air of gloom and deterioration (one notices this in the fine building of the Workmen's Hall at Mardy).

But capitalism cannot smother the efforts of the working-class to acquire culture. Many workers are seeking an answer to the problems of society, which are their own life-and-death problems. Mr. John Warner, the Chief Librarian of Newport, has declared that the period of the crisis has brought increased circulation to the lending libraries of that city, and he expected that the 1932 figure for books circulated would break all records at half a million books. Mr. Warner says that while the racing news page in the newspapers is always well-thumbed, "fifty per cent. of the working class of Newport who are unemployed read economics only. Manual workers browse on economics." He adds that while in 1931 forty-two per cent. of the books issued were fiction "a lot of that is first-class literature and classic fiction."[47] Certainly, the unemployed workers who flock to the public libraries like this will not be given Socialist, Marxist political economy to study; they will not be likely to find available revolutionary works—works which will really provide the answers to the questions which, maybe often only in a half-formed state, are stirring in their minds. None the less, the trend revealed in Newport is highly significant.

In South Wales the influence of reformism is stronger than anywhere else in the country. It is sufficient to recall the fact that not only was South Wales the one region to withstand the "National" landslide in the general election of 1931, but the Labour Party's vote actually increased. The significance of this lies in the special character of reformism in the Welsh valleys; and this special character is expressed most clearly in the leadership of the South Wales Miners' Federation. The older leaders of the Federation are the men who, a score of years ago, led the pre-war unofficial reform movement in the Federation—the stormy, Syndicalist movement whose faith was proclaimed in the famous pamphlet *The Miners' Next Step*. The younger leaders are those who for the most part passed through the school of the Labour College, and absorbed the barren, academic and opportunist dogmas which that institution palmed off as "Marxism." These leaders have shown in practice that they can offer the

E

miners nothing but further defeats, the acceptance of worse and still worse conditions at the hands of the coal monopolists whose allies they in fact are.   No one can under-estimate the effect of the defeats of 1921 and 1926 in shattering the miners' forces.   These leaders not only did nothing to try and rebuild the miners' fighting front, to infuse new hope and a new prospect of advance; they spread despair and the spirit of defeat, they helped the poison of demoralisation to do its work by the incessant propagation of the slander that the workers were "apathetic." With regard to the hours spread-over in December 1930, the January strike in 1931, the Schiller wage-cut award in March of the same year, the seven-hour day crisis in the summer of 1931 and again in 1932—on all these vital issues the leadership held the miners back from action, or brought action to nought once it had been begun.   At pits all over the coalfield they negotiated wage-reductions, unfavourable new price lists.   Militancy has been violently repressed (as in the expulsion of the Mardy lodge).

These leaders have played an essential part in bringing the miners down to the position which has been described in this chapter.   This is an inevitable result of their policy of co-operating with the coal monopolists in the work of capitalist rationalisation. Their policy is identical with that enunciated by Mr. Ebby Edwards, the national secretary of the Miners' Federation, in a recent speech whose whole theme was that it was possible to revive the coal trade under capitalism—as direct a flying in the face of every ascertainable fact as it is possible to imagine.   Mr. Edwards said:

> The coal trade is in very great difficulties and if I may say so, considering all departments of the trade, I am afraid the ship is without a captain. Yet the compass seems to be directed on a course that, with unity of purpose by all engaged in the industry, will bring the ship back to harbour and the passengers to safety. Internal war between employers and men can never solve the problems facing the industry. The problem the coal trade is facing to-day is the securing of a demand for coal at an economic price. [48]

That statement might have been made by Sir D. R. Llewellyn, Mr. Evan Williams, or any Welsh coalowner.*

In view of this it is not surprising that among the mass of the miners the once-mighty Federation is but a shadow of its old

* Here is a characteristic example of the depths of contemptible bankruptcy to which the policy of the S.W.M.F. leaders has sunk: in the early days of last December they circulated an appeal "to the generous British public" asking for money donations and gifts of clothing for the impoverished Welsh miners, whose terrible conditions they

self. The anthracite miners are alone in maintaining a strong union organisation, due partly to their different conditions, and partly to the greater organised strength and influence of rank-and-file militancy. In the Rhondda less than 20 per cent. of the miners, employed and unemployed, are organised. Yet even in areas where organisation has thus fallen away, the part played by the miners' lodge in the political and social life of the mining township is of considerable importance. The lodge is the backbone of the local Trades Council and Labour Party, and it plays a leading part in the Workmen's Hall or Welfare Institute.

And what of the Labour Party which dominates the principal local government bodies in the South Wales coalfield? During the past year it has pursued the policy of the "humane administration" of the Means Test. It is undeniable that in Glamorgan and Monmouthshire in general the Means Test has been less harshly administered than in the country at large. But to what end? The Labour Party no doubt retained prestige because it was able, for a time, to lighten the burden of the Means Test by strictly constitutional administrative methods; incidentally it helped to foster illusions that there was no need for the workers to fight against the Means Test, and thus assisted in keeping the unemployed passive. When the inevitable happened, and the Ministry of Health demanded that the Test be administered with the full brutality required by the "National" Government, the Labour Party's house of cards collapsed; they would have to administer the Test as required by the Government (in which case the shreds of "humanity" would be swept away and the Labour Party would follow); they dare not rally the workers to fight against the Means Test (which means hastening the development of the revolutionary spirit and movement). Typical of the whole line of the Labour Party was a recommendation made to a conference of representatives of Trades Councils and Labour Parties, and Labour members of Public Assistance Committees, which met in Cardiff last October to discuss this question. The recommendation was to the effect that if official pressure were yielded to in certain cases it should only be done in such a way as to protect the interests of the mass of those receiving public assistance; without concerning ourselves about the practicability of the involved manœuvres implied here, it may be noted

graphically portrayed; but on December 20th, meeting the coalowners in the joint disputes committee of the South Wales Conciliation Board, they agreed that all questions of wages and conditions should remain as they are until some time in 1934, "at the earliest." They help to perpetuate poverty, after begging for charity to relieve it!

that the whole case rests on the hollow and cynical assumption that by flinging some workers to the "National" Government's wolves their hunger can be appeased.

It is very noticeable in the Welsh mining valleys to-day that a real barrier exists between the employed and the unemployed. There are many reasons for this. Victimisation has weeded the majority of the most militant miners out of the pits, and the coal monopolists have certainly not been backward in selecting for employment those men whom they think least likely to show fight. The prolonged unemployment means that men will often stick at a job under conditions that once would not have been tolerated ("any job's better than the 'dole' "). But the existence of this barrier, which is of the first importance to the lords of the great combines, is objectively encouraged by the attitude of some of the most militant unemployed miners. This attitude may almost be described as treating the men still employed as if they were strike-breakers; because they are more backward, and because fear of victimisation makes them nervous of public association with the militants, they are dismissed as "spineless." It is not necessary to conduct a long argument to show that such an attitude is fatal: that its assumptions are groundless the facts cited below prove.

Revolt is growing among the miners. During the past year there has been an exceptional crop of pit strikes and struggles. Apart from the anthracite collieries, where the fighting spirit and organisation of the miners is at its highest point in South Wales (Cwmllynfell, Gwaun-cae-Gurwen and Gelliceidrim strikes), there have been strikes and disputes in the Rhondda (Tylorstown), in the Afan valley, at Ogmore and Bedwas. The anthracite miners are notably demonstrating the power of the "combine committee," the rank-and-file committee representing the miners at a group of associated pits, to enforce the men's demands. At a special conference of the South Wales Miners' Federation last November the delegates rejected the "re-organisation" scheme prepared by the Executive, with the aim of strengthening their own power at the expense of that of such bodies as the combine committees.

In every pit there is a surging under-current of discontent which only requires to be harnessed and given expression and leadership. Sir John Beynon, the chairman of the Ebbw Vale combine, said to his shareholders at their last annual meeting, "as regards wages being too high, I can only assure you that if you attempted to interfere with the South Wales agreement you would have the whole of the South Wales collieries on strike . . .

The men think they are too low as it is."[49] This is not to be interpreted as meaning that the coalowners will not "interfere with the agreement" and make a general attack on wages and conditions when they think fit, but it is of interest as an admission by a leading coal monopolist of the spirit of the miners.

The rising tide of militancy on every side is clear for all to see. Over seventy branches of the British Iron, Steel and Kindred Trades Association in South Wales have given their support to the unofficial militant movement which has developed, mainly in the West Wales tinplate area: the movement was strong enough to force the reinstatement of three of its leading members, whom the Executive of B.I.S.A.K.T.A. had expelled for their militant activities. The response to the campaign for solidarity with the Lancashire weavers during their great strike in August and September last far exceeded every expectation ; in a very short time over £150 was collected by the Workers' International Relief and ten and a half tons of food despatched by lorry in addition. Petitions against the Means Test have been signed in scores of thousands. There have been bitter eviction fights, as at Mardy, which resulted in the notorious trial for "riotous assembly" and the jailing of Arthur Horner and his comrades. The wave of sympathy for the Soviet Union is attested by such facts as the combining of twenty anthracite miners' lodges to send a delegate to Moscow for the fifteenth anniversary of the revolution last November. The local elections in March, 1932, showed a significant growth in the Communist vote in important areas like the Rhondda and Maesteg: in the first it rose from 3,048 (six wards) to 4,465 (seven wards) and in the second from 666 (one ward) to 1,559 (three wards) compared with the Labour Party's 2,413.

The unemployed are battling with new spirit for their urgent everyday demands, and are finding in struggle the antidote to the creeping canker of demoralisation. In Brynmawr, most derelict of all derelict areas, a militant united front movement has been developed among the unemployed and has succeeded in rallying wide support for a campaign against the Quaker "charity" cheap labour schemes. In Nantyglo and Blaina, scarcely less derelict, two thousand unemployed demonstrated to the offices of the Urban District Council against the Council's method of allocating jobs among the workless. A Communist councillor put the demand of the unemployed that the Council should interview a deputation on this question. The Council refused. The demonstrators, who had stormed the Council offices, and occupied the stairway leading to the council chamber, thereupon burst into the meeting, amid scenes of terrific pandemonium. The Council was compelled to receive the deputation and 'to accede to their demand that work should in future be allocated, not by the Council alone, but by a joint committee of councillors and unemployed representatives. [50]

The workers of South Wales have a fighting tradition second to none. Nearly a century ago it was the miners of the Monmouthshire valleys who were in the front ranks of Chartism, and who rose in armed insurrection in November 1839, marching down under John Frost's leadership to take Newport; those early heroes were defeated, but their spirit has never died. It inspired the fighters in countless strikes in the valleys since then, the men who built the Miners' Federation as a powerful fighting body and whose aim was the overthrow of capitalism. To-day, when the wheel of capitalism has come full circle, that spirit is more alive than ever; and when the influence of the allies of the enemy has been finally uprooted from the movement in South Wales, it will triumph.

CHAPTER II

LANCASHIRE: THE "CLASSIC SOIL" OF CAPITALISM

AFTER the land of coal, the country of cotton: we have now to study Lancashire, that "classic soil (as Engels wrote in 1844) on which English manufacture has achieved its masterwork . . . a country which, a hundred years ago chiefly swamp land, thinly populated, is now sown with towns and villages, and is the most densely populated strip of country in England. In Lancashire, and especially in Manchester, English manufacture finds at once its starting point and its centre."[1] Here, on this historic ground where capitalism and the factory system were first nurtured and grew to full estate, we shall expect to see more clearly and unmistakably than anywhere else what the final development of capitalism has meant to the teeming mass of working men and women crowded into this still unequalled concentration of industrial towns. It is inevitable that the mind should recall the early horrors of the factory system in Lancashire; the meaning of the industrial revolution of the eighteenth and early nineteenth centuries in fearful suffering for the many and fabulous wealth for the few; the unrestricted and unspeakable exploitation of women and little children; the grinding oppression, the squalor, disease and degradation of the workers' life. But these things have been told once and for all by Engels, and here it is not necessary to do more than refer the reader to him. What we need to do now is to sketch briefly the present position of capitalism in Lancashire, in order to have some background for our consideration of the condition of the working class.

This chapter will naturally be mainly confined to the cotton industry and its workers, though something will have to be said about the conditions in the other important industries of Lancashire; and it is cotton capitalism that will now claim our attention. Like coal, cotton has been in the limelight right through the post-war period; the bare facts of decline and depression are startling and clear to all; at the post-war peak production was roughly one-third below the pre-war level; and the crisis brought the industry in 1931 to a state of virtual paralysis, with one-half of its total labour force unemployed. From this depth there was a slight, and temporary, rebound in the concluding months of

1931 and the first part of 1932, but the figures for the latter half of 1932 indicate a renewed decline. The export slump is indicated in such facts as that the export of piece-goods in 1931 was less than one-quarter the immediate pre-war figure, and the export of yarn little more than one-half. For this the policy of British imperialism in the East, with its results in the fearful impoverishment of the peasantry in India and China (Lancashire's two biggest export markets), is responsible.

Around the neck of the cotton industry overwhelming capital charges hang like a millstone: "these excessive charges (said a notable memorandum of the Labour Research Department four years ago) are partly due to speculative over-capitalisation, partly to the monopolies established in certain sections, and partly to the multiplicity of capitalist interests and the general lack of organisation in the industry as a whole."[2] It is not easy to convey a just idea of the truly fantastic way in which the sheer dead weight of capital crushes the productive forces in cotton. The unparalleled speculative frenzy of the mill selling and reflotation "boom" of 1919-20 needs a book to itself; it resulted in over-capitalisation on so gigantic a scale that the average capital per spindle was increased from 14s. to 43s. 9d.; the cost per lb. of yarn showed that, comparing 1914 and 1925, the item "interest and depreciation" increased by 355 per cent., while the item "wages" increased by only 107 per cent. The lengths to which over-capitalisation went are illustrated by a spinning concern at Oswaldtwistle, which last November proposed to cut its share capital from £500,000 to £20,000. This same concern illustrates another fundamental point: in its latest balance-sheet the outstanding loan stood at over £137,000 and the bank overdraft at nearly £69,000.[3] For included in the over-capitalisation of 1919-20 was a more than doubling of the burden of loan capital in spinning; since then this burden has grown progressively heavier, until to-day the surplus-value extracted from the Lancashire cotton workers is mainly absorbed by fixed-interest bearing capital (debentures, bankers' loans and overdrafts). Four of the big mill combines alone have debentures totalling £9,200,000 and bankers' loans of over £6,000,000. Hundreds and hundreds of mills are in the hands of the banks. The grip of the usurer is fast about Lancashire.

Here is a true story about over-capitalisation—in the weaving section, this—which will help to make the process more real. It was told me a few weeks ago by a loom overlooker in one of the north-east Lancashire weaving towns. He was a shrewd, hard-headed fellow, expert in his exclusive and virtually hereditary trade, precise and dapper in his dress, with his high stiff collar and his tie drawn through a gold signet ring. I will call him Mr. Entwistle. Before the war he worked at —— Mill, a small and prosperous concern very typical of the industry; it had only 300 looms and a capital of £10,000, in which he, like all the other officials of the Mill, held shares; every year they received a fat dividend of 25 per cent., and every six months a gratifying bonus of 1s. in the £ in addition. Then came 1919 and the speculative scramble. "T'Forty Thieves rushed in from Manchester," said Mr. Entwistle, "and they paid £14 9s. for each £5 share. Shoved t'capital up to £64,000. Lad, ah *knew* it couldn't be done. If our 300 looms worked day and night they wouldn't pay dividend and interest on that lot. So when they came to me and said 'Of course, Mr. Entwistle, you'll exchange your shares for shares in the new company,' ah said 'No, ah'll take t'cash and clear out.' And where's those shares to-day, lad? Waste paper, that's all—and a £40,000 bank overdraft on top of it!"

Mr. Entwistle's astuteness stood him in good stead: but there were tens of thousands of cotton workers with shares in the mills who fell for the swindle of the "Forty Thieves," and who have lost a lifetime's savings in the subsequent calls on capital, which have totalled £25,000,000 between 1920 and the present day.

Mr. Entwistle told me the story of another mill in his neighbourhood, which had been owned by the same family for generations. "Bright lot *they* were," he said; "in t'owd grandfather's time a lot of grand folks came to look at t'mill. One lady thought rotten owd houses round t'mill weren't much for operatives. Grandfather said 'Oh, they only sleep there, they live in t'mill.' That's t'sort family were; and they each got £20 a week as sleeping partners (good pay for doing nowt but sleep). But they were caught out like others. T'firm went in tub [insolvent] and now t'bank runs it—and gets its interest allright."

The cotton industry is notorious for the multiplicity of middlemen it carries at every stage of the productive process; and it has been estimated that the annual toll, in a "normal" post-war year, extracted by these superfluous gentry (cotton brokers, yarn and cloth agents, shippers and so forth) amounts to more than £9,500,000.[4] At the same time the great number of individual concerns in the industry—there are over 600 in the American spinning section alone—engender a whole competitive chaos on the marketing side. On this point Mr. Entwistle was again instructive; he described a recent visit to Manchester and a casual meeting with the salesman of his mill outside the vast building of the Exchange. "'Ever been on 'Change, Entwistle!'

said t'salesman, and he took me in. We looked down on t'great floor at 'em—four or five thousand like him, buying and selling, all chaffering away. 'That's business for you, Entwistle,' he said, 'and mark, those're not £2 a week men neither; there's not a lad on that floor getting a penny less than £5 a week, plus commission.' 'Ah'm glad to know thy wages, Mr. ——,' ah told him, 'It's a damn sight more than ah earn, and a bloody sight more still than t'poor weaver gets for weaving t'cloth tha sells.' "

Monopoly has made but slow headway in the cotton industry; it is true that there are a number of combines in spinning (including also mixed spinning and weaving concerns), but they do not dominate the mass of small firms in the industry in the way that the big colliery combines dominate the mass of small pit concerns in the coal industry—as we have seen in South Wales. On the rock of this anarchy all large-scale rationalisation schemes, such as output restriction, production quotas, compensation for wholesale scrapping of spindles and looms, have hitherto founder-ed. The combines are financially top-heavy; and, whether new flotations (like the Lancashire Cotton Corporation or the Combined Egyptian Mills) or older ventures (like the Amalga-mated Cotton Mills Trust or the Crosses and Winkworth group), they are labouring heavily in angry seas. The Combined Egyp-tian no doubt hoped to emulate the consistent success of the forty-year old Fine Cotton Spinners' and Doublers' Association, a combine which cashed in early in the more specialised and more profitable Egyptian spinning section and which for long easily beat the others in riding the storm. Most interesting has been the ignominious career of the biggest combine of all, the Lancashire Cotton Corporation. This concern was floated early in 1929 with Bank of England money and prolonged flourishes of trumpets; its loudly proclaimed aim was to set the pace for the general rationalisation of the cotton industry; it acquired a hundred mills with near ten million spindles and 25,000 looms. But in the summer of 1932 it was announced that the policy of the Corporation had failed, due to "over-centralisation"; the three leading directors, who had been associated with the found-ing of the concern, resigned; and it was stated that a decentralised system of working the Corporation's mills would be adopted—presumably, a return to the old anarchy which the Corporation set out ostensibly to overcome.*

* At the last annual general meeting of the Corporation, Mr. Orr, the chairman, referred to the closing and dismantling of thirty-one of the mills acquired by the Corporation as illustrating their policy of retaining

But in one section monopoly has been almost traditionally all-powerful; and that is the "key" section of the various finishing trades. A handful of powerful combines rule the roost here. The Bradford Dyers, the British Cotton and Wool Dyers, the Bleachers' Association, the Calico Printers' Association, each controlling up to seventy-odd concerns, are able to fix their monopoly prices and compel the few unassociated firms to conform to their price-agreement. Thus they are able to hold the cotton industry to ransom and to enforce prices which may represent the largest single item in the costings for the manufacture of a yard of cloth. They have succeeded, despite greatly reduced turnover during the post-war decline, in recording large profits and building up impressive reserves.

THE WORKERS IN THE COTTON MILLS

The social bankruptcy of cotton capitalism is seen in one brutal fact: that for "normal" post-war trade its present equipment is surplus to the extent of no less than fifteen million spindles and 180,000 looms—which, in the capitalist view, should therefore be scrapped.[5] In this "normal" condition 15 per cent. of the cotton workers are unemployed. But in the middle of 1931 this figure rose to the staggering level of 45 per cent.; and at the end of 1932, even after the ruthless cutting of tens of thousands off the Labour Exchange registers under the Means Test and the Anomalies Act, it was near 30 per cent. What this means is that considerably over one third of the workers, men and women, in this basic industry are on the scrap-heap. The outward signs of this rotting of a whole industry are apparent to the most superficial observer. On the hoardings are the auctioneers' notices announcing the sale of weaving sheds with so many hundreds of looms here, of spinning mills with so many scores of thousands of spindles there. But who wants to buy? The machinery will probably be sold for scrap; and the empty shell of the mill will be left to fall gradually into ruin. Journeying through Lancashire by train, it is only necessary to glance out of the window to see these broken-windowed, gaunt wrecks in grim sequence. During the past year spinning firms with nearly one million spindles have closed down for good. In Oldham last October, as compared with a year previously, 10 per cent. of the spinners had permanently lost their jobs, with (says the official statement) *no hope of*

only profitable mills. One shareholder remarked that these closures flung 8,000 operatives "on the stones." (*Manchester Guardian*, January 27th, 1933.)

re-employment.[6] Look, too, at the unending forest of chimney stacks—and see how many of them are not smoking. There is bitter irony in the report of the Accrington sanitary inspector on smoke abatement, where he says, simply: "The number of weaving sheds in use has, however, steadily declined, and work under this head is being considerably lightened."[7]

Three elementary points have to be borne in mind in considering the condition of the Lancashire cotton workers. The first is female labour: the proportion of women to men in the industry as a whole is as seventeen to ten; and practically a third of the women cotton workers are married. The second is the traditional dependence on the income, not of one breadwinner, but of the whole family; husband and wife, or father, mother and one, two or more sons and daughters work in the mill; as a result individual wages are on a lower level than in other industries and in other parts of the country. The third is the geographical distribution of the industry: there are two main areas, the southern towns (mainly spinning) and the northern towns (mainly weaving). The outstanding spinning towns are Oldham for American (coarse) spinning and Bolton for Egyptian (fine) spinning; but the southern spinning belt includes the whole Manchester region, and is one of considerable industrial variegation. The northern weaving towns are almost exclusively dependent on cotton: in the main centres, Blackburn and Burnley, weaving the coarser cloths, up to 70 per cent. of the total number of the working population are in the cotton industry; and in Nelson and Colne, where the finer cloths are woven, the percentage is probably even higher. In these centres, and more especially in their satellite townships and villages, such as Great Harwood, Padiham, Rishton, Clayton-le-Moors and a dozen others, the collapse of the cotton industry produces a state of dereliction comparable to that we have already seen in the hardest-hit mining townships in South Wales.

We have noticed the heavy figures of unemployment; and much of this is unemployment of very long standing. A paragraph in a recent issue of the *Cotton Factory Times* told of a loom overlooker who had been unemployed for the past three years; in the same period his wife, a weaver, had had only twelve weeks work; that case, noted at random, is quite characteristic. But the unemployment figures only tell a part of the story. The cotton industry is notorious for under-employment, for chronic short-time working, which disguises the real extent of unemployment. Take the American spinning section: in the first half of 1932 there were 90 out of its 600 odd firms completely stopped, their spindles

totalling four and a quarter million; but in the same period the
short time worked by the remaining firms amounted to a total
stoppage of twelve weeks—that is to say, the spinners were on
the average working little more than one week in two. In the
weaving section under-employment takes the general form, not
of a general stoppage for so many days a week or any of the
other usual types of short-time working, but of stopping a certain
number of looms. The effect is to reduce the number of looms
per weaver, and therefore heavily to reduce earnings, while the
weaver has all the disadvantages of spending a full working week
in the mill. At the same time the percentage recorded as unemployed at the particular mill will only be one-third, one-
quarter, or even far less, what it would be if the weavers working
were operating their normal quota of looms. The *Industrial
Survey of the Lancashire Area* remarks:

> A weaver working two or three looms instead of four is regarded as
> fully unemployed; he pays a full contribution to the Unemployment
> Insurance Fund. Yet his wage may only be one half of the normal
> earnings for full capacity running. And in bad times a large propor-
> tion of the workers in the weaving section may be affected in this way.
> Repercussions upon family income are serious. [8]

This is a genuine anomaly; but it was not one with which the
Anomalies Act was concerned. That Act, precious offspring of
the Labour Government, had its most devastating effect in
Lancashire and made the repercussions of weaving under-
employment upon family income more serious still. Here is the
story of a young weaver and his wife which makes this point
clear. It was told me by the weaver himself last November.

This weaver, a young fellow of about twenty-five, had been
unemployed for a score of weeks, and had just got back to work.
During his first few weeks in work again he had frequently played
for warps, and his weekly wage had averaged 26s. The week I
saw him he had been able to earn the "large" sum of 31s. 7d.
He was fortunate; in his mill many weavers were consistently
working only two looms and were taking home £1 or less a week.
He had been married rather less than two years; and he and his
wife, also a weaver, lived in one of the miserable, unhealthy old
back-to-back houses, containing two rooms ("one up, one
down"), of which there are still many thousands in Lancashire;
their rent was 5s. 11d. But his wife was a frail girl, and shortly
after marriage she fell seriously ill and was ordered by the doctor
to give up work in the mill. After six months illness and con-
valescence she resumed signing on at the Labour Exchange; but
after a couple of weeks the Anomalies Act came into operation,

and as a married woman she was immediately disallowed benefit as "not having reasonable prospects" of employment. What were these young folks to do? The husband was either unemployed or earning a wretched wage. They were heavily burdened by the instalment payments on the furniture they bought when they were married. The wife, debarred from following her trade as a weaver, and having no other, was refused unemployment benefit. The only time they got a really solid meal was once a week when they visited relations. And they were luckier than many, for they had no children.

The story, however, does not stop there. The wife, in desperate need of a job of some kind, eventually took one as a canvasser. She was offered 25s. a week, plus commission, to go from door to door in the vain task of trying to book orders for somebody's £5 vacuum cleaner. Anything more hopeless in a poverty-stricken working-class area could not be imagined, nor anything more exhausting and depressing to one physically and temperamentally unfitted for it. But there was also a condition for the securing of this job; the canvasser had to agree to purchase a vacuum cleaner, paying 10s. deposit and an instalment of 10s. a month thereafter until the purchase price was met. This our unhappy young couple had had to do—to have a £5 cleaner, which they could not possibly afford, in their two-room back-to-back! And for the sake of an impossible job which would evidently not last more than a couple of weeks, after which the celebrated cleaner (plus their deposit and first instalment) would be taken back by the sharks who were peddling it, ready for another similar "sale." This may seem a digression from the cotton industry; but it is typical of the straits to which many unemployed cotton workers are being driven.

Lancashire has now had a dozen years experience of the efforts of the master cotton spinners and manufacturers to "restore" trade; those efforts have meant unprecedented unemployment, under-employment, repeated wage-cuts; they have also meant that the conditions of labour in the mills have been driven to a point that is worse than anything within living memory. Speed-up, the use of bad material, the exaction of higher and higher quality work while technical "economies" are enforced further and further, the badgering and baiting of workers on the job to an unheard-of degree, in brief, the intensification of labour to its utmost limit—this is the general picture in every mill and weaving shed in Lancashire to-day. And this drive is taking place in an industry which is for the most part an old industry, housed in factory buildings which are far below modern hygienic standards;

the workers breathe an atmosphere of cotton dust and dirt, and the effect on health is serious. This is particularly so in the preparatory processes, where the raw cotton is broken up, cleaned and carded; in these departments the workers toil in a fog of cotton dust, their clothing and persons covered with the flocculent fibre. It is not surprising that local medical officers report on the prevalence of respiratory diseases due to cotton weaving (Brierfield), or declare that bronchitis and asthma are common affections in those who have worked many years in the cardroom (Chadderton), that cotton workers are subject to bronchitis, rheumatism and catarrhal conditions (Crompton), and that the humid atmosphere of the mills has an adverse effect on the respiratory system (Haslingden).[9]

The cardroom is the first to feel the effects of bad material; for raw cotton is bought to-day in a condition where it loses an appreciable percentage of its weight in preparation from excessive dust and dirt, whereas a few years ago the loss would have been negligible. I met an old cardroom worker in Rossendale who said bluntly: "Conditions in t'cardroom, lad? They're too bad to mention. There's cotton coming in to-day so bad it can't be used. T'other day ah were collecting at mill and saw a fellow in t'cardroom come out all black, like a miner. T'firm'd bought up lot of raw cotton damaged in a fire, lot of it burnt, and were trying to make summat out o' it. When t'cotton we're working to-day gets spun and wound and to t'loom all ah say is God help t'poor weavers!" He added that that week he had seen several cardroom workers, married women, coming out after a full week's work with 19s. 4d. for their wages; and in the blowing-room and ring-room conditions are identical. The Cardroom Workers' Amalgamation was compelled to apply for the nonapplication of the latest reduction to a large proportion of their members who, even without the cut, were earning only from 15s. to 26s. a week. Subsequently the Amalgamation concluded an agreement with the employers which, for a number of grades of workers in the cardroom, fixed 22s. a week as the general level. Workers earning that sum or less are to be exempt from the reduction (though those earning less are not to be made up to this princely figure, which, it is explained, is not to be regarded as a minimum wage), while those earning up to 23s. 10d. are to be reduced to 22s.[10]

Traditionally the mule spinners (and the major part of Lancashire spinning is done on mules) are the aristocrats of the cotton industry, the relatively best-paid among its workers. Their position now is unenviable. The latest reduction has meant that some of them have lost as much as £1 a week in wages. A fine spinner, an experienced worker and trade unionist of long standing, chairman of his shop, explained to me the heavy extra strain imposed nowadays by the requirements to spin far finer counts of yarn than the grade of cotton warranted. "Years ago," he said, "we'd only be expected to spin 60's from a particular grade of cotton. 'Twas easy. Money for old rope. Now they want 80's from t'same cotton, and they see that they get it. To-day it's always t'same story—t'boss is out to make t'spinner conjure A1 yarn out of C3 cotton!" He went on to explain how the new institution of cleaning gangs was greatly increasing the actual productive time, while the spinner lost the 3½ per cent. on his piece price-list which he formerly received for cleaning. As an example of the speed-up involved, he told how, on that very day, a particular cleaning stoppage on his mules which used to take 180 minutes only took 52. Where he used to spin 860 lbs. of yarn he was now spinning 900 lbs. Payment for lost time is another grievance; a spinner is entitled to claim for lost time if he loses four hours or more on one of his mules; but it is rare nowadays for lost time to be claimed, for such a claim is equivalent to asking for dismissal.

If the position of the spinners is bad, the position of their assistants, the piecers, is far worse: it has always been an anomalous one, with the subordination of the piecers to the spinners (who pay them), and their organisation in the spinners' union without full membership rights. Piecing is youths' work, for youths' pay; but to-day the lad becomes a man, marries and has a family, and is still piecing—for the unparalleled depression has blocked the usual channel of promotion. The other day the *Cotton Factory Times* carried on its front page a story about one of its contributors, a young worker of twenty-two, who started piecing at sixteen and was still doing so, with little hope of advancement to a spinner's job. On an inside page of the same issue of the newspaper there was an account of the retirement of an aged spinner who, in his young days, got spinning when he was twenty-two. That is a suggestive sidelight on the worsened conditions of scores of thousands of workers in the spinning section now as compared with a generation ago. The piecers also suffer from bad material, and their work has consequently become vastly more arduous. A piecer told me grimly that if he only had as many halfpennies as ends he had pieced up these days, he'd be well off.

The ring spinners form an important section of cotton workers; the proportion of ring to mule spindles in Lancashire is roughly as one to three. The situation of these workers was described in these words by the *Cotton Factory Times* (December 30th, 1932):

The labour employed in ring spinning is mostly female, and the wages paid for this work are very poor; indeed, in some cases the ring spinner receives only £1 per week of 48 hours. The average wage for a ring spinner attending 600 spindles is in the neighbourhood of 25s. per week, and she is called upon to display a skill equal to any other female employed in a cotton mill. Far too much bullying goes on. . . . The condition of ring jobbers is even worse in some respects, as they are not governed by a list wage and conditions. As far as wages are concerned a favourite trick of some firms is to cut the rate every time a vacancy occurs, knowing that with aggravated unemployment they will find someone in such circumstances as will take the job.

In all the intermediate processes between spinning and weaving the same tale of sweat and drive is told. A woman doubler, on fine counts, described to me how the introduction of a special catcher on the doubling frame had made work hard that once was easy, since the catcher constantly filled up. "Running's been awful this last year," she said, "with the inferior and dirty yarn we're getting; and it comes from the same firm that we used to get good yarn from. Nowadays we're working harder than ever, and though we're supposed to get a bonus, we're actually earning less." Winders complain of frequent breakages and of a steady increase in speed; they commonly take home for a full week's work wages of only £1 or 25s.

This extreme intensification of labour reaches its culminating point in the manufacturing section of the industry, in the weaving shed. In the main weaving centres wages of 30s. a week and less for a full week's work on four looms are the rule. A Burnley weaver delegate told the last Trades Union Congress that he had been earning (before the wage cut) 35s. a week, "and I had five bellies to fill out of that wage. Now the employer has come along and says he wants 3s. 4d. out of that."[11] And these are the wages paid for work which imposes a maximum of mental and nervous strain. The nature of this strain can be readily comprehended by anyone who spends a few hours in the deafening racket of a weaving shed. Each weaver, penned in the narrow alley-way between his or her four looms, is in a state of constant tension; replenishing the shuttle on each loom every few minutes; stooping over the looms watching the thousands upon thousands of ends for breakages; stopping a loom to piece together a broken end. With inferior material breakages are unceasing; and the time lost on stopping the looms to "head pieces" means in the aggregate a serious loss in wages. Again, if a breakage has been missed and a portion of the cloth is faulty, the weaver has either

F

to "weave back" and rectify the fault if possible, which means so much unpaid work, or be fined for bad work. This is to-day an acute question. The employer supplies bad material; and then he fines the weaver sixpence or a shilling for the seam of faulty cloth which has resulted from the use of the bad material.

Here is an instance of the strain imposed on a weaver. Last December I was in the offices of the Nelson Weavers' Association when a woman weaver came in to report her case. She had had a new warp in one of her looms, and not all the ingenuity of herself and the overlooker could make that warp run aright. This went on for a week, with the loom stopped practically the whole time. "I couldn't eat nor sleep for thinking o'that warp," she complained; and at last, unable to make her wages and in desperation, she had asked for her cards. "May as well play for nowt as work for nowt," was her bitter comment.

This strain on the weavers is greatest in the weaving of the finer and more complex cloths, poplins, sateens, and so forth, and the various artificial silk, pure silk, and mixed weaves. This is work on which a weaver can earn, at the best, from £2 to £2 4s. a week. The need to watch hundreds of ends to each couple of inches, the extra breakages on the finer counts, and the extremely exacting inspection of the cloth (which is held up to the light to search for the tiniest flaw, though the weaver cannot examine his work so minutely) combine to make fine weaving a task with which only the most alert and speedy can cope. In mills which have gone over from weaving standard plain cloths, such as Burnley printers, to the fancy weaves, the old weavers have been unable to tackle the work, and have found themselves on the scrap-heap.

On top of all this the employers are up to all manner of tricks to evade the payment of list prices. The vast and unbelievably complicated price lists which operate in the cotton industry have many clauses prescribing the payment of extra percentages for special work. For example, an extra 5 per cent. should be paid for special care in pick-finding when there are 120 or more ends to the inch. This is evaded by the device of having 117-118½ ends to the inch, that is to say as far as it is possible to go without reaching the 120. The care required of the weaver is the same. The cloth is the same. But the payment of the 5 per cent. is evaded. Similar trickery is practised in regard to the weaving of coloured cloths. The lists contain special clauses relating to extra payment when there is 25 per cent. or more of colour in a warp. By having a fraction over 24.9 per cent. of colour these clauses may be evaded without any difference in the cloth. I

have been told of a case in which half a dozen ends of colour in
the particular warp would have made the 25 per cent. In this
way the weaver is robbed of no less than 1s. 8½d. on the piece of
cloth.

These are the conditions in which, after four years bitter
struggle, the "more-looms per weaver" system is being imposed
on the industry by agreement between the employers and the
cotton union officials. The "more-looms" system is a means of
rationalisation, of increasing the intensity of labour, without any
new capital expenditure, without any advance in technique.
It naturally involves a very large displacement of labour. Calcu-
lations have been made to show that a change from four looms to
eight looms a weaver would mean a displacement of no less than
45 per cent. in weaving labour, and of about one-third in the
total labour employed in the weaving sheds. The present agreement is for a general six-looms system, so the displacement will
presumably be slightly less, but still formidable—say, a minimum of one-quarter of the total labour, on the basis of the
same level of output. It has been estimated that the change over
to eight looms would only effect a reduction of from 2 to 7 per
cent. in the total costs of production per piece of cloth; on the
six-looms basis this sensational "saving" will evidently be even
less, and its effect on the competitive power of the industry
negligible, as the effect of the wage-cuts of the past three years
has been negligible.[12]

The six-looms agreement is highly unfavourable so far as wages
are concerned. There is a nominally guaranteed weekly wage of
41s.; but under the agreement this can fall to 37s. before even
"investigation" is possible. There is a "fall-back" minimum wage
of 28s. in the event of the weaver working only four looms; but
if he is working only three looms he can be dismissed and his
warps transferred to another weaver's looms. And the severe
strain on the weavers which has already been described will
be intolerably intensified by the minding of more looms.

The above lines were written before the six-looms system was
begun; the experience of its operation up to the end of February
has more than confirmed the justness of their criticism. The
employers' blatant trickery in the operation of the system has
become an open scandal. A description by a special correspondent of the *Daily Express* (February 14th, 1933) sums up the situation:

> The Lancashire weaver has been betrayed. . . . With the exception
> of a handful of manufacturers it is safe to say that the agreement has
> been honoured more in the breach than in the observance. . . .

Weavers in Burnley are in open revolt. . . . They were promised
42s. a week when the six-loom system was introduced. To-day many
of them are going home with not more than 25s. a week. . . . No
changes were made in the machinery, as promised. . . . Promises
to give better weft and warps to decrease the number of breakages
and the stoppage of looms have not been observed. Machinery was
not slowed down as agreed, and weavers found the conditions heart-
breaking. . . . I did not meet a single operative who has been reduced to four looms from the accepted standard of six who had drawn
a penny from the manufacturers to make his wages up to the minimum
of 28s. as promised in the agreement.

In an editorial headed "More work for weavers," in its issue
of December 2, 1932, the *Cotton Factory Times* drew attention to
some of the technical handicaps that the more-looms system will
impose on weaver and overlooker alike; for instance, the alteration of the shuttle to take a larger cop of weft will involve more
breakages and trouble with the "ballooning" of weft, meaning
more loom stoppages. The paper adds:

In some sheds the weavers are heading pieces every few minutes,
and it is obvious that where this rule applies they will require wonderful
skill and stamina to cope with the new conditions. . . . In cloths of
the satin, sateen and poplin weaves, something akin to perfection is
required of the weaver's output. Can this be achieved under the
more-looms system? Even in the plain-cloth sphere operatives are
now too familiar with the cloth-looker's comment, "they won't have
this at Manchester," on slight defects which mattered nothing ten or
fifteen years ago. . . . The new system will provide "more work for
weavers" in a very literal sense, but, unfortunately, the number of
operatives required will be considerably less. The surplus of labour
in the manufacturing section is very large now, but it must inevitably
become even greater.

This same issue of the *Cotton Factory Times* makes another point
clear—that the cotton industry is a dangerous industry. It
reports a whole series of accidents. A Rochdale weaver caught
her arm in the loom, sustaining a fracture below the elbow;
another weaver caught her jumper sleeve on the bottom shaft
when trying to put a runner of spare ends round the beam, and
she was lucky to escape with a bad sprain. A spinner at Shaw
had his left hand crushed in the headstock of a mule. A cardroom jobber at Chadderton caught his left hand in the machinery and badly mutilated two fingers. A stoker at a Middleton
bleachworks was fatally scalded through the bursting of a boiler
valve. These are one week's reports; they can be paralleled in
any issue of the same newspaper.

UNEMPLOYMENT, THE MEANS TEST AND POVERTY

No bare statistics of unemployment, of Means Test or Anomalies Act disallowances, can convey a picture of the frightful poverty and suffering of the mass of workless men and women in Lancashire. The ruthless assault of the "National" Government on the already miserable standard of life of the unemployed has caused some agitation among its local supporters. Thus the *Northern Daily Telegraph*, of Blackburn, in its issue of November 10 last, expressed its alarm at the "disconcerting" and "fatalistic" attitude of the Government; and in the course of a prominently featured "warning" to the Government it wrote:

> Here in Lancashire . . . we know of institutional church workers who will tell you, especially those whose labour is devoted to the helping of girls and the younger women, that a large part of the tale of unemployment is unprintable, and the rest almost too agonising. Last week we received a communication from a resident in a large town within a dozen miles of Blackburn who confesses that only now has she come to "an understanding of what unemployment is." She has been selling skirts for threepence and overcoats for sixpence at a jumble sale, and thereby has learned the ghastly realism of misery and its existence in our midst. And all those householders to whom in these days the suppliant on the doorstep has ceased to be a beggar scorned and become a human document well worth attentive study have acquired a new conception of the agonised hunger for a job that gives a wage.

Dr. Wilkinson, the Oldham medical officer of health, in speaking of the "tremendous amount of unemployment" in that town, remarks that especially in the case of those "who have been accustomed to live in moderately good circumstances, the loss of their employment has reduced many families to a very low state of poverty."[13] It was in Oldham, too, that the passer-by this winter could witness a strange example of the way in which the Means Test occupies the centre of the life of masses of workers. On the blank end of a building overlooking the Market-square in Oldham—the ground floor of the building was occupied by a cheap butcher's shop—there was a monster placard, its screaming black letters dominating the square. And it shouted:

"THE MEANS TEST MEAT SHOP.
Test your means *here!*
The cheapest meat in town."

Appropriately enough, the shop's window, as I passed by, was empty, like the larders of the victims of the Means Test.

Here is a typical Means Test case. In a family of three the father (a man over sixty) and son lost their jobs eighteen months ago. The son was called out on strike by the Weavers' Union against the introduction of the more-looms system in his mill. He received £1 a week strike pay. The father drew unemployment benefit for himself and his wife. Under the Means Test this benefit has been stopped. The family is told that the three of them can live on the son's £1 strike pay, plus a pension of 5s. a week that they receive for a son who was killed in the war.

The Means Test has nowhere been administered with greater severity, or with grosser discrepancies between one area and another, than in Lancashire. The percentage of claims disallowed has been considerably more than twice the percentage disallowed in the country as a whole. The local authorities themselves were compelled last summer to appeal for a less harsh administration. The Ministry threatened to supersede authorities which wished to allow more than 6s. for rent when assessing transitional benefit, though rent was in some cases from 12s. to 14s. As in other areas, the Labour Party helped to operate the Test. Mr. Tinker, a Lancashire Labour M.P., told the House of Commons, in the Means Test debate on July 13th last, that he had the "greatest difficulty" in getting the Labour Party councillors to do so. He had said : "If you are public men it is not right to refuse to carry out any Act of Parliament; . . . if injustices are being meted out we can call attention to the fact in the House of Commons and ask the Minister to remedy them." He asked, and got his answer. Sir Henry Betterton curtly stated that transitional payments were relief, and not benefit; and, in answer to Tinker's claim that up to February disallowances in the county area exceeded those in the county boroughs, he showed that in June the disallowances in a number of county boroughs largely exceeded those in the county. The Labour Party was in fact participating in an intensified cutting-off drive.

Reference has been made earlier to the operation of the Anomalies Act, and its particularly devastating effect in Lancashire, with a large number of married women unemployed. To the case then cited this one may be added. It helps to explain why Lancashire speaks, through clenched teeth, of the "wicked Act," and why Labour Party candidates received such severe defeats in the General Election of 1931. A young married weaver who had been very fortunate in never being unemployed right through her working life, in never missing a single stamp off her cards, left work to be confined. When her baby was nine weeks old she signed on at the Labour Exchange again. She was

a good worker and would no doubt have obtained work as soon
as it was available. She was at any rate in the labour market
again, looking for a job. But because she could not produce a
guarantee from her old mill that she would be immediately
re-engaged she was disallowed benefit, on the usual grounds
that she "had not reasonable prospects" of employment. The
Anomalies Act has its big tragedies also. Sarah McQuiggan was
an unemployed shop assistant in Liverpool. She was a widow
with two children. She was disallowed benefit under the Act.
She gassed herself. At the inquest a witness stated that she had
been very depressed after receiving notice that her unemployment benefit was to be discontinued.

The effect of the Means Test and the Anomalies Act is seen in
the increase of the number of persons on out-relief in the Lancashire County Council area from just under 18,000 in October
1931 to 21,000 in January 1932 and nearly 30,000 in January
1933. As additional reasons for the increase the County Public
Assistance officer instances "agricultural workers coming out of
work for the first time, retail traders who had given up business,
and the return of emigrants to this country."

Many unemployed workers in Lancashire are so hard put to it
that they cannot find the pennies to put in the gas meter. It
has therefore become a common practice to insert blank discs or
dummy rings, and then make the sum up when the meter is
emptied. This was stated recently in the Darwen police court,
when Arthur Reedy, an unemployed man, was fined five shillings for this "crime," with a warning from the bench that
further cases of the kind would involve imprisonment. Here is
the report:

> Reedy, who pleaded guilty, said he told the inspector he would pay,
> but he had had no money to pay with for eleven weeks. They had
> three children and had had practically nothing to eat. They had not
> had a penny in money from the Board of Guardians, but his wife was
> allowed 13s. per week in kind, which had to keep them. He had had
> a job on the market for the last three weeks, earning 5s. a week and
> sometimes 7s. 6d.[14]

But let Arthur Reedy and the scores of thousands in his position
take heart. Coincident with his case the newspapers were full
of great news for Lancashire. For it is planned to build the
biggest and most luxurious hotel in Britain, to cost over a million
sterling, on the exclusive North Shore at Blackpool. The curious
may read the rapturous details in the *Sunday Express* for December
4th, 1932—the 2,500 bedrooms (each with wireless), the 3,000
telephones, the ballroom covering a third of an acre, the garage

for 500 cars, the hydropathic baths and slimming installation. Lancashire workers may have "practically nothing to eat"; but Lancashire millowners and their etceteras, Lancashire brokers and middlemen, are to have a new palace for their pleasure, complete with slimming devices for their over-fed womenfolk. Mrs. Reedy, who has thirteen shillings a week in kind to keep five human beings, needs no slimming.

Blackpool, however, is not all the North Shore. Traditionally it is the playground of the Lancashire workers; but the poverty of the cotton towns has meant poverty for Blackpool. While the chatter about the new luxury hotel was at its height two hundred people were summoned at Blackpool for non-payment of rates.

> One woman said she had no money as her husband had only just started work after eighteen months' unemployment. They had had to sell their furniture to pay the building society. Another woman explained that her husband had just secured employment after being idle for twelve months. "We are all out of work," declared another defaulter, "and we have £2 5s. a week coming in to keep eight of us." A man stated that he had lost £110 in business since July. "I am not taking a shilling a week," he added. That he had to pay 15s. rent and keep a family of four out of 22s. a week was stated by another defaulter.[15]

Unemployment and misery weigh no less heavily on the workers in the much-boosted holiday resort of Lancashire than on the workers in the factory town.

Lancashire's Homes for Heroes (and Heroines)

The fact that large numbers of married women work in the mills makes the question of housing in Lancashire one of exceptional importance. To the woman cotton worker who has to rush back from the mill at breakfast time to feed and dress the children and get them off to school, and who returns home tired out at the end of the day, with an evening of housework before her, the condition and convenience of her house will quite evidently be a vital matter. And the position in Lancashire to-day briefly is that, as everywhere, there is an acute housing shortage, there is a vast deal of overcrowding, and there are scores of insanitary and unhealthy areas that are among the most shocking in the whole country. In regard to the elementary requirements of domestic sanitation, Lancashire is probably the most backward of the great industrial areas; it is still to a scandalous extent a county of middens, privies and ashpits.

In the older manufacturing areas housing conditions are worst.

Between Manchester and Oldham, for example, passing through Failsworth, the houses huddle together in narrow streets, their brick long since grimed black, roofs frequently sagging and slates displaced. These miserable dwellings jostle each other at the foot of the many-storeyed spinning mills, which effectively deprive many of them of light and ventilation. Dr. Wilkinson tells us that in Oldham in 1930 there was little alteration as compared with 1925; old and insanitary houses which ought to have been cleared long ago have not been dealt with; the high rents for Corporation houses prevent the poorer families taking advantage of them; and there are still 2,575 back-to-back houses and fifteen cellar dwellings.[16] The same is to be said of Stockport, another old cotton town, where the long rows of dreary houses sprawl without plan in all directions; "in the older parts of the town (says Dr. Gebbie, the medical officer of health) factories and dwelling-houses are in close proximity to each other and over the central area of the town there hangs a cloud of smoke from industrial and domestic chimneys." The houses built since the war have "only touched the fringe of the problem" of over-crowding, which is augmented "by the fact that married members of the family are unable to secure a house of their own, and are compelled to remain under the paternal roof" (the same point is noted by the medical officers at St. Helens and Kearsley: it is a general phenomenon). Stockport has nearly 1200 back-to-back and "single" houses and no fewer than seventy-five cellar dwellings. Dr. Gebbie cites the following cases of overcrowding, to illustrate its gravity:

(1) In a single house, consisting of two rooms, there were nine people —three over fifteen years and six under fifteen years of age. (2) In a single house of back-to-back type, consisting of two rooms, there were thirteen people—four over fifteen years and nine under fifteen years of age.[17]

A remarkable report of an investigation made by the Bolton Housing Survey Committee in the course of 1931 serves as a general indictment of housing conditions in the older areas. In Bolton there are sixty areas scheduled as insanitary. This report deals with the East Ward of Bolton, one of the oldest sections of the town, three quarters of whose houses were already built in 1844 (when Engels said of Bolton that it was "a dark, unattractive hole" and that "the older part of the town is especially ruinous and miserable"), and which has changed its character little since that date. The Committee, which included representatives of the Conservative and Liberal Parties, and the local churches, as well as the Trades Council, the Labour Party and the Co-operative Guild, made a thorough visitation of the 1,600 houses in the ward. They describe the houses "built in monotonous rows in dreary-looking streets, often bounded by the blank walls of factories," and speak of one district as "indescribably squalid and depressing." The percentage of overcrowding, they found, was over twenty-five. Over 90 per cent. of the houses had neither bath nor food store; in 55 per cent. there were no dustbins (that is, they used ashpits) in 40 per cent. there was no scullery. Twenty per cent. of the houses were verminous and 17 per cent. were grossly dilapidated. Some extracts from the report will make these figures more real:

Overcrowding. House containing two small bedrooms and twelve people, viz., father, mother, daughters aged 21, 18, 13, 10; sons aged 15, 11, 8, 6, 3, and baby aged 1. Father and daughter unemployed. Rent 6s. 2½d. Cannot afford more. House containing two small bedrooms and two families totalling nine people, viz., husband, wife, daughter aged 1; husband's mother, stepfather, sons aged 16 and 10, daughters aged 8 and 7. Rent decontrolled 12s. 6d. Could not afford more.

Lack of sunlight. The position of many streets and dwellings is such that some houses get practically no sunlight. As a result a tendency to rickets is induced and vitality is lowered.

Lack of Ventilation. This is often due to the faulty condition of windows which will not open, or of which only a small pane is made to open. Many of the houses are crowded together with very small yards.

Defective sanitation. In one house an unfortunate mother was nursing her baby in a room—kept beautifully clean—which had once been the scullery. A dismal procession of men and women passed all through the day to the communal sanitary convenience which constituted the entire outlook of the room. Such a picture of life lived under almost inhuman conditions is not easily forgotten. In another case a stream of liquid resulting from the defective pails reached to the door of a house and settled there. Sometimes the sanitary conveniences could only be reached through dark entries, where rubbish accumulated.

Dilapidation. Some had bulging walls so dangerous as to require props; some had unsafe bedroom floors and ceilings that necessitated the removal of beds and furniture to the ground floor (in one case the bed had already broken through the floor). . . . The most common defects were leaking roofs and damp walls. Constantly we were told that the small bedroom was unusable owing to dampness and rain coming in; beds had to be brought downstairs, or the family squashed in one bedroom.[18]

It is hard not to quote much more from this report on houses "unfit for human habitation" and workers' lives "robbed of decency, dignity and privacy" for the greater profit of a handful of landlords who simply collect the rent and let the houses go to ruin, who "gain notoriety by buying up property and charging extortionate rents at the first possible opportunity." But these quotations must suffice.

These horrible Bolton conditions are not exceptional. In Burnley Dr. Lamont reports the existence of 2,140 back-to-back and single houses, of which 1,748 were "unfit for human habitation or dangerous." Details of sanitary inspections of over 600 Burnley houses in 1931 indicate the large number of small rooms, the frequency of dampness in bedrooms, the vast number of defects of all kinds—windows that would not open, floors and walls out of repair, rooms without fireplaces. Of all these houses only seven had baths, and a mere handful had pantries. A significant sidelight on rents of Council houses is afforded in Blackburn, where Dr. Thierens reports that there were no applicants for the parlour type three-bedroom houses (rented at 17s. 4d.-18s. 2d.), but 587 applicants for the non-parlour type two-bedroom houses (rented at 10s. 6d.-12s. 4d.). Commenting on the houses let in lodgings, Dr. Thierens says: "The extortionate rents demanded by the landlords inflict such hardship upon the tenants that in many cases after rent is paid the tenant is left with only just sufficient money to provide the barest essentials of life." In Bury it is claimed that the general standard is "good," but Dr. Buckley admits that the older houses are crowded into squares "without any regard for sanitary accommodation," and that they are damp and ill-ventilated. Reviewing the position in Colne, Dr. Lobban writes:

> So long as rows of back-to-back houses exist, deficient in light and ventilation, aggravated by narrow streets, the absence of gardens or backyards, unventilated food stores, and sanitary conveniences a distance away from the houses, one cannot describe the general standard of housing as satisfactory.

Colne, which is a small town, has 1,175 back-to-back and single houses. Clitheroe, which is smaller still, has over 200. In Rochdale there are 2,300 houses classed as unfit and unhealthy. There are neither larders nor baths in 85 per cent. of the houses in Kearsley. In no fewer than forty-two districts of the administrative county of Lancashire the medical officers report overcrowding. Thus in Padiham, near Burnley, "overcrowding is mainly due to the inability of the inhabitants to pay the rents of available houses, which is due again to the large amount of unemployment." The formula is repeated almost verbatim for Chorley, Darwen, Great Harwood, Middleton and Ramsbottom.[19]

We have spoken of the primitive character of Lancashire's

sanitation. In the Urban Districts of the county in 1931, while there were over 300,000 fresh water closets, there were no fewer than 93,000 ashpits, middens, privy and pail closets, and 84,000 waste water-closets. A big town like Rochdale had, at the end of March 1931, over 3,000 pail closets. Mr. Hindle, the chief sanitary inspector of Accrington, in reporting on the conversion of dry ashpits to metal dustbin sheds, declares that "a borough possessing 9,000 'tippler' closets and 5,000 ashpits cannot justly claim high sanitary credentials." This is literally a foul state of affairs; and it is an ironic comment on the traditional boast of the bourgeoisie that Britain is a country whose domestic sanitary arrangements are so far, far superior to those of the benighted and backward foreigner.* After generations of this "superiority" we read in the latest report of the medical officer of Abram that "the privy system, so common in the district, is repulsive to those who have to use this type of closet, and must necessarily be detrimental to the health and well-being of those individuals." And in the sacred name of "economy" the work of abolishing these stinking abominations is held up. Dr. Butterworth, the Lancashire county medical officer, reports that "this work in some districts has been retarded by the prevailing economic conditions." In Tottington, for example, a scheme for the conversion of all privies was submitted to the Unemployment Grants Committee, "but when the grant was reduced the scheme was abandoned."[20]

In the larger cotton towns the privy is not so common; but the waste water-closet, which has taken its place, is not so very much better. In Nelson, where housing conditions are above the average, Dr. Markham observes that "the sanitary conveniences consist largely of the waste water closet, the rate of progress in conversion of this type to the fresh water closet being very slow. Similarly in regard to ashpit accommodation there is a large field for improvement." Dr. Lamont, at Burnley, puts the point plainly and what he says can be applied generally to Lancashire:

Although there are comparatively few privies [in Burnley] there is a very great sanitary drawback in the 18,293 waste water-closets. These are very unsatisfactory, the uncleanliness of the pans, the dirty

* It is significant to notice that the slow progress in conversion to the water closet is partly due to the regulations and restrictions with which slum clearance schemes are hemmed in by the existing property relationships. The view has been authoritatively put to me that the fear of "improving" insanitary property, and thereby prejudicing some future hypothetical slum clearance scheme, has led medical officers of health in Lancashire not to insist on this conversion.

water used for flushing, the accumulation of slime in and about the tipper, and the frequency of blockages causing serious nuisance. The smell from them is offensive at all times.[21]

The bad housing conditions in the cotton towns are repeated in the mining and other industrial centres of Lancashire. There are over 2,000 unfit houses in Wigan, and in 1931 the Council built only forty-one new houses, in place of the needed yearly average of 233. St. Helens has over 3,000 unfit houses, and Dr. Hauxwell, the medical officer, reports that "a very considerable amount of overcrowding still exists" because of the "inability to pay the comparatively high rentals of Corporation houses"; one third of the applicants for Corporation houses were living in overcrowded conditions.[22]

Among the worst conditions of all are those in the metropolitan cities of Manchester and Liverpool and their satellite towns. Engels spoke of the "shocking filth, and the repulsive effect" of the "multitudes of courts, back lanes and remote nooks" of Stalybridge, in the Manchester district. The courts are still there, with open middens in them, and children playing around the filthy place, because there is nowhere else to play. One may visit Moulders-yard in Stalybridge to-day and find it as Engels might have found it—the paving in a terrible state ("the big hollows," says one tenant, "remind me of the Somme, and the slush and mud is much the same, too"), the houses swarming with beetles and in the last stages of dilapidation (fireplaces falling in), the walls so damp that all the paper is peeling off, and no ventilation—but plenty of draughts. Manchester itself, as it was ninety years ago, was described in some of Engels' most scorching passages. And to-day what is the state of Manchester housing? It was stated in the City Council last July that there were more than 30,000 houses, inhabited by 132,000 people, not in a reasonable state of fitness. It is characteristic that the City Council has postponed the clearance scheme for the Medlock-street area in Hulme, one of the worst slum areas in the city, which was first reported by the medical officer of health in 1920, and which has been scheduled by the Ministry of Health as an insanitary area. In this area the infant mortality rate for the five-year period 1925-29 averaged 135, compared with ninety-one for the whole city; and the death rates from disease were two to three times those for the whole city. It was said in the City Council that the tuberculosis death rate in Hulme was twenty-seven per 1,000, while in the bourgeois suburb of Didsbury it was not one per 1,000. And even if the area is cleared, how can the poverty-stricken workers who live in it pay the high rents of the

new Council tenements?   The official view, expressed by the
medical officer of health, is that 80 per cent. of them can afford
the new rents (without indicating what the remaining 20 per cent.
are to do).   But Alderman Jackson, on the basis of a survey
made by the Hulme Housing Association, stated that 60 per cent.
could definitely not afford the new rents; while Lady Simon
pointed out that the application of the Rowntree "human
needs" scale, "which was not a generous scale," would show that
only 50 per cent. could pay the new rents.[23]

The Hulme survey, undertaken in 1932, has revealed that in
this one area of Manchester there exists the "gigantic problem"
of re-housing "at least 35,000 people, and quite possibly nearly
50,000."   Not only is transference to a Council housing estate
beyond the means of the majority of the inhabitants; two-
thirds of this number are unable to pay even their present low
rents if they are to maintain a barely adequate standard of
living. "We come," the survey emphasises, "to a problem which
goes beyond the consideration of housing conditions and are
brought face to face with the larger question of wages and living
costs."*   And, since there are far fewer children per family
among those who are able to afford the rents on a Council estate
than among those who are not, this is the position reached: if
outlying estates alone are to be relied on, then four out of every
five children in Hulme will be condemned to continue existing
in these vile slums.†

Liverpool and its neighbouring Merseyside towns illustrate
the inadequacy of municipal efforts to deal with the housing
question.   In Bootle, for instance, no further application forms
for Council houses have been issued since the end of 1929, and
Dr. Wood remarks that "much remains to be done before even
the accepted applications for municipal houses can be satisfied."
He adds:

* The same point has been made in an East London survey: see p. 128
below.

† This Hulme survey is one of a number, published by the Manchester
and Salford Better Housing Council, which have recently given an
accurate and detailed exposure of housing conditions there. *Some Housing
Conditions in Chorlton-on Medlock* records that many of the houses still in
use are the jerry-built hovels which Engels in 1844 said were only
intended to stand for forty years; it reports: "Several cases in which the
landlord . . . successfully evaded repairs by threatening the tenant
with eviction if the tenant complained direct to the medical officer of
health" (pp. 5-6, 10). Conditions in part of St. Clement's Ward—where
"large blocks date back to 1740. Most of it is in a shocking state of
disrepair"—are dealt with in *Under the Arches (Behind London Road Station).*
In *Angel Meadow and Red Bank* the area of that name in St. Michael's and

It is common knowledge that many of the worst cases of overcrowding are due to economic causes rather than to house shortage; such are the cases of poor people with large families, unemployed or in casual employment, who necessarily live in houses or rooms quite inadequate for their requirements, with resultant injury to their health and that of their families. As a class the housing needs of this poorest section of the community are greatest, yet such needs have been catered for only indirectly and inadequately by municipal efforts. [24]

The Social Survey of Merseyside, undertaken by the University of Liverpool, indicates a general percentage of overcrowding (for the sample families investigated) of eleven, rising in one ward, St. Anne's, to thirty-seven; and the survey notes that, in families where the principal wage-earner is unemployed, the percentage of overcrowding rose to twenty-one. The following cases of over-crowding, which are both of families below the low poverty line adopted by the survey, give a picture of the conditions of many workers in Liverpool:

> Coal carter with wife and five children. Head has not worked for last five years. Still signs on at Labour Exchange. Income 40s. Needs 37s. 6d. Rent 8s. 1d. (restricted) for two bedrooms. Parlour used as general shop by wife, who also sells vegetables; cellar kitchen let at 2s. 6d. as hairdressing saloon.

> Unemployed coal carter with wife and four children. Unemployment benefit has expired. Is receiving 32s. from Public Assistance Committee. Needs 32s. 10d. more. Rent 7s. 6d. (unrestricted) for one room, used both as living and bedroom. Nine families share one tap and ten families share four w.c.s and one yard. [25]

There are in Liverpool at the present moment two slum areas which have been scheduled, and where the City Council is purchasing the houses with a view to demolition. There are also eight unhealthy areas which it was resolved to proceed with as long ago as 1921, but on which nothing has since been done. Eight hundred unhealthy houses "of the worst type, mainly situated in courts," are scattered in various parts of the city; they are

Collegiate wards is described: "The whole area . . . is really unfit for habitation"; there are many houses let in furnished rooms, whose abominable regime can be guessed from the case of the woman "whose counterpane was stamped all over STOLEN (to prevent pawning)" (pp.6, 15). The seriousness of overcrowding in Manchester has been stressed by Sir Ernest Simon, who remarks that it is "far more widespread than the official figures of the Registrar-General would lead people to suppose"—being 25 per cent. of population on a reasonable standard, compared with the official 7.9 per cent. (*How to Abolish the Slums*, p. 10).

Attention may also be directed to Canon T. Shimwell's *Some Manchester Homes*, and to the publications of the Manchester and District Regional Survey Society. Nos. 5, 6 and 10 deal with health and housing in Ancoats, and Nos. 9 and 11 with housing in two Salford areas.

cramped together at the back of shops, built round so that they are absolutely sunless, and in one case that I know of an offal dump was right in front of the house. Let us visit the Gerard-street clearance area, one of the two slum areas mentioned. In a few narrow streets, "so arranged as to impede the free circulation of the air in or about the dwellings" (which are over a hundred years old), there is a population of 3,430 working men, women and children. The density of population is 403 persons to the acre, compared with the city's average of thirty-two, and with seventeen and three respectively in the middle-class areas of Wavertree and Woolton. And this mass of poverty, misery and squalor is in the centre of the city, immediately at the back of, and overshadowed by, the proud buildings of the Walker Art Gallery, the city's Museum and Library and Technical School. Boundary walls overhang the narrow rear passage-ways, and the removal of refuse is consequently difficult. There is much overcrowding. There is a "foul atmosphere" in the tenement dwellings, and the never-closed doors "destroy all privacy." Washing has to be dried in lobbies or living rooms where there is neither sun nor fresh air. The vital statistics for the period 1923-29 show that:

> The phthisis death-rate in this area is twice as high as the phthisis death-rate for the entire city; the infantile mortality rate in this area is almost double that of the city [i.e. 171, as against 98], the mortality rate from zymotic diseases is five times as high as that of the city; the mortality rate from respiratory diseases is almost three times that of the city; and the death-rate from all forms of tuberculosis (including phthisis) is more than twice the city rate.

The medical officer of health, Dr. Mussen, added the important note that "death-rates do not indicate the incapacity for work, extent of sickness, suffering and invalidity of the sick".[26]

Our examination of housing conditions in Lancashire has already led us to the point where we are considering the effect of housing on health; and to a more general examination of the state of health of the working class in Lancashire it will now be possible to proceed.

POVERTY AND DISEASE: FOOD THAT IS POISON

That the conditions of labour in the cotton mills predispose the workers to respiratory and other diseases has already been noted. It remains here to examine the general effects on the health of the Lancashire workers of the years of capitalist decline and crisis, of the years of ruthless capitalist attack on the standard of life and the resultant widespread impoverishment. First it is necessary to dispose of a certain comfortable official optimism, of which Dr. Butterworth, the Lancashire county medical officer, affords a good example when he says in his latest report that "there does not appear to be any direct evidence" that prevailing economic conditions "have seriously affected the health of the community." Curiously enough, the doctor prints, a few lines further down on the same page of his report, his own answer, from his Padiham colleague, who makes the obvious remark that "unemployment reacts on the health of the community owing to the consequent lack of proper nourishment."[27] To the layman this seems to be a point hardly worth labouring.

The effect of impoverishment can likewise be seen in the increased incidence of serious diseases. In Liverpool and Bootle there has been a marked increase in both the incidence and the number of deaths from diphtheria during the past five years. In Bolton Dr. Moffatt comments on the large number of scarlet fever cases, especially among adults. Dr. Sharpe, of Preston, in his 1931 report notes that "diseases of the circulatory system have risen by 10 per cent., due very probably to the increase of the strain on the mental and physical resources of the people. Circulatory diseases account for one fifth of the total deaths."[28] The death-rate from tuberculosis of the lungs increased in St. Helens in 1931; and Dr. Hauxwell, in discussing the reasons for this increase, says that it is necessary to take into account "the general financial depression in the town during the year, as evidenced by the higher number of unemployed and the greater amount of relief which the Public Assistance Committee found it necessary to grant." He adds:—

> One of the greatest difficulties in the treatment of tuberculosis is the disposal of cases after discharge from the sanatorium. Generally these cases return to homes where they have to exist on the bare necessities of life and where, owing to overcrowding, it is impossible for them to continue the treatment learned in the sanatorium. Further, owing to economic pressure, they return to work before they are properly fit.

Precisely the same point is made by Dr. Osborne, at Salford; while Dr. Ratner, the Stockport tuberculosis officer, writes:

> The housing conditions of many patients who have been visited by the tuberculosis officer are deplorable. It may perhaps be far-fetched to say that the abolition of the slums would abolish tuberculosis. There is little doubt, however, that poor housing and especially overcrowding play a definite and important part in the spread of tuberculosis. It is impossible to insist on a separate room for the patient; it is unfortunately frequently impossible to insist on a separate bed.[29]

G

What is being done to tackle this grim situation? Well, it is stated that Salford is spending more than £20,000 a year on the treatment of tuberculosis, but only £10,000 a year on the improvement of housing. Dr. Whitehead, at Wigan, writes with some natural exasperation in his 1931 report that "once again it must be reported that nothing has been done to provide a new tuberculosis dispensary, although it was pointed out at length in the 1924 report, and frequently since, that the present dispensary building . . . was altogether unsuitable for the purpose." And in Salford Dr. Osborne reports on the blackguardism of some employers whose workers suffer from tuberculosis; he is explaining the successes of the pneumothorax treatment for tuberculosis, which consists in the introduction of air into the chest to form a kind of air-cushion round the lung. This treatment takes some time to have effect, and at intervals of a few months the chest has to be refilled with air. But some employers, the doctor reports, have refused permission to tubercular workers undergoing treatment to have time off to attend for air refills, and have dismissed them. Such is the humanity and charity of the capitalist in our "enlightened," "civilised" age! [30]

Of the first importance for health is the condition of the main foods. Lancashire affords some striking evidence that, so far as milk and meat are concerned, the present position is a disgraceful one. The general figure for tuberculous milk is 8 per cent. to 10 per cent. of all samples examined. Mr. Locke, the Manchester veterinary inspector, says bluntly that "no headway is being made towards a reduction in the incidence of tuberculosis in dairy herds in this country," and points out that the percentage of dairy farms supplying Manchester affected by tuberculosis in 1931 (over 16 per cent.) has only once been exceeded in the past thirty years. His Preston colleague, Major Finch, an exceptionally conscientious and outspoken official, declares that the Tuberculosis in Cows Order of 1925, "a public health measure of the first importance, is a dead letter," since it depends on notification by the owner of the animal, and subsequent inspections often reveal tuberculosis which "must have been known to the owner." [31]

The percentage of milk samples found dirt-contaminated ranges from over thirty to nearly fifty. The medical officer of Rawtenstall remarks that "some improvement in the methods of producing and handling milk has been made, but this is not taking place as quickly as is desirable. Very bad samples from farms which are well equipped for the production of clean milk were too common." [32]

In regard to meat Major Finch has some strong things to say. He reports that though for years he has criticised the lack of canteen and washing accommodation and effective lighting in Preston's public abattoirs, nothing has been done. Beasts continue to be slaughtered in conditions which are unhygienic and which prevent proper inspection of the carcases. There is a growing tendency for butchers to import meat slaughtered outside the borough, from places where the inspection is often perfunctory. Major Finch is critical of the shortcomings of the present system of meat inspection by public authorities (a point worth remembering when reading the optimistic reports of the average municipal veterinary inspector). He describes the difficulty of controlling the slaughter of diseased beasts, and tells of "attempts frequently made to mask signs of disease." In Blackburn the numbers of beasts found affected with tuberculosis was nearly 3½ per cent. of those slaughtered in 1931; and this percentage has been steadily rising since 1923, when it was less than half the present figure. The Blackburn veterinary inspector stresses another serious meat problem:

> For several years I have pointed out that "liver fluke" in cattle and sheep has become a national scourge. The year 1931 [when 6,579 livers were condemned, as against 2,335 in 1926] will stand out as probably the worst year we have yet had, and if more active steps are not taken to suppress it the results will be progressively worse in the future.

In Preston it is also noted that a number of the premises used for the manufacture of ice-cream are "in a very poor sanitary condition," and regulations for the registration of such premises and the fixing of standards of purity for their products are "urgently required."[33]

MOTHERS AND CHILDREN

Lancashire is the classical area of female labour; and we have seen that a large proportion of the women cotton workers are married. Lancashire is also the area with the blackest record for maternal mortality, for deaths of women in childbirth. Of all the towns in the country with a maternal mortality rate of over five deaths for every 1,000 births, half are in Lancashire. And in Lancashire itself the heaviest mortality is in the manufacturing areas. For the five-year period 1927-31 the maternal mortality rate in manufacturing areas in Lancashire averaged 5.62, while in residential areas it averaged 4.58.[34] And for this abnormally high rate in the cotton towns, for this avoidable slaughter of working-class mothers, the general social and industrial conditions are responsible.   The Ministry of Health's departmental committee on maternal mortality made this fact perfectly clear.   They dealt at length in their report with the Lancashire position, and concluded that there was "an excessive amount of difficult midwifery, much of which is probably due to disproportion caused by pelvic contraction," of which "rickets is the most common cause" (and rickets is notoriously a disease of bad housing, poverty and malnutrition).   The committee added that work in the mills "when combined with household duties is likely to prove injurious," and stressed further the effect of generations of social development in environment generally bad and unhealthy.[35]

In the last couple of years the maternal mortality rate has not only shown no tendency to fall, but on the contrary it has tended to rise, as the following table indicates:

MATERNAL MORTALITY RATES

			Average 1923-29	1930	1931
Bolton	..	..	5.2	6.7	6.5
Burnley	..	..	5.1*	4.5	5.1
Bury	..	..	6.8	5.4	7.1
Blackburn		..	6.7	4.4	3.9
Oldham	..	..	6.8	5.2	6.4
Preston	..	..	5.9	6.6	5.3
Rochdale	..	..	7.0	9.6	7.4
Stockport		..	5.3	1.7	6.1

*Average for 1924-28.

Only in the case of Blackburn does the rate for 1931 show an appreciable reduction on the average for the seven-year period 1923-29; and Dr. Thierens curtly comments that, "as, however, the Blackburn maternal mortality rate has been consistently high over a period of forty years, and has further exhibited wide fluctuations year by year, it is not improbable that the reduction, though welcome, is fortuitous, and therefore unlikely to be maintained."   It is significant that the Blackburn rate was higher for the decade ending 1930 than for the decade ending 1900.   This is a general characteristic of maternal mortality in Lancashire; over a period of twenty or forty years motherhood has become, not less, but more dangerous.   In Preston the maternal mortality rate for the five-year period 1926-30 was 6.32, while for the five-year period 1911-15 it was 4.51.   Comparing these same two periods, we notice that the incidence-rate of puerperal fever increased more than six times, and the death rate of puerperal fever increased three times.[36] It is a staggering and infuriating reflection upon the development of capitalist society, with its boasted science and culture, in Lancashire, that the young married weaver (let us say) who leaves the mill to-day to be confined runs a greater risk of an agonising death in child-birth than her mother, or even her grandmother, did.

How can maternal mortality be reduced? Sir George Newman, the chief medical officer of the Ministry of Health, says, by "skilled personal attention and the provision of necessary services . . . clinics, attractive, popular and thoroughly efficient." He might have added by increasing wages, by improving the general conditions of life and work; but perhaps those are not sufficiently medical considerations. However, let us take him on the "necessary services"; in Lancashire fully equipped and free maternity homes are even more necessary than they are in other parts of the country. Are such institutions general in Lancashire? There is such a home run by the Nelson Borough Council; but the fee, for borough residents, is three guineas a week*; and while this fee may be reduced or waived on application, only four patients out of 210 were admitted free in 1931.[37]

As with the mothers, so (even more so) with the children. The infantile mortality rate in Lancashire has risen steeply over the last two recorded years, as we have seen it rise steeply in South Wales. The reflection of worsened conditions is unmistakable. Here are the principal figures:

INFANTILE MORTALITY RATES IN LANCASHIRE INDUSTRIAL TOWNS

(a) County Boroughs

	1930	1931				1930	1931
Bolton	67	80	Oldham	..	..	67	106
Burnley ..	.. 76	86	Preston	..	..	68	89
Bootle ..	.. 79	95	Rochdale ..		..	66	66
Bury ..	.. 69	73	St. Helens ..		..	79	88
Liverpool	.. 81	94	Salford	..	..	75	101
Manchester	.. 79	85	Stockport ..		..	57	79
Warrington	.. 65	100	Wigan	..	..	106	103

* The comment of Dr. Thompson, the medical officer of health of the Metropolitan Borough of Lambeth, is apposite: referring to the Maternity Home in that London area he says, "all economies to pay the fees mean that some of the family go without necessaries, and the expectant mother herself is the main sufferer. In her unselfishness for the benefit of the other children she overlooks the fact that in depriving herself she is acting in a way detrimental to the best interests of her unborn baby" (Lambeth Health Report, 1930, p. 25).

(b) Municipal Boroughs and Urban Districts

Ashton-in-			Leigh	57	98
Makerfield ..	70	87	Middleton	46	99
Atherton.. ..	61	82	Newton-in-		
Colne	51	110	Makerfield ..	65	79
Darwen	70	82	Prestwich	77	86
Eccles	64	85	Radcliffe	48	80
Farnworth ..	70	84	Ramsbottom ..	64	96
Haslingden ..	69	95	Royton	87	120
Hindley ..	69	115	Widnes	55	82

The average infantile mortality rate for Lancashire Urban Districts rose from sixty-four in 1930 to seventy-two in 1931; those given under (b) in the table above have been selected as the districts which are at once above the county average and which show the biggest increase between the two years. It is true that there are towns where the rate has fallen. Nelson is such a one; and the comment of Dr. Markham, the medical officer, can apply to others in a like position. He writes that "although it is pleasing to report a low infantile mortality rate, it would be a matter of greater congratulation if this figure could be maintained or even show a reduction over a period of years"; and he considers it advisable to omit any comments until future reports shall have shown whether this low figure is an exception or not.[38] In Nelson's neighbouring town of Colne the infantile mortality rate has more than doubled; and it is with an eye on the local conditions that Dr. Lobban says:

Among the important external causes of infant mortality are domestic insanitation in its widest sense, unsatisfactory systems of disposal of excreta, the unfavourable conditions of urban life, employment of pregnant women in factories, overcrowding, unpaved yards and streets, ineffective scavenging, poverty and filth. All these circumstances contribute, directly or indirectly, to a high death-rate among infants.

Dr. Whitehead, at Wigan, remarks on the bad housing conditions in some districts of that town, and emphasises that "there are approximately twice as many infant deaths in insanitary dwellings as in healthy dwellings." He declares that:

Not many towns have been harder hit by trade depression than Wigan. It is difficult to keep the infant mortality low under such conditions. Although there is no actual starvation going on, there is undoubted lack of clothing and home comforts generally. Babies are not wanted in many poor homes, owing to inability to keep them in reasonable comfort.[39]

A significant point about the Lancashire infantile mortality figures (which is stressed by Dr. Sharpe, of Preston) is that the much-proclaimed reduction during the past ten years—up to the

present increase—is almost entirely among infants over one
month old. The death-rate among infants under one month,
the "neo-natal" death-rate as it is called, remains at the same
level; its main causes are premature birth and congenital defects.
That these latter causes are actually on the increase is suggested
by the Warrington figures, which show the infant deaths from
these causes increasing in 1930-31 from twenty-six to forty-nine;
in twenty-eight cases of infant deaths in Warrington the home
conditions were found to be unsatisfactory, and in six cases there
was definite overcrowding.[40]

When we turn to examine the infantile mortality rates for the
different wards in the principal Lancashire towns we notice at
once that the general rate for each town does not reflect the full
gravity of the situation in the most thickly-populated working-
class quarters. Thus in Blackburn (the one manufacturing town
where the rate has declined) the rate is above the town average
in six wards, each of which has a high density of population.
In Oldham exceptionally high rates (over 140) are recorded in
seven out of the twelve wards, embracing more than half of the
population of the town; and in four wards the rate exceeds the
appalling level of 170—the average rate for the whole of England
and Wales in 1931 was sixty-six. Five wards in Burnley have
rates considerably exceeding the general town rate of eighty-six,
and three of them have rates of 101, 131 and 133 respectively.
In Stockport there are five wards with rates exceeding 100 (the
town average is seventy-nine), which represent double and treble
the rates in those particular wards for the previous year. And so
these examples can be multiplied. But there is something else
that these ward statistics vividly illustrate, that is, the vast difference in infantile mortality between the working-class wards and
the bourgeois—the middle-class residential wards. Manchester
and Liverpool shall show us the class distinction in terms of the
lives of little children:

INFANTILE MORTALITY RATES IN 1931

(a) Working-Class Wards

LIVERPOOL		MANCHESTER	
Everton	113	Ardwick	120
Exchange	117	Collyhurst	120
Abercromby	133	Bradford	101
		Collegiate	143
		New Cross	121
		St. Clements	120

(b) "Residential" Wards

Wavertree	68	Didsbury	49
Woolton	50	Levenshulme	44

In Everton the density of population is 174 to the acre, in Wavertree·it is seventeen, in Woolton it is three. These are not figures that call for explanation; they call for action.

THE HEALTH OF THE SCHOOL CHILD

If the Lancashire worker's child survives infancy successfully, how does it fare? Sir George Newman, in his latest report as chief medical officer of the Board of Education, particularly cites Lancashire in support of his statement that "the depressed state of industry and the need for national economy does not appear to have exerted, as yet, any measurable physical ill-effect upon the child population." That is to say, he quotes Dr. Butterworth (whom we have already met) as saying that in the administrative county of Lancashire there is a "significant improvement" in nutrition.   As the Lancashire county area, for educational purposes, excludes all the important industrial towns, and includes only a minority of the population of the area, this statement is misleading as a guide to the state of child health in Lancashire. Sir George goes on to quote the case of Blackburn, where nutrition was definitely worse in 1931 than it was in 1930, and where the medical officer says that "the standard of nutrition continues to decline, and in the case of boys shows but small improvement over that of the war period." He also notes that in Bury nearly 10,000 more school meals had to be provided than in 1930.[41]

But there are many things that Sir George Newman does not mention. He has no word to say of the significant fact that in Blackburn the percentage of "normal" nutrition has declined considerably more among school entrants than among school children as a whole. He does not cite the increase in malnutrition among St. Helens school children, nor the remark of Dr. Hauxwell that the fact that nutrition is as good as it is "is due to the excellent school feeding arrangements"; he does not refer to the large increase in the provision of free school meals in Rochdale (meals incidentally provided in cookshops or private houses, where "unfortunately adequate supervision is far from easy"); he does not quote the statement of Dr. Markham, at Nelson, that the provision of school meals "contributes to a large degree in the maintenance of the good physical standard shown by the school children as a whole."   On the contrary, it appears that this eminent and comfortably placed medical gentleman wishes to reduce school meals and increase malnutrition; what other inter- pretation is to be placed on his suggestions for "economy," in which he asks: "Can we be satisfied that all the expenditure on school meals is being wisely incurred and that it could not with advantage be more closely related to the medical needs of the children?"[42]

Even where children do not come within the extreme classification of malnutrition the actual state of their nutrition may be very unsatisfactory. Sir George Newman himself has previously emphasised that children should have an obligatory pint of milk a day, as well as fresh vegetables and fruit. What a mockery such excellent counsel is for the children of the workers of Lancashire to-day! Dr. Lamont, at Burnley, reports that:

> There are many children who do not appear to have a sufficiency of fresh vitamin-containing foods. In the present state of unemployment the efforts of the mother of a family must of necessity be directed more towards supplying a sufficiency of food of the less expensive variety, and consequently there is a danger of children getting too much starchy food . . . and too little fresh milk, fresh vegetables, fresh fruit and fresh eggs. Fresh milk, unfortunately, plays too little part in the dietary of the schoolchild.[43]

The relatively greater decline in normal nutrition among school entrants (noted above, at Blackburn) is an indication that the burden of growing impoverishment is falling particularly heavily on the pre-school child, the toddler. In Preston Dr. Elizabeth Critchley reports that "the general health of the children showed a uniform decline throughout all the centres in the last quarter of the year, the unprecedented trade depression and consequent unemployment being the direct cause. The chief sufferer was the toddler." In Liverpool, where 192 pre-school children were referred for special treatment:

> Home visits were paid in each case, and all the children were found to be unable to obtain the necessary treatment from private practitioners on account of poverty, or from hospital out-patient departments on account of the already long waiting lists, necessitating loss of time and consequent risk of irremediable defects.[44]

Children have to be clothed as well as fed. But in Blackburn in 1931 the numbers of children satisfactorily clothed declined by 8 per cent. in the case of boys and 7 per cent. in the case of girls, as compared with the previous year. The St. Helens school medical officer sheds light on one aspect of parental poverty and children's clothing when he points out that "many children are now wearing Wellington boots owing to their low price . . . (but) their wear all day and every day should be discouraged. They prevent the natural evaporation of perspiration, so that the feet become sodden and the circulation interfered with."[45]

The incidence of defects found in the medical inspection of Lancashire school children naturally varies; it may be as high as 81 per cent. (Blackburn elementary school girls); and in all cases the incidence is far higher among elementary school children than it is among secondary school children—in Rochdale it was three times as great in 1930. And what chance do the children stand? Dr. Greenhalgh, the Accrington school medical officer, wisely remarks that "improvement in the hygiene of the bedrooms of the children, where they should spend more than one-third of their time, is an item calculated greatly to reduce this story of defects." Such hygienic improvement is very likely and possible indeed in the housing conditions that have been described earlier in this chapter, with children and adults crowded by poverty into one bedroom! While the percentage of defects is high, the school medical service is frequently most inadequately equipped for dealing with them. In Burnley, for instance, there is only one school dentist. He treats 4,000 children a year, though 1,500 is considered to be the maximum if treatment is to be thorough. ·An average of 3,000 children a year do not receive treatment; and the many thousands of fillings needed cannot be done, with the result that there is excessive extraction. [46]

Finally, on the state of the schools. In Burnley out of twenty-six schools many are old, with bad lighting, closely surrounded by other buildings and lacking play and air space; twelve have old-fashioned, unhygienic closets; floors are worn and dirty; there is an insufficient supply of towels and soap; and there are still very many antiquated desks, which foster round shoulders and flat chests. In Rochdale schools "it cannot be said that the cleanliness of the rooms, and especially the lavatories, is up to the necessary standard." Lighting, ventilation and general sanitary accomodation are unsatisfactory in several of the older schools in St. Helens; "some of these older schools are also badly overcrowded and one still finds classrooms divided only by curtains. This is a most unhygienic procedure." Open-air schools, so essential for delicate children, are a rarity; though the experience of Nelson shows that in such a school children's weight increases at a notably greater rate than when they are in an ordinary school. [47]

THE OTHER BRANCHES OF LANCASHIRE INDUSTRY

What has been written of the extreme intensification of labour in the cotton mills applies with equal force to the other industries of Lancashire: it applies notably to the toilers in the coalfield, which is one of the principal coalfields of the country. The Lancashire coalfield is characterised by a mass of many under-takings and small collieries, less than one-fifth employing over 1,000 men; and the four principal monopoly concerns, which have been formed by amalgamation within the past four years, account for something under 50 per cent. of the total output, two of these concerns accounting for almost 40 per cent. of the total output. This recent development towards monopoly has been accompanied by the keenest speeding-up in the pits; since the 1926 lock-out the number of conveyors in use in Lancashire pits has more than doubled.[48] Typical of the process that is going on in the bigger collieries is the position at one of the most important collieries of the largest of the new combines, the Manchester Collieries Limited. Here, says the secretary of the local branch of the Miners' Federation, the introduction of machinery has meant that four hundred fewer men are employed than there were three years ago, while the output per head has doubled. The youngest and strongest miners are put on in conveyor-runs as price-fixers, and the prices per ton have been cut in some cases from 2s. to 1s. 6d. Machines are being used in the brutal condi-tions of the exceptionally thin seams (no more than twenty-one inches) which are common in Lancashire. Like the Scottish miners, the Lancashire men find that they are compelled to stop and clear the whole of the coal that the machine has cut, no matter how long the overtime may be, sweating in the danger and cramped space of the working.

Lancashire was the scene of the two worst colliery disasters of 1932. Within a few weeks of each other nineteen men were killed —drowned in the sump—when the cage at the Plank Lane col-liery, Leigh, crashed, and twenty-seven men were killed in an explosion at the Edge Green colliery, Ashton-in-Makerfield, owned by the Garswood Hall Company, one of the recent combines.

Engineering of all kinds is the other great Lancashire industry. In general engineering there has been a particularly heavy decline in the numbers employed in the past ten years, and since the onset of the crisis the unemployment figure has trebled, reaching over 40 per cent. The extent of speeding-up is shown by figures, supplied by engineering employers, which reveal an increase in output per head over the period 1923-30 amounting in many cases to as much as 25 per cent.[49] A real "trembling system," as an old tool-maker in the Manchester district pun-gently described it to me, operates in the engineering works of Lancashire to-day.

Engineers are mainly on piecework. They are especially hit by the extensive short-time that is worked, and by the fact that there are now only a few jobs where there used to be many. But the piece-rates were fixed on a basis of a large number of jobs per man; and so now in very many cases engineers can only make their bare time-rate. The extent of short-time can be judged from the example of the biggest electrical engineering works in Manchester, where some departments never work Saturday mornings, and are laid idle two weeks out of every eight, while others only work one week in two. This same establishment is an example of the large proportion of women now employed in the engineering industry; nearly one-third of its 7,000 workers are women. In other works women and girls are largely employed on press-stamping and other automatic machines; their wages range from 12s. to 28s. a week.

Lancashire is the great centre of textile engineering. Here the falling-off in home demand and the collapse of the export trade (which is one-half, and less, of the pre-war level) have brought acute depression. It is common knowledge that if it had not been for extensive orders from the Soviet Union the industry would almost have disappeared. Monopoly has made big strides in the industry in the past two years. Six of the largest firms have combined to form Textile Machinery Makers Limited. Some idea of the conditions of the textile engineers is afforded by the fact that one of the combine firms which used to employ 3,000 now hardly employs a third of that number; and boy labour has been extensively introduced. The combine has displaced labour by concentrating its production in the most profitable works of its constituent firms.

As in the country as a whole, the minor, "new," industries have shown some expansion in Lancashire; but the "decline of the older industries has been much greater than the expansion of the newer." Similarly, there has been a parasitic enlargement of the distributive trades at the expense of production. Monopoly has grown here also; nine large chain stores in the Lancashire area had 599 shops in 1923 and 734 in 1931. But the increased employment in distribution up to the crisis "has gone along with increasing numbers, and an increasing percentage, of unemployed"; there is much casual labour in the large stores.[50] The parasitic development of the "new" industries and the distributive trades offers no more hope to the workers in Lancashire than to the workers in any other industrial area.

THE COTTON WORKERS IN THE CLASS STRUGGLE

In the stormy 'forties "the cotton workers," declared Engels, "pre-eminently stand at the head of the labour movement." Chartism, the first great independent and revolutionary political movement of the British working class, had its greatest strength in Lancashire. The strikes of 1932 showed the cotton workers once more standing at the head of the labour movement. This is a fact of fundamental significance, not only for the movement in Lancashire, but for the working class throughout Britain. It is significant because no section of the working class was more corrupted during the period of British capitalism's industrial, and then colonial, monopoly than the Lancashire cotton workers.

Writing in 1885, Engels noted the "permanent improvement" in the position of the cotton workers since the 'forties. "The fixing by Act of Parliament of their working-day within relatively rational limits," he wrote, "has restored their physical condition and endowed them with a moral superiority, enhanced by their local concentration." Discussing the reasons for this improvement in the position of a "privileged minority," he added, in a celebrated passage:

> During the period of England's industrial monopoly the English working class have, to a certain extent, shared in the benefits of the monopoly. . . . With the breakdown of that monopoly the English working class will lose that privileged position; it will find itself generally—the privileged and leading minority not excepted—on a level with its fellow-workers abroad. And that is the reason why there will be Socialism again in England.[51]

Since the war the colonial monopoly has gone the way of the industrial monopoly. What that has meant in the catastrophic decline of the cotton industry, in unemployment and short-time, in low wages and universal impoverishment, in intolerable working conditions, we have already seen. And what is the effect of all this upon the cotton workers and their movement?

It is necessary first to examine the peculiarities of trade unionism in the cotton industry. After the collapse of Chartism the cotton workers began to establish and consolidate their autonomous local unions of the different crafts (spinners, weavers, cardroom, etc.), the form of organisation which still exists. A later step was the formation of federations of these local unions, generally called amalgamations. The spinners led the way, in 1853, and it was not till thirty years after that the weavers and the cardroom workers followed suit. As the leaders of these unions there grew up the most extraordinary caste of officials that the trade union movement has ever known. Many years ago the Webbs described with enthusiasm, in their *Industrial Democracy*, how the "cotton men" were chosen by competitive examination for their mathematical and technical ability in interpreting the voluminous and incredibly complicated piece price-lists which governed cotton wages. The work of the cotton union official, they said, was "a service which, like that of a legal or medical professional man, could, with equal propriety, be rendered to either client."[52] So, on the basis of the sharing in the fruits of monopoly, the spirit of class collaboration found its most naked expression in the leadership of the cotton unions over whole generations.

These traditions of class collaboration in its extremest form, of officials who (to quote the Webbs again) "accept too implicitly the employers' assumptions, and do not sympathise with aspirations of a more fundamental change than a variation of wages or hours," are the background of the present generation of Lancashire cotton union leaders.[53] The old basis has gone for ever. The cotton workers face Engels' alternative, "starve or rebel"—and they have given clear testimony in the last four years that they are not prepared to starve. But the present leadership acts as a brake on their movement, holding them back from struggle and surrendering the struggle to the employers when once it has begun. Indeed, the quotation from the Webbs above needs to be modified; not only do the union leaders fight against a "fundamental change," but the only variation of wages that they offer to the workers is a variation downwards.

When a historical turning-point has been reached, all that has led up to it appears in a newly vivid light. The Midland Hotel agreement, by which the weavers' strike was concluded last autumn, is such a turning-point. It illuminates the whole previous policy of the union leaders, of which it is the natural outcome. The agreement conceded the employers a wage-cut of 1s. 8½d. in the £, accepted the more-looms system (later detailed in a separate agreement, to which reference has already been made), and provided for a system of "conciliation" to ensure "peace" for three years. A pious clause was also inserted relating to the reinstatement of weavers victimised for taking part in mill strikes against the more-looms system; it has proved to be empty of meaning.

All along the cotton workers had shown the most invincible determination to fight wage-cuts; the Burnley weavers voted in January 1932 by 8 to 1 for a strike; the weavers' county ballot in

June was 4 to 1 in favour of a strike; the spinners' and cardroom workers' ballots 20 to 1 and 15 to 1 in favour respectively; but the officials agreed to wage-cuts. All along the weavers had demonstrated their implacable hostility to more looms; the solidarity of the Burnley strike of January 1931 against more looms and the general lock-out which followed had compelled the employers to withdraw the demand; but the officials, who had agreed to the "experimental" working of more looms in 1929-30, and who had confined resistance to the employers' calculated mill-by-mill more-looms attack in 1931-32 to isolated mill strikes, accepted finally the more-looms system.

The big fact in Lancashire to-day is this divorce between the militant temper of the cotton workers and the reformist policy of their union leaders, who nevertheless still retain their influence over the decisive majority of the workers. This was shown once and for all in the strikes of 1932. It is not possible here to tell the story in detail. But it may be recalled how the line of the union leaders was, from June (when the existing agreement terminated) onwards, first to prevent any strike and to continue negotiations at all costs, and second to localise the strike in Burnley, when the weavers there finally forced its calling. There were the confusing ballots, which never put the straight issue—for or against a strike. There were the prolonged and complicated manœuvres of the Central Board of the Northern Counties Textile Trades Federation and the Central Committee and General Council of the Weavers' Amalgamation to avoid calling a general Lancashire strike and to negotiate—on the basis of a 6¼ per cent. wage-cut (the employers demanded 12½ per cent.). In this way Burnley fought alone for a month, until the rest of the county could be held no longer, and the strike became general on August 27th.

When the Burnley weavers forced their leaders to call the town out, on July 25, they received from those same leaders the advice to keep away from the mills. That advice was sensationally disregarded. Never had Burnley seen such mass pickets. Strikers rallied in their thousands on the streets leading to the few mills which endeavoured to keep working. The demonstrations were so fiery that the whole atmosphere became electric, charged with enthusiasm for the strike, hatred for the employers, and fierce contempt for the "knobsticks" who, despite the efforts of the police, both home and imported, were in instance after instance chased right through the town. In three days Burnley was solid as a rock. Employers and union leaders alike were astounded by the response to the strike call.

A month afterwards Burnley's experience was repeated all over Lancashire. The strike swept the northern weaving towns like a flame. Whole troops of pickets marched out from the big centres to "wipe up" the weak spots. Buses conveying "knobsticks" were stoned. Mill managers had to be escorted home under strong police guard, followed by booing crowds. Tradesmen whose relatives went to blackleg were boycotted. Since the insurrectionary general strike of 1842 Lancashire had never known such a movement. Equally, the strike represented the highest point reached by the class struggle in Britain since 1926 ; and the spontaneous wave of solidarity with the cotton strikers which arose among the workers all over the country was a sign of this.

The strike was remarkable for another thing: the unlimited use of the forces of the capitalist State against the workers. Police were imported wholesale, especially into Burnley. Baton charges were an everyday affair; pitched battles took place between mass pickets and police, as at Hargher Clough mill, Burnley, on August 16. Young and old, women and girls as well as men, were clubbed. There was in fact a police pogrom which enraged every worker in Lancashire, which evoked protests from Trades Councils, and which forced heated debates at Town Council meetings. The "blacklegs' charter," the Trade Disputes Act of 1927, was constantly invoked. Even the secretary of a local weavers' union, Mr. Ashworth, a J.P., was jailed for "intimidation," though the case was so grotesque that he was subsequently released. One Burnley weaver, taken to court under this Act, said: "We are fighting for our rights and for our bread and butter. I always thought this was a free country." That worker, and many thousands more, got a new insight into "freedom" under the dictatorship of the capitalist class.

There is a widespread feeling in Lancashire to-day that things cannot be allowed to continue in the old way, that the policy which has led to the present situation must be ended. "People can't go on like this," I heard a young woman winder cry at a union meeting; that is a cry which is being echoed more and more. But how to break with the past? That is the problem. Lancashire is widely disillusioned with the Labour Party. The cotton workers remember the lock-out of 1929 and the wage-cut awarded by the arbitration board set up by the Labour Government. They remember the attitude of Labour Cabinet Ministers to the more-looms system during and after the victorious strike of 1931. They have the bitter experience of the Anomalies Act. They know that the policy of the Labour Party during the last strike, as evidenced by the campaign of the *Daily Herald*, was to call for intervention—by the "National" Government (and when that intervention came it helped to fasten the Midland Hotel agreement on the backs of the workers). It is not surprising that the slump in the Labour vote in the general election of 1931 was particularly marked in Lancashire. Yet the influence of the Labour Party is still an important factor in Lancashire, and will remain so while the influence of the union leaders continues to be strong.

The plain fact is that unless the break with the past is carried through in the unions it will not be carried through at all. The last strike showed that the cotton workers were adopting the leads of the revolutionary workers, of the Communists, for militant struggle, especially in the mass picketing. At the same time there is a growing sympathy with the aims and policy of the Communists. But this influence lacks any corresponding organisation (as election results have shown). And of the development of a real, wide opposition movement in the unions there is as yet barely a beginning. The basis for a movement exists in the general disgust with the Midland Hotel and more-looms agreements, a disgust which compelled a number of local weavers' unions, on the initiative of the Nelson Weavers' Association, to participate officially last November in a conference of local union committees whose aim was stated to be the organisation of a campaign against the agreement (a campaign which has not since materialised). The structure of cotton trade unionism, with its autonomous local unions, and committees consisting of workers in the mill, facilitates the development of an opposition movement. It is the sectarian weakness of the revolutionary workers which has hitherto prevented full advantage being taken of this.*

The union leaders do not hesitate to try and mask their own bankruptcy and betrayal by provocative abuse of the Communists; thus the Blackburn Weavers' Committee, in their latest quarterly report, speaking with the voice of their secretary, Mr. Luke Bates, review the strike in a deeply pessimistic fashion, and

---

* A scheme has latterly been prepared by the leaders of the Weavers' Amalgamation for its transformation from a federation of autonomous local unions into a centralised body, with the suggested title of the "National Union of Weavers and Allied Workers." This scheme is now under discussion. The establishment of mill committees is proposed, which gives possibilities for rank-and-file development; but it is equally proposed that all organisers and area officials should be appointed by the central Executive, which indicates that the leaders' aim is not democratic, but bureaucratic, centralisation. Details of the scheme were given in the *Manchester Guardian* of January 23rd, 1933.

H

declare that in such acute trade depression strikes are fought "with the dice loaded against the operatives," adding:

> These facts are ignored by shallow-minded critics. They fail to comprehend the difficulties created by the state of the industry. There are adverse critics of our policy less concerned for the welfare of cotton operatives than creating disunity in our ranks and furthering the cause of an avowed insurrectionary movement, financed from doubtful quarters. Happily, these mischievous individuals are persons without influence among cotton operatives. The high character and intelligence of our members enable them to effectively resist the malicious propaganda of the persons referred to.[54]

On the contrary, it is precisely the "high character and intelligence" of cotton workers, coupled with the "difficulties created by the state of the industry," or in other words capitalist decline, that offer to the Communists the best guarantee of winning the widest support. But to achieve this the revolutionary workers will have to tear out, root and branch, the evil old tradition of sectarian isolation from the mass of trade unionists. Not many weeks ago I was present when a deputation of angry women winders and doublers visited the weavers' union office in a Lancashire town; and in the course of a heated discussion on the failure of the union officials to assist the women in a dispute one burst out: "Well, if we want owt done, we mun be Bolsheviks and non-unionists, ah see!" That woman was not exceptional; to many cotton workers, and among them some of the most militant, "revolutionary" and "trade unionist" seem to be a contradiction in terms. To show that, far from this being so, they need at all costs to be complementary, and that only so can the workers of Lancashire advance, is the vital necessity of to-day on the "classic soil of English manufacture."

CHAPTER III

CRISIS ON CLYDESIDE

THE basin of the river Clyde is outstanding as a compact and concentrated area of heavy industry. Here, centred on Glasgow and its satellite towns of Clydebank, Paisley, Dumbarton, Port Glasgow and Greenock, is one of the greatest shipbuilding and heavy engineering centres of the world. Within a brief radius lie big iron and steel works, at Motherwell, Coatbridge, Rutherglen; the whole is encircled by coalfields, reaching out north-east to Stirling and Fife, east to the Lothians, south and south-west to Lanarkshire and Ayrshire. Clydeside is the industrial heart of Scotland; and to-day that heart is scarcely beating.

The statistics speak loudly enough. They reveal a paralysis that is absolutely without parallel. Shipbuilding in Scotland has 77 per cent. of its workers unemployed, and marine engineering 65 per cent., the latter being the highest figure for the whole of Britain. Clyde shipbuilding output in 1932 only reached the infinitesimal level of 67,000 tons; and two-thirds of this tonnage was built by one firm. This output is the lowest since 1860, which was before the modern shipbuilding industry had developed seriously. It is little more than one-third the output of the previous blackest years in the Clyde's history—1886 and 1923. It compares with the pre-war peak of 757,000 tons, and the post-war average of 550,000 tons.[1]

Even worse is the position of the iron industry. There are eighty-nine blast-furnaces in Scotland. At the end of 1932 there were only two in blast; the maximum number in blast at any one time during the year was seven, and at one period in August it even sank to one. In general engineering the unemployment percentage is 42, the highest in Britain. The output of coal in 1932 was only two-thirds the pre-war level, falling back to the level of the nineties, and in Lanarkshire the output was little more than half the pre-war level; the number of miners employed in Scotland last year was some 87,000, compared with 140,000 before the war and at the post-war peak.[2] In December 1932 there were 130,000 registered unemployed in Glasgow. Allowing for the numbers not recorded at the exchanges, the Glasgow workless with their families account for half the population of that city.

A trip along the Clyde to-day is like visiting a cemetery. Mile after mile the empty slipways succeed each other. Over the whole length of this great shipbuilding river there are but three or four insignificant little boats on the stocks. To see this desolation is to understand the grim meaning of the latest Lloyds' return that the new tonnage commenced in all British shipyards during the concluding quarter of last year was only 7,410—the lowest ever recorded. And this is the end to which monopoly capitalist control of Scottish heavy industry has led. Clydeside has been for a generation and more a classic centre of the operation of capitalism in its final, most "advanced" form of finance-capital, the fusion of monopoly industrial capital with monopoly banking capital.

It is not possible here to unravel all the intricate ramifications of capitalist ownership in Scottish heavy industry, nor to analyse in detail the contradiction between the handful of huge monopoly concerns, with an advanced technique, and the anarchic mass of smaller concerns, with a very backward technique. The main feature that requires to be noted is the financial integration of the principal concerns in the different branches of heavy industry—shipbuilding, heavy engineering, iron and steel, coal. This trustification process reached its height in the period immediately following the war; but it has not stopped still since then, and, on the other hand, it had its origins in much earlier developments.

From the early years of this century the noted Clyde firm of Beardmore's, owners of Parkhead Forge and the Dalmuir shipyard and works, were linked with the gigantic Vickers combine; they were prominent members of the notorious "armaments ring," together with Vickers, Armstrong-Whitworth, Cammell Laird and the Sheffield steel, coal, and heavy engineering grouping of John Brown's. John Brown's (the product of the reinvestment of Lancashire textile profits in the sixties by a group of Manchester magnates) were at the same time large shipbuilders on the Clyde ; and their associates in the opening-up of the South Yorkshire coalfield, the Markham family, were linked with the Dalmellington Iron Company in Ayrshire. Beardmore's later joined with the big Tyneside shipbuilding firm of Swan, Hunter & Wigham Richardson (controllers of Barclay, Curle, shipbuilders and marine engineers on the Clyde) to acquire the Glasgow Iron and Steel Company, who were also coalowners in Lanarkshire.

Other Clydeside shipbuilders and engineers followed suit. A. Stephen & Sons (a subsidiary of the P. & O. shipping combine) joined with Yarrows, the builders of destroyers, and two other firms to take over the Steel Company of Scotland. Lithgows, of Port-Glasgow, bought up James Dunlop, coal and ironmasters, and the Calderbank steel works.[3] David Colville & Sons, the iron and steel lords of Motherwell, owners of the famous Dalzell iron and steel works, the largest individual steel works in Britain, had been steadily absorbing allied concerns, and also the important Lanarkshire and Stirlingshire colliery concern of Archibald Russell. They themselves became a subsidiary of the powerful Clyde and Belfast shipbuilding firm of Harland & Wolff, who control the well-known Clyde shipbuilding concerns of D. & W. Henderson and A. & J. Inglis, and who are associated with John G. Kincaid, the Greenock marine engineers, their licensees for building Diesel engines on the Burmeister & Wain system. Harland & Wolff's, in their turn, are part of that shipping monopoly *par excellence*, the £80,000,000 Royal Mail combine, embracing over thirty companies, which was formerly headed by the notorious Lord Kylsant.

Recently Colville's fused with Dunlop's and took over the steel business of Beardmore's. The Dalmellington Iron Company and the Ayrshire collieries of William Baird, big coal and ironmasters, were combined to form Baird's and Dalmellington Limited, who control 75 per cent. of the output of the Ayrshire coalfield. The Colville-Beardmore deal was the sequel to the enforced "reconstruction" of Beardmore's in 1928. The effect of that operation, in brief, was that the banks and the Treasury stepped in in order to make sure of their interest. The ordinary shares, of which practically the whole £2,000,000 worth were held by William Beardmore, first Baron Invernairn, chairman of the company, were slashed to the extent of 19s. of each £1 share; and, as the *Manchester Guardian* wrote on October 8th, 1928, "the banks and the Treasury assume absolute control of the business."

But let no one shed tears over the poor industrialist trembling in the clutches of the usurious bankers. We have already remarked that Scottish heavy industry is notably characterised by the development of finance-capital, the combination of bank and industrial capital. And prominent on the boards of two of the three banks which in effect foreclosed on Beardmores were two typical Scottish heavy industry magnates, Charles Ker and Allan Macdiarmid. Mr. Ker, a director of eight companies, is on the board of Lloyds' Bank and its subsidiary, the National Bank of Scotland; he is a director of Baird's and Dalmellington

Limited, of the L.M.S. Railway, of the monopoly Clyde Valley Electric Power Company and of insurance companies. His partner in the firm of M'Clelland, Ker & Co., chartered accountants, is none other than Lt.-Colonel J. Beaumont Neilson, descendant of the noted Scottish ironmaster of the same name, who, in 1830, first introduced the hot blast for smelting; and Colonel Neilson is one of the outstanding lords of heavy industry, a big figure in the Baldwins and Vickers concerns and chairman of the latter's child, the English Steel Corporation. Mr. Macdiarmid, also a chartered accountant, is an even more important person. He is a director of thirteen companies and chairman of six. He is on the board of the National Bank of Scotland. He is chairman of Stewarts and Lloyds the vast steel and tube-making combine, whose monopoly position dates from their formation thirty years ago by the fusion of Stewart and Menzies (of Rutherglen and Coatbridge, in Lanarkshire) with Lloyd & Lloyd (of Birmingham), and who are to-day the unchallenged rulers of the tube industry. He is also chairman of large-scale colliery companies, such as Wilsons & Clyde, with big pits in Lanarkshire and Fife, and the Robert Addie collieries, with three big pits in Lanarkshire. In addition he has a whole string of other directorships in subsidiary tube concerns, investment trusts and ironstone mining.*

Three points now arise from our sketch. The first is that the process of vertical trustification, from the raw material up to the finished article, is far advanced in Scottish heavy industry; coal mines in Scotland and iron ore mines in Spain, iron and steel works, shipyards and engineering shops, are brought under a single capitalist control. The second is that there is much horizontal interlocking between coal, iron and steel concerns which are not in the same vertical combination. The third is that the little clique of industrial magnates are at the same time big bankers and financiers, are largely concerned with insurance companies, investment trusts and similar financial ventures. To which we may add that they exhibit their characteristic imperialist concern in the drawing of tribute from abroad and from colonial exploitation by their frequent ownership of foreign trading concerns, of industrial concerns (for instance, mines) operating

---

* Stewarts and Lloyds are to-day directly linked with the "Big Five" Banks and the Bank of England itself, through the Bankers' Industrial Development Co. They are likewise integrated with the three monopoly concerns of the Lancashire Steel Corporation, the United Steel Companies, and Babcock & Wilcox (boilers). The facts are given in *Labour Research*, February 1933, pp. 32-33.

abroad, and of plantation companies (rubber and tea). Further, the divorce of the industrialists from industry, their metamorphosis into parasitic coupon-clippers, is particularly striking here, where a remarkable number of the "captains of industry" are accountants and lawyers.

In the light of the foregoing a survey of some of the most typical figures in Scottish heavy industry is instructive. The case of Mr. Macdiarmid and Mr. Ker we have already examined. Associated with the coal interests of the former gentleman are Major W. B. Rankin, an Edinburgh lawyer, W. A. Wilson, and W. Hamilton Telfer; all three are on the board of Wilsons & Clyde, and the first two are also directors of the Robert Addie collieries. Major Rankin is a director of fifteen companies in all, and chairman of four, including chemicals, insurance, investment and plantation companies. Now comes the horizontal interlocking. Mr. Wilson and Mr. Telfer (the latter has twelve directorships of colliery, insurance, iron ore mining and other companies) are both directors of the Coltness Iron Company, which describes itself as the largest manufacturer of locomotive steel castings in Britain, and which owns eleven collieries—the big Blairhall pit in Fife, a couple of pits in West Lothian, and eight in the Shotts area of Lanarkshire. On the Coltness board they are joined by no less a personage than Lord Invernairn, ex-chairman of Beardmore's; and Peter Rintoul, yet another accountant, who is the chairman of Coltness. So the finance-capitalists who, as we have seen, were interested in the taking over of Beardmore's by the banks are indirectly interlocked with Beardmore himself.

Lord Invernairn holds nineteen directorates and eight chairmanships, a whole string of engineering, coal, finance, and sugar-growing concerns; he is on the board of United Collieries, which is, with its sixteen pits in Lanarkshire and the Lothians, the second largest colliery concern in the whole of Scotland; here my lord is joined by A. C. Strathie, another accountant, director of a steel and an engineering company.

Peter Rintoul is the king of the Scottish accountant magnates. He is director of no fewer than twenty-six companies and chairman of nine. He links directly back to the interests of Mr. Macdiarmid, under whom he sits as deputy-chairman of Stewarts & Lloyds. Coal, iron, steel, iron ore mining, insurance, real property are all prominent among his interests; and he is on the board of the Union Bank of Scotland.

The next big horizontal interlocking has coal for its core. It will be appropriate to trace it outwards from the Fife Coal Company, which, with its twenty-six collieries in Fife and its 4,000,000 ton output, easily heads the list of Scottish colliery concerns and is one of the dozen principal mining monopolies in Britain. Sir Adam Nimmo, chairman of the Scottish coal industry board and vice-president of the Mining Association, is the chairman of this Fife colossus. He is also heavily interested in two of the largest Lanarkshire colliery companies, being on the board of the Shotts Iron Company (which also owns pits in the Lothians) and chairman and managing director of the family concern of James Nimmo & Company; he is likewise chairman of a small Ayrshire company.

Sir Adam has some interesting associates on the board of the Fife Coal Company. There is J. A. Hood, for instance, the chairman and managing director of the Lothian Coal Company and a director of Edinburgh Collieries; these are the two biggest companies operating in the developing coalfield of Mid and East Lothian, aggregating ten pits and more than 2,000,000 tons output. There is also Alexander Wallace (another Edinburgh lawyer), who ornaments the boards of eleven companies, including numerous insurance and finance companies and investment trusts; he is chairman of the Shotts Iron Company, a further link with Nimmo. And Mr. Wallace sits on the board of the Bank of Scotland cheek by jowl with John Craig, the chairman of the steel-monopolising Colville's and of eight other companies. Mr. Craig is a director of fourteen coal, steel and engineering concerns, including Colville's colliery subsidiary, Archibald Russell, and Harland & Wolff, the shipbuilders, by whom, as we have observed, Colville's are themselves controlled. It is not surprising that Mr. Craig occupies a foremost place in the national councils of capitalism, and is a member of the Council of the Federation of British Industries.

From Colville's we can retrace our steps to Sir Adam Nimmo and his immediate associates. It may be remarked in passing that Colville's are interlocked with the Lochgelly Iron & Coal Company, third in order of importance of the Fife coal companies, through their control of Archibald Russell, which members of the Thorneycroft family link with the board of the Lochgelly Company. We have noted that Colville's recently effected a fusion of interests with James Dunlop's, the iron, steel and coal concern controlled by Lithgow's the shipbuilders. A prominent member of the Dunlop board is one R. T. Moore, a doctor of science, who is to the fore in half-a-dozen important Scottish colliery companies and also in the Clyde valley electric power monopoly (with Charles Ker). These companies include the

Edinburgh Collieries, of which he is chairman (thus connecting him with Nimmo through J. A. Hood) and Baird's & Dalmellington, the lords of Ayrshire (which connects him with our previous acquaintance, Charles Ker and the Ker interests). He is a director of the third largest Lothians concern, the Niddrie & Benhar Coal Company, with their two big pits near Portobello, and also of several companies mainly operating in Lanarkshire.

Other Nimmo associates include John Alston, a Coatbridge solicitor, who is a director of James Nimmo & Company, and who numbers structural engineering, tinplate, insurance and other coal companies among his nine directorates. There is likewise Lt.-Colonel Alexander Mitchell, co-director with Sir Adam Nimmo and Alexander Wallace of the Shotts Iron Company, who is the chairman of the Alloa Coal Company, owning four pits in Clackmannan and two in the Lothians, and who is interested in collieries abroad and in shipping.

In conclusion, a word should be said about that strange phenomenon the Wemyss Coal Company, the second largest colliery concern in Fife, and owners of the biggest, most modern, most rationalised pits in Scotland. This company has gained some current notoriety by its opposition to the plan of the Coal Mines Re-Organisation Commission for compulsory amalgamation of all the Fife collieries. It presents in some ways a curious reproduction of feudal ideas in a thoroughly up-to-date dress. Its pits are completely mechanised, the last ounce is sweated out of its miners in the most "advanced" manner possible, its output per head is (I should guess) among the very highest in the whole of the British coalfields. It is not interlocked with other collieries, remaining a family concern. In this splendid isolation—which has proved profitable, too, for the Wemyss seams are rich, and the pits have Methil docks literally on their doorstep—the family utters the truly feudal-flavoured boast that for five and a half centuries coal has been mined on their estate and that the laird of Wemyss has always been, as of right, the head of the mining enterprise.[4]

We have now pictured in broad outline the complex capitalist structure of Scottish heavy industry, centring on the Clyde, stretching out from shipbuilding and engineering to iron and steel, and embracing the major part of the coal industry of the whole country. The picture is far from complete. Space forbids consideration of many large-scale shipbuilding and engineering firms whose names are household words on the Clyde—Fairfield's, Denny's, Scott's, Rowan's, Weir's. Equally it is impossible to do more than list such concerns as Sir William Arrol & Company,

one of the biggest structural engineering establishments (a
Vickers subsidiary), the North British Locomotive Company (one
of the biggest locomotive builders in Britain), Singer's sewing
machines (whose vast Glasgow works is among the very largest of
British engineering plants) and the Albion Motor Company (one
of the principal makers of heavy commercial vehicles). It should
be remembered, too, that Paisley is the domain of J. & P. Coats,
the cotton thread monopolists.

Keeping in mind this sketch of the little clique of interlocked
monopolists who hold Scottish heavy industry in the hollow of
their hands to-day, we shall now see what has been the fate to
which these parasites have condemned the workers who carry
them on their backs.

MEN, SHIPS AND STEEL

The shipyard workers, one-time aristocrats of labour, have
been brought to the lowest depths by the rationalisation drive of
the shipbuilding monopolists. Equipment has been modernised,
wages cut, work speeded up, so that larger vessels can be built in
less time with fewer workers. In the past ten years the labour
force in shipbuilding has undergone a catastrophic contraction,
and recruitment has virtually ceased. The figures for 1929, the
last pre-crisis year, show that while the total tonnage produced in
British yards exceeded the 1921 level, there were over 72,000
fewer men employed. On the Clyde the displacement of labour
in some sections of the industry has. been as high as 30 to 40
per cent.[5]

Precisely the same process has marked the Clydeside steel
works associated with shipbuilding. One steel plant employed
2,400 men for an output of 2,400 tons of ship plates a week; after
reconstruction only 800 men were required for an output of 4,500
tons a week. In two rolling mills 500 men were employed to
produce a weekly output of 3,000 tons of sectional material for
shipbuilding, rails and so forth; one of the mills was reconstructed
in 1931 and is now able to yield the same output as the two
formerly did, with only half the number of men. Furnace output
has been practically doubled without any addition to the number
of men employed.[6]

The big shipbuilders have openly come out in the role of
machine-wreckers. Unable to employ their productive capacity
at a profit, and careless of the future of the scores of thousands of
skilled shipyard workers flung on to the scrap-heap, they have
cynically organised themselves to buy up and demolish "redun-

dant and/or obsolete yards." This was the objective of a concern
entitled National Shipbuilders' Security Limited, which was
established, with the assistance of the banks, just three years ago;
it has since purchased for a song and dismantled some dozen
yards in various shipbuilding centres, including the recently
built and modern yard of Beardmore's on the Clyde. Could there
be a more striking instance of the manner in which capitalism
to-day is not only unable to develop the forces of production, but
actually destroys them; that, as Marx said, "the monopoly of
capital becomes a fetter upon the mode of production, which has
sprung up and flourished along with, and under it ?"

This machine-wrecking organisation, too, is a real gathering
of the "heid yins" of the Shipbuilding Employers' Federation.
Its chairman is Sir James Lithgow, who built in his yards two-
thirds of the Clyde's 1932 output, and who is a past president
of the Federation of British Industries and of the National
Confederation of Employers' Organisations. On its board sit
representatives of the Vickers-Armstrong combine, of Swan,
Hunter's and of such prominent Clyde firms as Harland &
Wolff, Barclay, Curles, Fairfield's and A. Stephen & Sons.

Activities of this kind have reduced the shipbuilding capacity
of Britain from 3,000,000 tons a year to round about 2,500,000
tons or less; but in 1932 the actual output was not one-tenth of
the latter figure. It is to this figure of productive capacity, as
well as to the figures of displacement of labour due to rationalisation, that the forecasts of increased shipbuilding activity in the
present year need to be related. The Shipbuilding Employers'
Federation announced on January 26th last that orders for
fifty-eight vessels (more than half of them very small boats)
had been placed with British shipyards since November 1st,
1932; they claimed that "it is extremely probable that the figures
for new tonnage commenced in British shipyards for the March
quarter will exceed the tonnage commenced during the whole of
1932." Of course, there is nothing surprising in the fact that,
once the bottom has been reached, there should be a rebound.
But what serious difference is there likely to be made in the
volume of shipbuilding unemployment? On the Clyde even a
boom would not mean that, according to the rosiest estimate,
more than 60 per cent. of the workers employed in 1929 would be
re-employed—and there were over 20 per cent. unemployed in
that year. Some Clyde shipbuilders do not go above 40 per cent.
as their estimate of the proportion of the present labour force
that a boom would employ. And the Federation's statement is
careful to stress that "there is no desire to raise false hopes that

British ship-building and ship-repairing are on the eve of any boom." So much for the "Shipbuilding Spurt," as the *Daily Herald* headlines screamed.[7]

The years of crisis, culminating in the fearful collapse of 1932, have seen the rationalisation offensive pressed forward more intensively than ever. We have this on the authority of Mr. J. B. Hutchison, the president of the Shipbuilding Employers' Federation, and a director of Scotts' Shipbuilding & Engineering Company, a big Clyde concern. Mr. Hutchison states that during the past year the membership and scope of the Employers' Federation has been "considerably extended"; and the Federation statement, quoted above, remarks that since July 1931 shipbuilders and steelmakers "have established closer co-operative arrangements" among themselves. What is the reason for this drawing together of the capitalist forces, for this strengthening of monopoly capital? Mr. Hutchison shall answer:

> There has been a concentration of effort on the overhaul of all methods of production, systems of remuneration and payments and allowances of all kinds. No general reductions in the national uniform time rates of wages have been made, but short of this everything possible has been done within the industry to stimulate and secure the maximum productivity to enable British shipbuilders to supply all their clients with the cheapest ships possible.[8]

Wages, that is to say, have been driven down to the bare time rate. Some idea of what that means is shown by the recently published Ministry of Labour figures, which return 51s. 7d. as the average weekly earnings in shipbuilding in the latter part of 1931. That is the pittance, barely enough to keep a family above the harshest poverty line, earned by skilled workers for arduous and exacting toil. And the process which the president of the Employers' Federation dignifies with the name of "overhaul of systems of remuneration"—it is "overhauling" the children's ration of bread, Mr. Hutchison, but to you it is merely the adjustment of another piece of machinery!—means this: in 1932 the wages of 28,000 shipyard workers were reduced by an average of 3s. 5d. per head per week.[9] What this "overhaul" of "all payments and allowances" involves can also be deduced from longstanding demands of the employers for the general reduction of overtime rates and a slash of allowances which would mean in certain cases—for instance, men working on the repair of oil tankers—cuts up to 23s. a week.[10]

It is by a further advance along these lines to a grand assault on the already shockingly low standard of their workers that the shipbuilding magnates, the heavy industry monopolists, plan to "restore prosperity." Such a pre-eminent Clyde capitalist leader as Sir James Lithgow has propounded this plan with brutal candour in a New Year review of "Scotland's Industrial Future," which is a regular manifesto.[11] He declares that "in an impoverished world it is idle to talk of maintaining our standards of remuneration"—a plain admission that the capitalist "remedy" for poverty is to make more poverty—and adds that the "first problem" of all the heavy industries "is the question of wages costs"—when the average weekly earnings in shipbuilding are 51s. 7d. He takes the familiar line that the wages of Government employees and of workers in the "sheltered" industries must be brought down; in the degree, no doubt, of the 15 per cent. cut which the master printers are now demanding of their "sheltered" workers. He makes special reference to marine engineering, where, he avers, "the handicap of our high wage standard" is "apparent"; the average weekly earnings in marine engineering are considerably below even the shipyard workers' miserable level, and stand at the very "high" figure of 45s. 11d.*

This wealthy monopolist is not concerned with the condition of the workers, except to worsen them; indeed, the working class do not enter into his picture at all, save as victims; but he is characteristically anxious to endorse the alliance of the trade union leaders with himself and his fellows, in order that wage-cuts may be successfully put over. He says that industrial "recovery" depends on "the three main parties to our industrial life—the capitalist, who provides the resources for initiating and carrying on our industries, great and small; the trades union leader, who by wise advice may maintain conditions of stability which are within the reasonable possibilities of industry to provide; and the public administrator," whose task is to "adjust" the "financial burdens" on industry. That is a candid and revealing statement of the division of labour between the capitalist and his labour lieutenant; the one enforces the wage cuts, the other holds the workers back from struggle against the cuts—by "wise advice maintaining conditions of stability."

What does Sir James Lithgow offer to the great mass of the workless in heavy industry? "We must look forward," he says, "to a smaller percentage of our population being employed in what have hitherto been regarded as our heavy basic industries"; the "balance" he relegates to "the lighter and more specialised

---

* It would be interesting if Sir James Lithgow would reveal the connection between his singular good fortune in securing the major part of the Clyde's 1932 tonnage and the wages and conditions in his yards.

industries associated with articles of domestic consumption, ranging from tinned tomatoes to electric fires." This is insolent and loathsome mockery of the misery of the working class with a vengeance. Talk of electric fires, notoriously expensive to run, to the hundreds of thousands of workers condemned to live in the vile slums of Glasgow, and with difficulty able to afford coal for their hearths! The fundamental contradiction here leaps to the eye. Wages are to be cut, impoverishment increased, but the "superfluous scrap" of heavy industry's labour force are to find work in manufacturing articles of domestic consumption which the mass of the population cannot consume, because they cannot afford to buy them. The point is a childishly obvious one; so obvious indeed that it is noticed even by the genteel economists of the University of Glasgow, in the *Industrial Survey of South-West Scotland* prepared by them for the Board of Trade. They anticipate that "there will be a slackening off in the intensity of consumption. After all, our standard of living is high (!) in comparison with that of our continental rivals. And it is more than doubtful if the maintenance of its present level can persist much longer."[12] For the nonce the dons are more honest than their capitalist master.*

The whole prospect of a permanently changed balance in British capitalist economy between the basic and the light industries is, of itself, a prospect of a devastating lowering of the workers' standard of living. The issue is summed up in the *Industrial Survey of the North-East Coast*, which deals with an area exactly analogous to the Clyde; it says:

> In our view it is highly improbable that any expansion of these [light, distributive] industries and services can take place on such a scale as to make up for a continued loss in the heavy or basic industries, for which the area is so favourably situated. It is on these that Britain's position in the economy of the world depends. If that goes permanently it seems to us that the general standard of life in the country must fall.[13]

This prospect is at the same time one of advancing social parasitism. The 1931 census figures for Glasgow show that metal workers, who in 1921 led the way with nearly 18 per cent. of the occupied population, have dropped to less than 13 per cent. First place is now taken by "commercial occupations," which

* The powers of logic and general intellectual profundity of these hacks of the governing class are really astonishing. Thus they will observe the "curtailment of spending power forced upon a large portion of the general public by the loss of remunerative work" (*Industrial Survey of S.W. Scotland*, p. 114), and later aver that "there has been an appreciable improvement in the standard of living" (ibid., p. 120).

have risen from under 11 to nearly 14 per cent. "Personal service" shows an increase from just over 7 to nearly 10 per cent.

But we have still a few more rounds left in the magazine for Sir James Lithgow! Recall his reference to "the capitalist, who provides the resources for initiating and carrying on our industries great and small." Set that against the fact that Sir James is the chairman of the shipbuilders' wrecking organisation, which only exists to buy up shipyards and put them out of action, to destroy the forces of production. To define such operations as "providing resources for carrying on our industries" is preposterous humbug. And what of the notorious backwardness of the Scottish pig-iron and steel industries?

The technique of the Scottish iron industry is of a very low order. Its average furnace capacity is only 300 tons, compared with 500 tons on the north-east coast; in 1929 the annual average output of British blast furnaces was 48,000 tons, of South Wales furnaces 101,000 tons, but of Scottish furnaces only 23,000 tons. These facts are well known; and so are the measures required for the needed radical reconstruction, both geographical and technical, of the Scottish iron industry. Nothing is done, because the capitalist does not and will not "provide the resources," since the inducement of profit is lacking. But the capitalist "provides the resources for initiating industries." Indeed! On Clydeside and in its surrounding areas industrialisation has been at a dead stop throughout the post-war period. True, 155 firms started operations; they were concerns of such magnitude that they only employed a total of less than 17,000 workers, or one-tenth of the numbers now *unemployed* in Glasgow and its adjoining towns; and of these firms only a handful, employing not more than 3,000 workers all told, were in the basic industries.[14]

"That Iron-Hearted Carl, Want"

The unemployment figures cited at the beginning of this chapter afford some indication of the depth of poverty and want on Clydeside. Glasgow itself reproduces, on the enhanced scale of a big industrial city, the ghastly symptoms that we have seen in the derelict mining villages of South Wales. Of its 130,000 registered unemployed the great majority, over 90,000, are on the Means Test; and 16,000 of these have been refused any benefit whatever. The scourge of unemployment, and long-term unemployment at that, is felt most keenly by the skilled workers. Just on half the Glasgow district membership of the Amalgamated Engineering Union, for instance, are signing the unemployed book. Craftsmen who at one time had a tolerable standard of living sink deeper and deeper into the mire as the months and years drag by; the trim clothes become shabbier and more and more threadbare, the collar and tie is abandoned; if they had been able to get decent housing accommodation that has to go too, and the family is driven into a noisome one- or two-room apartment in a Cowcaddens or Anderston slum.

An engineering Trade Union official in Glasgow recently told me a typically tragic story of this kind. "When I was a youngster," he said, "there was an engineer here, a keen crafts-man, who was quite a noted character because of the invariable smartness of his dress. He was always a bachelor, and was univer-sally nicknamed for his smart appearance. Now he is middle-aged, and has long been unemployed. The smart lad of my apprentice days is so sorely hit that I was glad to be able to give him an old suit of my own when he was up in the district office the other day."

Here is the case of an unemployed Clydebank riveter. He happens to have been recently left a widower, with a little girl two years and odd to look after. His weekly benefit from the Exchange is 17s. 3d., out of which 7s. goes in rent. In order to be able to go out and look for work he is having a young girl in to look after the child, for which he will pay 4s. a week. That leaves 6s. 3d. to spend on everything necessary to sustain life for two people, father and little daughter; two human beings, that is to say, have rather less than 11d. a day to keep them in food, heat, light and clothing. The child's only toy is an old brick. Faced with the blank impossibility of maintaining the child's bare physical health under such circumstances, the unhappy father is desperately afraid that she will have to go to some institution, and he will lose her.[15]

Faced with a growing mass of predominantly male unemploy-ment, the Glasgow bourgeoisie have tried to develop some sort of a movement for the employment of male domestic servants. I forbear to offer any comment on what Sir James Lithgow would doubtless think an admirable method of helping to dispose of the "balance" of the working class, for whom there is no place in the basic industries; instead I reproduce the following letter to the editor of the Glasgow *Evening Times*, printed in that news-paper on January 16th, 1933:

SIR,—Regarding male domestics and also in advice to "Unemployed," who is anxious to gain such a post, I advise him to seek other employ-ment. I, like himself, was willing to accept anything, and when the opportunity came along for a cook I gladly accepted. But what an

awakening! Having interviewed my prospective employer, I was
engaged as cook, not cook-general. My duties commenced at 6 a.m.,
ceasing at 9 p.m. On my second morning I was surprised to find on the
kitchen table a large order board, having been placed there the
previous evening by my employer. Here were the orders: Rise 5.30,
light kitchen fire, dust drawing-room and clean out drawing-room fire,
clean boots and shoes, at seven o'clock take tea to master and mistress,
set breakfast table for breakfast at eight o'clock, wait table, clear table,
have own breakfast, sweep stairs, clean brasses, wash breakfast dishes,
clean kitchen, dust hall; lunch, 1 p.m.; in afternoon prepare dinner;
tea, 4.30; dinner, 6.30; wait dinner table, clear table, wash up. On the
days mentioned the following had to be thoroughly cleaned: Monday,
hall; Tuesday, bedrooms; Wednesday, drawing-room; Thursday,
silver; and Friday, kitchen. And all this came under the duties of a
cook!—I am, etc.,   NEVER AGAIN.

The smell of poverty is in the air in every working-class quarter
of Glasgow. "That iron-hearted carl, Want," as Burns sang,
stalks down every grey and grimy street. In the course of a brief
walk the passer-by is struck by the extremely impoverished
appearance of the women, especially the old women. It fills the
heart with black rage against the social order to see these white-
haired grandmothers exhibiting in their every lineament, from
frail bodies and shrunken aged faces, to the soiled and tattered
shawl which is their only protection against the bitter wind, the
squalor and misery to which capitalist society condemns them.
The half of Glasgow's population which is in the grip of
unemployment has not only to exist on a diet that is meagre to
the point of famine, that excludes the foods most vital to health,
but one that is often actively harmful. Apart from bread and tea*
(plus the cheapest skimmed condensed milk, devoid of all nutri-
tive value) the main items of the Glasgow unemployed family's
menu are the bacon, sausages, and mince that one sees everywhere in the cheap, and very nasty, butcher's shops and on the
barrows in the numerous poor markets. These items should
really be specified in inverted commas, for their common price—
threepence a pound—is eloquent of their atrocious quality. The
chemical redness of the mince tells its own story; and one can
read in the health reports of the city year by year the analysts'

* Compare the observation of the school medical officer for Roxburgh
that "it was found by questioning the children and others that bread and
tea is in many cases the regular diet both in urban and rural areas, and
the old instinctive sense of the necessity of butter, milk and eggs is being
gradually lost" (*Annual Report of the Department of Health for Scotland*, 1931,
p. 51). He adds that such a diet "affects nutrition in such a way that a
marked weakness develops in the mucous membrane and glands of the
throat."

I

reports on the relatively high percentage of adulteration in sausages and sausage meat, and the illegal use of sulphite as a preservative for mince.[16]

After food, clothing (a very long way after, so far as the Glasgow workless and their families are concerned). On a recent visit to the city I passed a clothing shop outside which a large crowd had gathered. Flaring posters in the window proclaimed that this establishment was conducting a "sale at throw-away prices for the benefit of the unemployed." On production of an unemployment card it was possible to purchase here men's trousers for 4d. a pair, boy's trousers for 1d., and a lounge suit for 1s. 6d. What was behind this venture I do not know; it certainly received extensive editorial publicity in the local newspapers.

But I have in my hands something which is infinitely more significant than this isolated stunt. It is a document entitled "Glasgow (North) Condemned Street List," issued by one of the large credit clothing and supply concerns to its local agents. Consisting of five closely printed sheets, this remarkable document is a real directory of poverty; for the purpose of its issue is to indicate those streets and houses whose inhabitants are so poor that it is not a commercial proposition to allow them even the smallest credit. And who should be in a better position to construct such an index of a city's impoverishment than the doorstep men of a "two-down-and-one-a-week" organisation? It is enough to add that the six sections into which this grim directory is divided list a total of over 500 streets; in some cases individual numbers, or series of numbers, in a street are specified; but for the most part it is entire streets that are marked off as "condemned." Sometimes the directory becomes peremptory, as in the entry "London-road, absolutely all backlands." Each section, too, after its long list of streets, invariably terminates (it is like a refrain) with the words: "Also all courts, alleys, backlands and slum clearance schemes."

"Burn It Down!"

" 'Burn it down!' is the classic reply of the eminent traveller to questionnaires regarding this or that city. The recommendation is the only one that meets the case of certain large areas of a city like Glasgow, where in 1931 there were more than 148,000 dwellings of two rooms or less, containing half the population." The quotation is from an organ of the Berry brothers, the coal, iron, steel and newspaper monopolists—the *Sunday Times* of

January 15th, 1933. Glasgow, the "second city of the Empire," has an appalling record as the city with the very worst housing conditions; a century ago the Glasgow workers were housed unspeakably—and a description of conditions then is interchangeable with a description of conditions to-day. Engels quotes the following from a newspaper of 1842:

> The working class forms here some 78 per cent. of the whole population and lives in parts of the city which exceed in wretchedness and squalor the lowest nooks of St. Giles and Whitechapel, the Liberties of Dublin, the Wynds of Edinburgh. There are numbers of such localities in the heart of the city, south of the Trongate, westward from the Saltmarket, in Calton and off the High-street, endless labyrinths of lanes or wynds into which open at almost every step, courts or blind alleys, formed by ill-ventilated, high-piled, waterless and dilapidated houses. These are literally swarming with inhabitants. They contain three or four families upon each floor, perhaps twenty persons.

J. C. Symonds, a Government Commissioner in the 1830's, wrote as follows after a visit to Glasgow:

> I have seen wretchedness in some of its worst phases both here and upon the Continent, but until I visited the wynds of Glasgow I did not believe that so much crime, misery and disease could exist in any civilised country. . . . This quarter consists wholly of narrow alleys and square courts, in the middle of every one of which there lies a dung heap. Revolting as was the outward appearance of these courts, I was yet not prepared for the filth and wretchedness within. . . . No one seemed to take the trouble to cleanse this Augean stable, this Pandemonium, this tangle of crime, filth, and pestilence in the centre of the second city in the kingdom. An extended examination of the lowest districts of other cities never revealed anything half so bad, either in intensity of moral and physical infection, or in comparative density of population.[17]

Against this we may set the report of the Government Commissioner sent to enquire into a Glasgow slum clearance scheme in 1926. The Commissioner wrote:

> It is impossible to draw any picture which could adequately describe the conditions under which we found human beings living in practically the whole of the houses which we inspected. There were, it is true, differences in degree, but all were hopelessly unfit for habitation. . . . The majority of the houses were dark, many of the tenants having to burn gas all day, winter and summer. Large numbers of tenements were built in the middle of hollow squares, hard up against high buildings on all sides, with no proper ventilation or light. Damp was present everywhere, the walls and ceilings in a large number of houses being literally soaking. Everywhere we noticed an almost total lack of sanitation, conveniences being few and for the most part out of repair, and in some cases leaking down the stairs and even into the houses. . . . Dilapidation is rife throughout the areas. Ceilings are

falling down, woodwork is rotting away, there are holes in the walls of houses through which the street can be seen, and the plaster-work of the walls is loose and broken. The houses are a hunting-ground for vermin of every description. Fleas, of course, abound, but we found also that practically every property we inspected was absolutely bug-ridden. The tenants complained that they could get no peace from these pests, which drop upon their faces and crawl over their persons and beds at night, and which fall into their food during the day. The food itself will not keep in many of these tenements . . . owing to the damp and verminous condition of the holes in the wall in which it is kept. In addition to the insects which I have mentioned we found evidences of a perfect menagerie of animal life, including lice, rats in great numbers, mice, cockroaches, snails and even toads. Can it be wondered that such places breed an unhealthy and discontented population? Crowded together, we found as many as eight persons living in one small house [i.e. a "single-end," or one room], cold and damp; neither adults nor children have much chance of health. Vital statistics do not prove much, but I was painfully struck by the information which the tenants gave me repeatedly of having recently lost one, two or even three children, of relatives in hospital and of continued ill-health, all of which were attributed by them very largely to the conditions in which they lived.[18]

Anyone who visits Glasgow to-day and spends a few days in the working-class quarters will see that this description of the indescribable cannot be bettered. That nearly a hundred years separate the first two quotations from the third is once again a scorching revelation whither the "culture," "progress" and "civilisation" of capitalist society lead.

A walk through Cowcaddens, Anderston, Gorbals and Calton reveals the barbarous condition of living to which capitalism in its final stage drags down hundreds of thousands of working-men, their wives and children. Sometimes the gloomy, grey, five-storeyed blocks look solid enough when seen from the street; but pass through one of the closes into the court at the back, skirt round the filthy overflow from a blocked drain, and the picture is very different; without exception the common lavatory and staircase windows are broken, save in those cases where they have been taken right out and iron bars substituted, adding to the general jail-like atmosphere (though prisons are vastly cleaner). The stairs are precipitous and often as dark as a mine gallery. I recollect my astonishment, after a morning groping up and down stairs like this in Cowcaddens, when I came across a light and well-maintained stairway; but there was no cause for astonishment—the stairs led to the factor's office.

No fewer than 40,000 dwellings in Glasgow, or one-sixth of the total, consist of only one room. Engels has described how the continental system of building five- and six-storey blocks, as adopted in the Scottish cities in contrast with England, where each family as far as possible has a separate house, means that "the crowding of human beings upon a limited area is thus intensified." When this is coupled with the "single-end," as the one-room dwelling is called, the overcrowding is frightful. In the Central Division of Glasgow there are six tenements where the density is at the rate of 367 houses and 1,399 persons to the acre, compared with the city's average of 8.7 and 37 respectively.[19] I have been in a court in Anderston, consisting of nine closes, with from thirty to forty families living in each close, at the rate of five to six one-room apartments on each landing. And for the refuse of more than three hundred families there was but one ashpit in the middle of the court. So bad were conditions here that the ground floor had been condemned and the windows bricked up; on the street side the ground floor was a basement, the windows abutting on a gully not more than two feet wide—and a few years ago human beings were living in this detestable dungeon!

In many cases when one penetrates the dark passage-way of a close, it is not to emerge into a court, but into what is little more than a blind alley. There, facing you, is yet another squalid block, and through that, finally, what remains of the court. These are the "backlands," which we have seen figure on the "condemned list" of the credit clothiers. If you wish to be filled with hatred for the social order which flings the producers of wealth into these foul warrens, visit Whitehall-street and White-hall-court, in Anderston, and their backlands. The savage irony of the name will not be lost on you. Equally ironically named and equally vile are Piccadilly-street and Rotten Row—the latter only a few paces from spacious and imposing George-square, the city's centre.

Altogether there are over 13,500 houses in Glasgow whose condition is so scandalous that they are officially classed as "uninhabitable." This, as can be seen from the figure of houses of two rooms or less, which is more than ten times as great, is only a small part of the problem. Nearly 50 per cent. of the houses in the city have no separate water-closet accommodation, and nearly 100,000 water-closets have to serve three or more families each.

Side by side with general overcrowding there exist, in the northern division of the city for example, numbers of larger houses standing empty because the rent demanded is too high. Sometimes these houses are sub-divided. But the sub-division is a farce. All it means is that rooms are sub-let, partly furnished (the emphasis is on the "partly"), at rents of from 6s. to 8s. a week. For one house so sub-divided there is usually only one water-closet and one water tap.[20] I have heard of a case where a factor cleared out the existing tenants and converted the house into a warren of "single-ends," let to young married couples "furnished"—meaning a couple of chairs and an apology for a bed—for 10s. a week.

On the internal state of the houses I have little to add to the 1926 Commissioner's report, already quoted. I have been in houses in Tradeston where the tenants had had to plaster the ceiling themselves to prevent it collapsing on their beds in the hole in the wall, where the thin floors varied from the horizontal by as much as six inches, where the walls were porous, where the windows either could not be opened at all or else lifted right out of their rotten frames, where the food store was a damp recess adjoining the stinking common lavatory. It was noticeable that the workers living in these houses were far indeed from being slum proletarians; they were solid working-class types, politically keen, and spirited in their determination to fight the landlord's exploitation. As a result of an organised rent struggle a number of them had won a reduction of their rent to the pre-war level.

A significant sidelight on the extent of overcrowding is provided by the report on the medical inspection of school-children. Dr. Arbuckle Brown reports that there are to-day "still more than two-thirds of the pupils living in houses which provide on the average no better accommodation than at the rate of 2.7 persons per room," and "13.3 per cent. of the children inspected were living in one-apartment houses, in which the average number of inmates was above 5." Of the children five years of age there were 17.4 per cent. living in one-apartment houses. No comment is needed on the further fact that the percentage of children coming from one-apartment houses was higher in 1931 than it was in 1912; and the average number of inmates in one-apartment houses was similarly higher.[21] That is a striking index of the real worsening of housing conditions, despite all the municipal schemes and the new Council houses.

It is possible to show the direct connection between housing (and the economic position that it connotes) and the physical condition of the children. We may note, by the way, that only 54 per cent. of the Glasgow school-children examined in 1931 were classified as "good" for nutrition. The following table, showing the heights and weights of boys and girls aged thirteen, related to the number of rooms in their home, speaks for itself—and how bitterly!:

GLASGOW HOUSING CONDITIONS AND CHILDREN'S PHYSIQUE IN 1931[22]

| | | Heights (in inches) | | | | Weights (in lbs.) | | |
| | | Number of Rooms | | | | Number of Rooms | | |
	1	2	3	4+	1	2	3	4+
Boys	55.3	55.7	56.6	57.6	77.1	78.2	81.4	84.9
Girls	56.0	56.8	57.5	58.5	79.5	82.0	84.3	88.3

The boy who comes from a home with four rooms or more is on the average nearly 2½ inches taller than the boy who comes from a one-room home; and the girl who comes from a home with four rooms or more is on the average just on nine pounds heavier than the girl from a one-room home.

Capitalist society inflicts on the workers of Glasgow the barbarous living conditions that have now been sufficiently exposed; and in this way it bears the criminal responsibility for the brutal fact that Glasgow has traditionally had an infantile mortality rate far greater than that of any other big city. This rate is rising higher with the crisis, as in every other centre; from 101 in 1930 it rose to 105 in 1931 (when the average for the whole of Britain was 66, and for London 65). Actually this real "massacre of the innocents" in Glasgow's working-class quarters is worse than these figures indicate; for the city rate is artificially depressed by the low rate prevailing in the bourgeois, residential areas. For the twelve wards of Glasgow where more than 50 per cent. of the population is officially returned as overcrowded (and this is on the excessively low standard of more than two persons to a room), the average infantile mortality rate in 1931 was 116. For the five wards where less than 10 per cent. of the population is returned as overcrowded, the rate was only 54. Between 1930 and 1931 the infantile mortality rate in a number of the principal working-class wards, where overcrowding is severe, has risen as follows (the 1930 figures are in parentheses): Dalmarnock 127 (96), Provan 124 (101), Townhead 129 (87), Anderston 126 (105), Ruchill 109 (96). In two comfortable bourgeois suburbs, on the other hand, the rate actually fell—in Pollokshields from 66 to 34, and in Cathcart from 50 to 46. We may sum up the connection between housing and health in Glasgow in tabular form:[23]

GLASGOW HOUSING AND VITAL STATISTICS, 1931

	Rooms per house	Percentage of population over-crowded	Mortality rates p/1,000			
			Infant	Respira-tory	Tuber-culosis (Phthisis)	Gene-ral
WORKING-CLASS WARDS						
Dalmarnock	1.71	69.3	127		*	16.6
Calton ..	2.07	58.4	140	average 2,000	1.389	17.9
Anderston ..	2.26	51.6	126		*	15.9
Cowcaddens	2.02	58.8	119		*	18.0
Gorbals ..	2.32	52.5	127		*	17.3
Exchange ..	2.14	50.0	150	2.494†	1.497	19.2
BOURGEOIS WARDS						
Kelvinside ..	6.01	1.8	34	average .400 to .600	.135	11.7
Pollokshields	4.83	7.0	34		*	10.5
Cathcart ..	4.20	9.0	46		.344	9.9

†Pneumonia rate only.   *Figures not available.

There, in cold statistics, is class distinction in its most ferocious form. Up to twice as many people die in the working-class areas as do, say, in middle-class Cathcart. Death will take four babies of the working-class in these Glasgow wards before they are a year old, for every one baby of the bourgeoisie. The respiratory diseases claim five proletarian victims to every one bourgeois. In 1842, we have seen above, Calton was condemned for its "wretchedness and squalor," its "ill-ventilated and dilapidated houses": the condemnation applies with redoubled force to-day, ninety years after; and our table shows that in Calton now ten times as many people die from tuberculosis of the lungs as die in Kelvinside, Glasgow's "West End," on whose fine, broad streets a good number of the lords of Clydeside, the heavy industry monopolists, have their handsome villas.

THE WORKERS' MOVEMENT ON THE CLYDE

The metal workers in the shipyards and engineering works of the Clyde have written some of the most inspiring pages in the history of the working-class movement in Britain. The great struggles during the war and the deportation of the militant leaders, the forty-hour strike of 1919, the rent war, the development of the Shop Stewards' Movement and the Clyde Workers' Committee—these come readily to the mind. It was the workers of Glasgow who gave the Labour Party its greatest triumph in the general election of 1922; and the keenest hope was aroused, to be subsequently signally falsified, that the "Clyde Brigade" would form the nucleus of a real Socialist working-class leadership in the Labour movement.

Clydeside, and industrial Scotland in general, may be compared with South Wales from the point of view of the influence that the Labour Party had won. But whereas South Wales remains the outstanding stronghold of reformism, as the 1931 general election showed,* the position in Scotland is far different. The Labour Party's Scottish losses in 1931 were severe, even in Glasgow constituencies that had been considered impregnable. At the same time, Clydeside has for long been the strongest centre of the Independent Labour Party. And it is therefore natural that on Clydeside the play of the forces which have produced the present acute differentiation and ferment in that party should be especially marked. The principal strength of the avowed reactionary supporters of the Labour Party in the I.L.P. lies in Scotland, where they have formed a new party, the Scottish Socialist Party, as a breakaway from the I.L.P., and control *Forward*, the former Scottish organ of that party.

Disillusion with the old movement spreads on the industrial field too. In Clydeside engineering shops where there used to be, say, from thirty to fifty shop stewards, there are now only a handful, perhaps none at all. But the spirit of the workers is unbroken, and there is a growing urge to forge new weapons, that will be able to carry the fight for emancipation from the present diabolical conditions to a triumphant conclusion. This urge, of course, is a nation-wide thing; but Clydeside, and Scotland in general, are significant in that it has there developed further than it has hitherto in other centres.

What are the signs of this development, of this growth of a revolutionary movement? First we may instance the demonstrations of 1931, which were on a greater relative scale in Glasgow than perhaps in any other major industrial centre. Since then the unemployed movement in Glasgow has continued to grow; and numerous demonstrations have been carried through with notable success. Glasgow, indeed, has learnt the technique of demonstration very thoroughly as a result of the unemployed turn-outs and the fight for free speech on Glasgow Green.

Second, is the growing influence and organised strength of the Communist Party. Scotland unquestionably leads the whole of Britain in building a really mass revolutionary party of the working-class. In Glasgow considerable successes have been achieved in the fundamental sphere of factory organisation; in some of the biggest railway works Communists have won leading

* See pp. 47-48, above.

positions, and in one recent case were able to rally decisive opposition to an attempt to expel a leading Communist from his place on the works committee.   In the municipal elections of 1932 the Communist vote in Scotland rose to 29,000 as compared with less than 12,000 the previous year.   Nearly 11,000 votes were polled last year in Glasgow alone; and in some wards the increases were striking.   Thus in Cowlairs the Communist candidate polled 1,206 votes (232 in 1931), in Gorbals 1,615 (989), in Springburn 1,239 (383), and so generally thoughout the city. The Communist vote, in these three wards, approached 50 per cent. of the Labour Party vote, and in each case far exceeded the votes received by the candidates of the Independent Labour Party.   High votes were likewise recorded in some of the mining areas, such as Fife, where Communists have been elected to the County Council and to local councils.

Testimony to the deepening influence of the Communist Party is also afforded by the success which has attended a campaign of public reporting on the recent congress of the party.   Many working-class organisations, including trade union and I.L.P. branches, have accepted Communist Party speakers to report to them in this way.   And a West of Scotland conference, with the same aim, was held in Glasgow in January; it was attended by 125 delegates from 54 organisations, including the district committee of the Amalgamated Engineering Union, several A.E.U. and other trade union branches, and branches of the I.L.P.   The significance of this initial success for a practical effort to translate into current terms the famous saying of Marx and Engels—that the Communists "have no interests separate and apart from those of the proletariat as a whole"—hardly requires emphasis.

A word must be said in conclusion about developments in the Scottish coalfield.   Four years ago a revolutionary miners' union —the United Mineworkers of Scotland—was founded as a result of the refusal of the old leaders of the National Union of Scottish Mineworkers to give up office when their members had voted in Communists and other militant miners.*   The reformist leaders had split the miners' ranks from top to bottom rather than give way to revolutionary fighters who had won the support of the men.   In consequence trade unionism as an organised force in

* The revelation of this classic flouting of trade union democracy and splitting of the union by the reformist leaders, rather than surrender their power, is given, in elaborately documented detail, in *Barriers of the Bureaucrats: Fife Breaks Through,* by D. Proudfoot and J. McArthur (London, 1929) or *The Fife, Kinross and Clackmannan Miners' Union Dispute* (Dunfermline, 1929).

the Scottish coalfield is at its lowest ebb. Seventy per cent. of the miners are unorganised; in Lanarkshire, where the rump of the old County Union does not claim more than 4,000 members out of the 30,000 miners employed there, the percentage is even higher.

This is the position in a coalfield where the rationalisation and speeding-up drive of the owners has been pushed ahead with exceptional ruthlessness. At the commencement of this chapter we noted the heavy fall in the numbers of miners employed. In Lanarkshire there are to-day only half the number working in the pits that were working before the war, and in Fife only two-thirds. Mechanisation has reached its highest pitch; three years ago 66 per cent. of the total Scottish output was machine-cut, compared with only 26 per cent. for the coalfields of England and Wales, and in Lanarkshire the percentage rose to 74, in Fife even higher. Output per man per annum has risen from 276 tons in 1925 to 345 tons in 1932;[24] and during the same period the wages cost per ton was slashed from 11s. 8½d. to 6s. 11½d.

It should be recalled that the miners of Scotland have fighting traditions second to none. The Fife men in the seventies won the eight-hour day by direct action, a historic achievement which the annual Fife gala still commemorates; and the Fife miners' union was one of the little gathering of pioneer organisations which founded the Miners' Federation of Great Britain at a conference in Manchester in 1888. It was among the miners of Lanarkshire and Ayrshire that, with Keir Hardie's early efforts, the idea of independent working-class political action first struck root. In the great struggles of 1921 and 1926 the Scottish coalfields, especially Fife, were in the forefront. So complete was the control exercised in the General Strike by the Council of Action in Methil, covering the eastern section of the Fife coalfield, that workers were beginning to raise, in the second week of the strike, the question of power.

During the past two years there have been a whole series of strikes, embracing single pits, groups of pits, and the entire coalfield. There was the Scottish strike of December 1930 against the hours spread-over; the strike of 10,000 miners in Fife in July 1931, which compelled the Fife Coal Company to reopen their pits on a 7½-hour day and to reduce wage-cuts they were demanding from 1s. 4½d. to 4¾d. a shift; the strike of 5,000 miners in Fife in May 1932, led by the Bowhill pit committee, which stopped the imposition of cuts ranging from 6d. to 2s. 2d. a shift. The unremitting drive of the individual colliery managements against ton and shift rates, the starting of men below the recognised rate, and the scores of similar attacks on the miners' conditions which can be found reported in every issue of the executive minutes of the United Mineworkers of Scotland have produced a steady crop of pit strikes. Of these the most important in the past year have been in Fife (Lochore), Stirling (Millhall), Lanarkshire (Auchengeich and others) and Ayrshire (Dallars).

The United Mineworkers of Scotland has played a leading part in these strikes, particularly in Fife, where its biggest strength lies. At two of the largest Fife collieries, the Bowhill and "Peeweep" pits, U.M.S. leaders have been elected as workmen's inspectors under the Coal Mines Acts; and the thoroughness with which they have conducted their inspections, resulting in important improvements in the safety conditions in the pits, has certainly made a deep impression.* Another interesting feature of the activity of the U.M.S. is the issue of periodical papers, in duplicated form, at certain pits in Fife; these papers have circulations among the miners at the particular pit ranging up to thirty dozen copies per issue. With their contents mainly consisting of letters from miners in the pit covered, and their vigorous homely cartoons and pungent comments, these papers are certainly a force.

There is no difference in policy between the old reformist leaders in the Scottish coalfield and their colleagues elsewhere; the criticism which was made in the chapter on the South Wales coalfield applies with equal force to Scotland. It is against the hopeless prospect offered by reformism that the United Mineworkers of Scotland raises the banner of the miners' revolt. The problem of the U.M.S. lies largely in the transformation of the mass influence it has won into strong organisation; for up to now it has been more like a union in the old French sense of a grouping of the most advanced and most militant spirits, the spearhead of the movement, than an organisation embracing the decisive mass of the miners within its ranks.

* The election of workmen's inspectors at Bowhill was a significant instance of the collaboration of the colliery management with the officials of the reformist union. When two U.M.S. leaders had been duly elected by ballot of the men the management refused to recognise the ballot, and claimed, in total defiance of the Coal Mines Act, that two reformist officials were the inspectors. They were compelled to abandon this illegal position and on a second ballot the U.M.S. men were overwhelmingly re-elected.

CHAPTER IV

LONDON

ONE-FIFTH of the total population of England and Wales, and more than one-quarter of the urban population, is concentrated in London. In the conditions of this unparalleled, this colossal centralisation, which makes the whole situation in London unique, the specific characteristics of British capitalist society are most clearly exemplified; and the inherent contradictions of that society reach their tensest point. The reflections which London inspired in Engels ninety years ago are apposite to-day:

> After roaming the streets of the capital a day or two, making head-way with difficulty through the human turmoil and the endless lines of vehicles, after visiting the slums of the metropolis, one realises for the first time that these Londoners have been forced to sacrifice the best qualities of their human nature, to bring to pass all the marvels of civilisation which crowd their city; that a hundred powers which slumbered within them have remained inactive, have been suppressed in order that a few might be developed more fully and multiply through union with those of others. . . . The brutal indifference, the unfeeling isolation of each in his private interest becomes the more repellent and offensive, the more these individuals are crowded together within a limited space. And, however much one may be aware that this isolation of the individual, this narrow self-seeking, is the fundamental principle of our society everywhere, it is nowhere so shamelessly barefaced, so self-conscious as just here in the crowding of the great city. The dissolution of mankind into monads, of which each one has a separate principle, the world of atoms, is here carried out to its utmost extreme. [1]

As the capital, the centre of government, of finance, and trade, not only of Britain, but of the British Empire, London has always borne a strongly parasitic character. This has been most marked in the imperialist epoch. From the eighties onwards London was no longer the shop window of the "workshop of the world," but the counting house of the world's creditors. The whole of London's economy and life is profoundly influenced by this fact. The census returns tell their own story. A large proportion of the occupied population is covered by the categories of commerce, finance and insurance, clerks and typists, and personal service. Transport and communication easily head the list of industries, followed by metal-working and engineering, building, wood-working and furniture making, clothing, printing and paper. A random instance will make the general tendency clear. Here are the figures for one London borough, St. Pancras:

PROPORTION OF POPULATION IN CERTAIN OCCUPATIONS
(Metropolitan Borough of St. Pancras: 1921 Census.)

Males	%	Females	%
Transport	18	Personal Service ..	15
Commerce and Finance ..	10	Textile Goods and Dress	6
Personal Service	7	Clerks and Typists ..	5
Metal Working	7	Commerce and Finance..	3
Clerks and Typists	6		
Wood and Furniture ..	5		

The picture that these figures reveal is one of a whole process of parasitic and socially retrograde growth; and of this process the population changes of the past decade have been but the vehicle. The 1931 census showed that the direction which population had followed in its growth for generations past had been reversed. In 1921 the classic industrial areas still headed the list of population increases; to-day it is London and the satellite region of the Home Counties which have decisively taken the lead; the old industrial areas register decreases, the heaviest of all being in South Wales. Eleven counties have recorded a population increase of more than ten per cent. between 1921 and 1931; and the leading five, with increases ranging from fifteen per cent. to over thirty per cent., are the Home Counties of Middlesex, Surrey, Hertfordshire, Essex and Buckinghamshire. Of the twenty-eight large towns where the population has increased during the period there are fifteen in the Greater London area, and of the twelve which lead the list ten are in the Greater London area, while a number of others are in the Home Counties or adjacent areas in the South of England. The most sensational increases have taken place in London's suburban outer ring; Hendon shows an increase of 101 per cent., Kingsbury (Hendon's western neighbour) one of 796 per cent., and Dagenham, where a township of 9,000 has swelled into a city of 90,000, one of 879 per cent. And London is growing, not at the expense of the rural areas, but of the industrial centres in South Wales and the North of England, where a real process of depopulation has been going on. It is significant to note that this process was not evenly distributed over the decade, but mainly concentrated in its latter half, becoming most marked after 1926.[2] The changes outlined express, in terms of population, the fundamental fact that British society is suffering from congestion at the heart and anæmia at the extremities.

London has been the lodestone alike of the much-discussed "southward drift" of population, and of the parallel development of industry of which the human migration has been the accompaniment. These two movements mark a radical change in the whole balance of British economy. For what is the character of this industrialisation of Greater London, which has meant that in the northern and western sectors of the region alone there are between 120,000 and 130,000 workers in industry, where ten years or less ago the numbers were insignificant?

We may note, first of all, the general reflection of industrialisation in the growth of the insured population, which rose in London and the south-east by 21.4 per cent. in the period 1921-31, while the increase in population was less than 10 per cent. Thus the labour force for the new factories of Greater London has been drawn from existing sources within the region as well as from immigration; it has been drawn from workers not previously in insured trades (for example, from agriculture or domestic service), especially from women, boys and girls. Between the years 1923-24 and 1930-31 the percentage of men to boy entrants into industry in London dropped from 121 to 24, and of women to girls from 89 to 45.[3] This already points to the fact that the "new" industries of Greater London are cheap labour industries run on modern rationalised lines; more will be said on this later.

The industries themselves include such traditional London lines as light engineering, clothing and furniture-making; in addition there are a host of miscellaneous trades producing what Dr. D. H. Smith, a recent investigator, calls "a wonderful array of desirable devices that add to our comfort and efficiency." The same writer gives the following "few items" from the list of Greater London manufactures: "fire extinguishers, gyroscopes, figures for corsets, artificial limbs, billiard tables and cues, caravans, trams, surgical instruments, films, tooth-brushes, sporting guns, stationery, typewriting materials, office equipment, helmets, dairy machinery, refrigerators, water-softening machinery, refining of precious metals, organs, pianos, paints, foodstuffs, fine chemicals, suit cases, electric motor equipment of every kind."

Thus the industrialisation of Greater London has been directed to the production of consumption goods which the vast mass of the population become less and less able to consume; many of these goods are of a luxury character and find their market among the bourgeoisie and the middle class, whose biggest concentration is in London. Here is a particular parasitic element in the growth of the "new" industries in the London region. But over and·above this, as Dr. Smith concludes, "is the important influence of the concentration of commercial activity in London. London is the hub of industrial and commercial control. With the amalgamation of firms and the creation of combines, the controlling offices are established in London."[4]   This indus- trialisation of the capital, in other words, is a reflection of the development of monopoly capitalism in Britain and of the general parasitism which that development connotes.

We can now turn to review the conditions of the workers in this vast, overgrown metropolis; and we can best begin by seeing in what kind of houses and quarters they live.

THE HOMES OF LONDON'S MILLIONS

Housing, and all that it implies, is a dominant issue in the life of London workers. The main facts can be simply stated. Rents are the highest in the whole country. Overcrowding is general, chronic and of the most abominable character—and is on the increase. The shortage of houses is hyper-acute. The slums are virtually untouched. "Housing provision," wrote the *Evening Standard* on January 27, 1933, "is not even keeping pace with the *increase* of London population, to say nothing of the needs of the thousands who are already sunk and settled in the slums."

The high rents are the direct result of the land monopoly, to which reference is made below, and of the always soaring land values in the metropolis. Compared with the pre-war level, controlled rents have increased by something under fifty per cent., whereas decontrolled rents have risen from 85 to 100 per cent. And the rent burden falls most heavily on the poorest- paid workers; it has been calculated that such workers pay over 20 per cent. of their income in rent, while the handful of highly- paid workers (earning over £6 a week) pay only 10 per cent.[5] An average figure of this kind, however, can convey no idea of the actual situation, which is that the landlords' tribute is extracted in effect by taking the bread out of the children's mouths.

That this is no exaggeration may be seen from the latest report of Dr. Howell, the Hammersmith medical officer of health. He says that many families are to-day paying no less than 50 per cent. of their income in rent, compared with an average of 16-17 per cent. before the war; consequently—

the amount available for providing food, etc., is greatly reduced, resulting in parents and children being underfed and improperly nourished. . . . Many families are being forced to live on a food allowance of two or three shillings a week. Mothers and fathers are going without themselves to provide more food for their children, but in many cases their self-sacrifice does not leave the children adequate nourishment.

Dr. Howell cites the case of a barman who earned 45*s.* a week and had to pay a rent of £1 a week for three rooms. He had four children; his wife who had just been confined, was urgently ordered extra nourishment, which he was totally unable to provide.[6] This case is characteristic for these hotel, restaurant or domestic workers, who are relatively more numerous in London than anywhere else. In Paddington Dr. Oates refers to the glaring contrast between the miserable wages of such workers and the high rents they are forced to pay. He says:

> With wages of anything between 20*s.* and 40*s.* per week, plus food, a rent of perhaps 15*s.* to 20*s.* per week to meet and a wife and children to maintain, the difficulty can be appreciated. . . . The high rent factor is too well-known to call for much comment. A so-called furnished room will rent at from 15*s.* to 27*s.* 6*d.* per week and an unfurnished room (difficult to obtain) will realise 8*s.* to 16*s.* weekly.[7]

Casual workers, such as dockers, and low-paid labourers of all kinds, suffer similarly from the exactions of the landlords. Dr. Connan, the Bermondsey medical officer of health, reports that in that typical riverside borough "rents range from 5*s.* for one room to 35*s.* per week for six rooms. Having regard to the average wage in the borough, which cannot be more than from £2 2*s.* to £2 5*s.* per week, I regard the rents as being high . . . often exorbitant." Of St. Pancras Dr. Sowden writes, in almost identical terms, that:

> There are large numbers of unskilled labourers and other workers in the borough, usually with numerous children, who are earning wages of about 50*s.* per week. In order to avoid overcrowding . . . these families require flats with at least three bedrooms. The rent of such flats in a central area is about 18*s.* 6*d.* per week, an amount it is quite impossible to pay out of such an income.

Here is the case of a St. Pancras worker. He lives with his wife and six children (their ages ranging from ten years down to two) in one furnished room, for which he has to pay rent of 15*s.* a week out of his wages of £3. Right in the very heart of London, in Soho tenements which are devoid of all amenities, where the sole sanitary convenience is a w.c. in the tiny back area, rents range from 7*s.* 6*d.* to 20*s.* a room.[8]

What of the loudly-trumpeted housing efforts of the London County Council and the Metropolitan Boroughs since the war?

K

The plain fact is that these have foundered over the rent question; it is notorious that the rents for these municipal houses or flats are far too high for the workers who are in most need of them to pay. The L.C.C. will only accept tenants for its suburban estates who are in a position to pay, not only the rent, but their fares to and from work. Examples of the way in which this automatically rules out the most needy cases occur with monotonous regularity in practically every one of the reports of the medical officers of the twenty-eight London boroughs. It was on this ground that four-fifths of the Lambeth applicants for L.C.C. houses in 1930 were mainly rejected; and of the families so turned down 137 were living in one-room tenements, no fewer than seventy-five of these families numbering five or more (up to nine in one case). In Shoreditch the typical case is cited of a family of four living in one tiny room—its capacity was only 500 cubic feet, though their minimum need was 1,200 cubic feet—to whom the L.C.C. was "unable" to offer accommodation because they could not afford to pay a rent of 17s., plus fares. Of the large number of overcrowded families in Greenwich, at least 50 per cent. cannot afford to pay L.C.C. or municipal rents. Dr. Lennane, of Battersea, reporting on the "serious local overcrowding," remarks that "there has been no very material decrease in this unhappy state of affairs," because "very little attempt has been made to provide for that element of the population which is unable to pay the rents demanded for the new houses."[9]

A survey of conditions on the Isle of Dogs (Poplar) by two expert women estate managers led to the conclusion that practically three-quarters of the families housed there could not even "hope" to pay the L.C.C. rents, and there was such "a high percentage of acute poverty" that 23 per cent. of the families were not in a position to pay rent at all, except by starving themselves. Among these casual riverside workers, there was an "overwhelming demand" for municipal houses or flats at their present rent standard (averaging 3s. a room) or less; and the writers concluded, in suggestive words, that "this is not a housing problem, but a problem of unemployment, casual labour, and low wages." A problem, in other words, of the impoverishment of the workers under capitalism.[10]

The contribution of the L.C.C. to the solution of this high rent obstacle is typical. They propose to build a block of "experimental" flats, at lower rents, at Brockley. Mr. H. R. Selley, builder and estate manager, Tory M.P. for South Battersea, and chairman of the L.C.C. Housing Committee, describes this as "a successful endeavour to provide suitable hygienic dwellings for the poorer classes." The motto is cheap—and nasty; for it is stated that "economies proposed in the new flats are smaller rooms, no kitchens, stained woodwork instead of painted, absence of plaster in the lobbies, open balconies, no drying rooms, and one common washhouse to each three tenements." The washhouse will contain the bath and copper; so cleanliness will be purchased at the cost of a draughty, exposed journey across an open balcony. The Deptford Borough Council has been driven to register a strong protest against this impudent proposal.[11]

Workers who have been "fortunate" enough to secure a house on one of the big L.C.C. estates at Dagenham, Becontree, Watling, or Downham, are not long in finding that rent is the bugbear of their lives. A war widow, who was evicted from Becontree for arrears, had an income of £2 4s., out of which she had to pay 19s. 9d. rent, leaving her with a trifle over 24s. to maintain herself and six children.

The fact that so little is left for food can be coupled with the remark of Dr. Thomas, the Finsbury medical officer of health, à propos the removal of families from the centre to these outlying estates; he observes that "the town children, transferred to the healthy tonic environment of the country, develop enormous appetites and seriously increase the food bills of their parents."[12]

Two further points arise in connection with these L.C.C. estates. The first is that workers who have moved out to them are driven back to the slums as an inevitable consequence of their inability to pay the high rents. This Bermondsey case is characteristic:

> A man in regular work, and living in overcrowded conditions, is accepted by the L.C.C. as a tenant on an outlying estate. The premises are regularly visited in the interval, and on one of his visits the sanitary inspector finds that the family has returned and the premises are again overcrowded. The father states that he has lost his work, fallen in arrears with rent, and has had to leave the estate.

The second point is the abject failure of the so-called "filtering-up" process. It was argued that, as families left for the suburban L.C.C. estates, the rooms they vacated would become available to ease overcrowding in the more central working-class districts. The simpletons who talked thus reckoned without the landlords. Dr. Sowden (St. Pancras) points out that directly houses have been vacated in this way they of course become decontrolled and rents rise to a "prohibitive level." The same process in Stepney means that "the profiteering landlord promptly raises the rent, and again the lowest wage-earner is defeated, or alternatively he is forced to pay a quarter or a third of his income on rent, or go short on food."[13]

We can already perceive the obvious connection between house shortage, high rents and overcrowding. Dr. Connan, in Bermondsey, records his "general impression . . . that overcrowding is ubiquitous" and that "the position is getting worse rather than better." That applies, not only to Bermondsey, but to every working-class quarter in London. It is unnecessary here to spend time over the much-discussed question of overcrowding standards,* but it is significant to note that even a low and grossly inadequate standard shows that one-quarter of the total population of London are overcrowded. A general figure of this kind does not indicate the extent of overcrowding in the working-class quarters, for it includes the extravagant accommodation enjoyed by the bourgeoisie. The same applies to the minute fall in the general average of persons per room in London during the past decade, which is hailed by the authors of the *New Survey of London Life and Labour* as "welcome evidence that some effect has already been produced on overcrowding."†

The staggering fact is that the most acute form of overcrowding, that of more than three persons to a room, has increased between 1921 and 1931. In the area of the *New Survey* there are now 176,000 people living under these appalling conditions. The

* "The so-called administrative standard of legal overcrowding is such a ridiculous and scandalous farce that when an old-fashioned, large-roomed house is divided up amongst several families you can find a father, mother and eight children living in two rooms without transgressing the standard." (*St. Marylebone Housing Messenger*, January 1932, p. 17. See also *Fourth Annual Report of the Bishop of London's Housing Committee*, p. 1). This refers to the regulation of the number of cubic feet per head in tenement houses. The best discussion of overcrowding standards is in Sir E. D. Simon's *How to Abolish the Slums*.

† Since the general line of Sir H. Llewellyn Smith and his colleagues is to extract comfort for the governing class, and confusion for their enemies, by assembling vast masses of statistics without penetrating to the reality of the social relationships behind those bare figures, I commend to them the following passages in the annual report of Dr. Porter, the St. Marylebone medical officer of health, for 1930. The doctor records how an overcrowding survey he undertook produced the surprising statistical result that in small houses accommodating three, four or more families the average number of persons per room was less than 1.7. He adds, "such a figure is very comforting *until individual cases and the conditions as to overcrowding in particular families come to be investigated*" (p. 68, my italics). The statistics of the *New Survey* may be "very comforting . . . *until*, etc.!"

highest proportion is in Finsbury and Shoreditch, where it amounts to over 10 per cent. of the population; then comes Stepney with 7.5 per cent., Bethnal Green 6.9 per cent., Bermondsey 6.5 per cent., and Southwark 6.2 per cent., while a number of other boroughs are in the neighbourhood of 5 per cent. The rise over 1921 has been greatest in West Ham (where the figure has doubled), followed by Bermondsey, Shoreditch, Poplar and Bethnal Green.[14]

Many quantitative indicators of the extent and intensity of overcrowding can be given. Over one-third of the population live two or more to a room in St. Pancras, Holborn, Finsbury, Shoreditch, Bethnal Green, Stepney, Poplar, Bermondsey and Southwark—a total of nearly 400,000 people overcrowded, on this basis. The proportion is far greater if the calculation is made on the rather higher standard (but still one that falls far below what would be considered a very ordinary middle-class standard) of not more than one "equivalent adult" to each room. On this basis children are allowed for as fractions of an adult, who is counted as a unit. The result is that in three such solid working-class boroughs as Bethnal Green, Shoreditch and Stepney the proportion of families overcrowded is 52 per cent., 60 per cent. and 53 per cent. respectively—an average of 54 per cent. In Bermondsey, Poplar and West Ham the proportion is 44-45 per cent.[15] Worst of all are the cases of overcrowding in single-room tenements. There are in London 30,000 people, in families of from five to eleven, each herded into one room.

It would be instructive to examine in detail the London figures of the 1931 census from the overcrowding point of view; but such a study would be far too lengthy for our present purpose. It will be possible, nevertheless, to obtain some important indication of social tendencies from the examination of even one borough. Let us take Islington, the second largest of the Metropolitan Boroughs, which embraces a large working-class area in its south and centre, and has a middle-class belt at its northern extremity, where the land rises towards Highgate. The extent of overcrowding in Islington may be gauged from the fact that 14,956 of its inhabitants live more than three to a room (an increase in percentage over 1921), 34,493 live three and more than two, and 56,531 live two and more than one and a half to a room. These three categories together account for roughly one-third of the total population of the borough. There are 15,359 families (27,084 persons) living in one-room tenements, and 552 of these families live five or more to a room. There are 26,805 families (80,505 persons) living in two-room tenements. At the other end of the scale 1,241 families (5,870 persons) have eight to nine rooms apiece, and 561 families (2,823 persons) each have ten rooms or more. Within walking distance of each other are families of five or more human beings jammed into one poky room, and families each member of which has a ration of two rooms to play with! The past ten years have seen merely microscopic changes in this gradation of families. The proportion of families in three-room tenements has increased 2.1 per cent., which is the biggest change. An increase of a fraction over 1 per cent. in the two-room families offsets an identical decline in the one-room families. The four-room families are stationary; while the families with five to ten and more rooms register slight decreases, of the order of one-half to four-fifths of 1 per cent. It is clear that here is a picture of stagnation and decline, so far as housing is concerned.

All that has been said so far has told us nothing of the *quality* of overcrowding; by which I mean that all the figures are based on the number of persons to a room, without saying anything about the size of the room. The importance of the point needs no labouring. It may be met by saying that the average size of rooms has not changed during the past forty years—that is to say, they are disgracefully small. Cases of over-crowding are common in which six or more people are crammed into a space which is insufficient for two, even according to the extremely low standard of 300 to 400 cubic feet per adult person prescribed by the regulations for tenement houses. It may be noted, also, that in the thirty years up to 1921 the numbers living in small tenements rose by 25 per cent., while the numbers living in larger tenements declined by 17 per cent. Consideration of this point makes us realise, as Dr. Howell of Hammersmith puts it, that there are "very many cases in which, although not legally overcrowded, the families are living under conditions prejudicial to their health—the standard laid down as to cubic capacity being a very low one." Dr. Keith (Deptford) remarks of his borough:

> The housing shortage necessitates many of the inhabitants living under badly overcrowded conditions, and even where overcrowding does not exist, the unavoidable practice of letting, to two or more families, houses originally constructed for only one family creates great hardships for the occupiers . . . [including] . . . defective ventilation or lighting, and lack of adequate provision of sanitary conveniences, such as proper provision for food storage, washing, etc.

The magnitude of this latter problem is witnessed by the statement of the L.C.C. Housing Committee that one-half the working-class families in London live in houses not structurally sub-divided and occupied by two or more families.[16]

One fact remains to record—the most terrible, in many ways, of all. There are at least 100,000 London working people living in the thirty thousand unhealthy basement dwellings that still disgrace the metropolis, though such underground dens have been virtually wiped out of many of the biggest provincial cities. And a London slum basement, a recent observer notes, "often means a place where, in the darkness and the damp, the paper hangs in sodden tatters from the walls; where rats and insects abound; where the inhabitants are seldom free from illness." Children living in basements are twice as liable to ill-health as children living above ground level—and their liability to rheumatism is three times as great. The grimmest and most graphic comment is afforded by the following table, displayed by the London Housing Societies at the 1932 Public Health Congress and Exhibition:

BASEMENTS AND THE CHILDREN'S HEALTH
(Percentage Incidence of Defects)

			Basement Dwellings	Non-Basement Dwellings
Defective Nutrition	..	..	35.7	19.1
Nose and Throat Defects ..	..	..	7.4	3.3
Diphtheria	..	..	5.1	2.5
Rheumatism	..	..	2.2	0.8
Subnormal Progress in School	..	..	43.6	24.8
Irregular School Attendance	..	..	11.8	5.9

These figures are collated from those of the boroughs where basement dwellings are most numerous, namely, Kensington, Paddington, Westminster, Islington, Finsbury, Poplar, Stepney and Southwark. It should be noticed that the problem of base-ment dwellings is actually far wider than even the dreadful total given above indicates. For "basements" in the sense used here means basement dwellings with ceilings at or below street level. Evidently these are the worst; but there are many other basements, not coming within this category, which are little better from the standpoint of lack of light and air. Thus in Islington there are 1,460 basement dwellings falling within this strict category, but a grand total of nearly 13,600 basement dwellings; and of this total nearly 3,600 front on an area only three feet or less in width.[17]

A typical case of basement-dwellers in Westminster is the following: "husband, wife and two children occupy two base-ment rooms and pay a rent of 18s. a week. One child has suffered from nervous disease ever since basement was flooded in January 1928. No alternative accommodation." Those last three words ring like a knell over the workers condemned to dwell in these detestable holes, and render farcical the nominal illegality of the use of basement rooms for sleeping apartments. In Marylebone some years ago a number of basement dwellings were closed; but in 1925 they were found to be again occupied, and have continued in this illegal occupation ever since; the medical officer of health comments helplessly that "on account of difficulty in obtaining other accommodation it is often impossible to deal with cases that should be dealt with." The same situation prevails in Wandsworth, where the number of underground rooms illegally occupied is increasing: it was 27 in 1930 and 55 in 1931. In view of this there appears to be positive optimism about the gloomy estimate of the London Council of Social Service that "at the average annual rate at which unhealthy basement dwellings in London are at present being closed, it would take more than a century and a half to close all of them."[18]

As with basements, so with overcrowding in general—the law which purports to give powers to check these horrors remains a dead letter. Dr. Allan Young, the Poplar medical officer of health, commenting on overcrowding in his latest report, remarks that "thirty-eight of the more serious cases were reported to the Public Health Committee, but owing to the inability of the overcrowded families to find alternative accommodation, the Committee decided that it was impossible for them to take action." Every Public Health Committee in London has made similar decisions.[19]

THE EAST END: "PRACTICALLY ALL SLUM"

The East End really begins in the centre of London. From Finsbury, through Shoreditch, Hackney, Bethnal Green, Stepney and Poplar, to West Ham beyond the county boundary, there is an unbroken mass, mile after mile, of squalid streets where millions of working people are forced to dwell. "Practically all Stepney," says an L.C.C. official, "is a slum." No experienced Londoner would hesitate to extend the description to the whole chain of boroughs named. Here is the biggest and most intense concentration of the working class that exists in any city in the world; let us see in more detail how they are housed.

Finsbury and Shoreditch cover some of the oldest working-class quarters in London. Damp and dilapidated hovels are huddled together in narrow streets along courts and alleys. A walk round Clerkenwell is enough to make one realise that Finsbury has the worst overcrowding in London—over half the population, even on the lowest standard. Shoreditch is the traditional centre of the cabinet-making trades and is the most Cockney quarter of all: it has the highest percentage of London born population of any Metropolitan Borough. It was in olden time the refuse dump of the city; and its houses, most of them over a century old and, as Dr. Maitland Radford, the medical officer of health, says, "literally falling into ruins," are built on layers of rubbish several feet thick. A population of 100,000 is crammed into a square mile. Half the houses, built for one family, are now occupied by two or more families. Dr. Radford grimly comments that if the sanitary inspectors were to take measurements of the cubic space in the rooms many more cases of gross overcrowding would come to light than are at present officially known, but they would be cases "in which it was not practicable for the Sanitary Authority to take effective action." In 1919 six unhealthy areas in Shoreditch were scheduled, but eleven years later a housing scheme had only been approved for part of one, and that scheme had not been completed.[20]

Last November Sir Edward Hilton Young, the Minister of Health, made a tour of Finsbury, Bethnal Green and Stepney, visiting basement rooms and generally inspecting housing conditions. The *Daily Telegraph* of November 17, 1932, carried the following report:

In some of these underground rooms he found families living in a perpetual twilight below the pavement level. Through a grating near the ceiling feet could be seen passing in the street above. Although it was daylight outside very little penetrated to alleviate the gloom. A pathetic feature was that on one overcrowded, crockery-laden dresser, sunless withering flowers had been placed to brighten a room in which the whole family lived by day and the children slept at night. But overcrowding is by no means confined to the basements. "We have lived here for twenty-three years," a woman in one street told Sir Edward. "My two daughters, aged 23 and 16, and my boy of 22 sleep in this room, while my husband and I and the two little boys are upstairs in the other room. We pay 10s. 3d. rent." Very often a family shares one room. Some of the alley-ways were so narrow that the walls were almost within an arms-length of each other. There were "communal" taps used by several families, and in some places sinks or wash-basins had been fitted outside the bedroom window so that washing—in chilly contrast to the basement rooms—has to be done leaning out of the window!

That report was published on the same day that the Ray Committee presented its notorious "economy" report, whose recommendations for stopping even the small housing efforts that the municipalities have made, the Government, and Sir Hilton Young in particular as the responsible Minister, are now carrying into effect.

Bethnal Green and Whitechapel were specially mentioned by Engels as "the most extensive working-people's district" in the 'forties of last century. He quotes[21] a contemporary description, by Mr. Alston, preacher of St. Philip's, Bethnal Green, of the "mass of misery" there, such "that a nation like ours must blush that these things can be possible." Overcrowding, said Mr. Alston, was such that "it is nothing unusual to find a man, his wife, four or five children, and, sometimes, both grandparents, all in one single room, where they eat, sleep and work." And a special correspondent reports, in the *Evening Standard* of January 27, 1933, that an analysis of 1;500 individuals living in Bethnal Green, Hackney and Poplar shows 22 per cent. living five or more to a room. He adds this ghastly picture—of 1933, remember, not 1843:

> There were several cases of ten adults and children living in one room. And what "rooms" some of them were! One top room, with six people, was just under a railway, and its one window had to be kept closed because the engine sparks flew in and set fire to the bedclothes. A family (parents, four girls from 13 to 21, and two boys aged 6 and 9) who had lived in the same basement for nineteen years were all under the doctor. I was shown a slum cottage where the children slept in the attic in winter to avoid the rats in the basement and in the basement in the hot weather because the rats downstairs are less fearful than the bugs upstairs. . . . When a death occurs there is often no place for the coffin but the one table. It releases the bed, where the living and the dying need no longer be together.

Thirty years ago the population of Bethnal Green and Stepney was at super-saturation point, with one-third of the population overcrowded; to-day hundreds of families are living well below even the mean official overcrowding standards. "The greater part of the housing," says Dr. Vynne Borland, the Bethnal Green medical officer of health, "is seriously below modern standards, badly designed, dark, lacking in proper lighting and ventilation, and much of it worn out in structure. To deal with this situation by way of notices to remedy some particular 'sanitary defects' is nothing more than continually giving 'first aid' to a patient who has long needed the surgeon's knife." Here is a typical Stepney case. A family of eleven live in two small rooms, each measuring ten feet by nine, one upstairs and one down. The walls of the downstairs room are dripping with moisture. There is a double bed and a single bed in the upstairs room, occupying the whole of the floor space; here the mother and seven children sleep at night, two boys sleeping in the damp downstairs room, where the family live and eat and keep their food. The father, who is a night-worker, sleeps in the upstairs room during the day. The mother and several of the children are attending the local tuberculosis dispensary.[22] Another Stepney case was described in these words by Mr. Howard Marshall in a recent B.B.C. talk:

> The mother showed me over the three rooms—all about eight feet square, no larger. The very ill-fitting front door opened straight into a bedroom; beyond, there was a kind of kitchen-living-room from which a door opened into a tiny yard, and up a flight of extremely shaky stairs was another bedroom. You could feel the damp on the walls, and through the cracks in the doors and round the window came a perpetual draught. The woman was ailing, her throat was wrapped up in flannel, and her voice was husky. It was her chest, she said—none of them was ever free from colds and rheumatics—and how could you expect it in a place like that? Her children were attractive little people with big brown eyes and curly hair, but most of them had rickets, and she'd had two more and lost them with pneumonia. Her husband had done his best—he'd rigged up a sort of match-board screen round the door, and boarded over the tap and the sink out in the yard, but the wind still came in and the moisture still soaked through those porous walls. The place was a death-trap, and there were plenty of others like it.[23]

A little further east we come to Poplar, and, at its southern extremity along the riverside, the Isle of Dogs. Here is a cluster of small cottages, built on swampy soil without any damp courses, liable to flood (their ground floors were flooded feet high in the great Thames flood of January, 1928) and many with water permanently under their floor boards. Their damp, decayed and unhealthy condition may be imagined. Their roofs leak, plaster is crumbling away from the walls, woodwork is rotting, the air within them is tainted with the smell of mildew, they are over-run with vermin. In a ground floor back room in Claude-street a family of eight sleep, packed into two double beds and one chair "bed." The ground floor rooms of Ingleheim-cottages are too damp to be slept in: but in the two first-floor rooms of one of these cottages ten people sleep; the man, his wife, a girl of 17 and a boy of 10 occupy the back room—the two children sleeping in one single bed; in the front room six sons sleep in two beds, and they would be joined by a seventh son when he came home on leave from India. The kitchen was too small for the family to feed together, so they took their meals in relays.[24]

It is impossible to give a full picture here of the horror of East

End housing. Cases might be multiplied indefinitely. We shall have to pass by the slums of Canning Town and Silvertown in West Ham, where 15,000 houses need major repairs; we cannot do more than notice the swarming warrens of the Whitechapel back-streets; we can only record the general infestation of these rotten old houses by loathsome vermin of all kinds, from rats* to bugs, which drive thousands in the summer months to drag their beds out into the streets in order to try and secure some sleep, until the police drive them indoors again.

Our survey may be rounded off with Hackney, where 22,000 houses are between fifty and a hundred years old, 1,500 have passed their century, and many thousands are classed as "of very poor type." In 1901 the then medical officer of health of Hackney, Dr. King Warry, spoke strongly of the failure of attempts to reduce overcrowding; and his words are endorsed and applied to conditions to-day by Dr. Dart, his successor. One instance of overcrowding, cited at random, is that of a family of six who slept in one basement room, well below the legal space minimum. The family included boys of 10 and 4, and girls of 11 and 7 years of age: "the mother stated that indecent behaviour had occurred between the two eldest children owing to her inability to make separate sleeping arrangements." I do not know of a more revolting instance that the more capitalist social relationships "change," the more they remain the same; nothing worse can be found in the annals of housing squalor a century ago.[25]

Hackney is honeycombed by a score of slum areas, which Dr. Dart described elaborately and with great fidelity (accompanied by a whole series of horrifying photographs) in a section of his 1930 Report—the fullest and most objective survey of the kind that has been made in recent years in London.[26] These areas are a formless tangle of streets that are scarcely more than paths, of tiny yards, courts and culs-de-sac from 8 feet to 11 feet wide, frequently approached by a covered passage from the street not more than 4 feet wide. Light and air is cut off by the railway embankments which bisect the neighbourhood, and by the high buildings of the many factories. The houses, which were often "very poor in initial construction" and have since had only a minimum of "indifferent maintenance," are generally

---

* The Rats and Mice (Destruction) Act of 1919 characteristically threw the onus of dealing with these pests on the occupier of the house; though in the houses most infested the worker-occupier is far too poor to buy traps or take any other practical steps towards eradicating the vermin (*Poplar Health Report*, 1931, pp. 141-147).

below street level, and are universally damp. W.c.'s are usually at the end of a yard, or the other side of a narrow street; in every way the normal decencies and conveniences of life are lacking. In many of these areas the houses have no internal water supply and not even a sink; the inhabitants have to make use of a common tap in the yard. The houses in Morning Lane and round about are built on marshy soil, and it is shortly remarked that "many of the adults are chronic invalids."

To read Dr. Dart's description of these conditions inevitably recalls the early abominations of workers' housing under capitalism—the tumble-down maze of reeking courts of which Engels made such a burning exposure. Here to-day in Hackney are the back-to-back houses (it is a courtesy title only) of East-street, Pear Tree-court and Queens-court. At one end of a narrow yard are the unscreened communal w.c.s, dilapidated and stinking. Near the front doors of the houses, which have no through ventilation, stand the dustbins. Dr. Dart makes a pungent comment on the "mentality" of the builders who provided, as the sole washing convenience, a copper in the middle of the open yard, devoid of any protection from the elements; it is naturally disused and in ruins, and the housewives have to do their washing with the maximum of difficulty and discomfort in the cramped conditions of their poky airless rooms.

Over by Hackney Marshes, on low-lying land and liable to floods, are groups of cottages in the High Hill Ferry and Middlesex Wharf areas. These unsavoury hovels were ordered to be closed in 1918. They are still open and occupied—"no alternative accommodation." Worse still is the case of one of the most notorious of all the Hackney slums, Duncan-square. This was "represented" for action in 1900. Thirty years after it still remained untouched. The characteristics of this spot and its purlieus are those generally described above; and bang in the middle of the neighbourhood is a chemical factory whose activities, Dr. Dart notes, do not improve the atmosphere—but, he adds, most of the Duncan-square workers are employed in this factory, and this may account for the lack of complaints. Capitalist "freedom"!

Yet Duncan-square is not the most barbarous of these hellholes. It is beaten by some of the courts in the East-street area, by the only too appropriately named Bones-cottages, by the unspeakable 500-year old Heywood Buildings in Banister-street (originally a cowshed, according to local tradition), whose inhabitants have to cross the road to reach their w.c.s, and by Devonshire-place, where there is so much timber in the aged cottages that insurance companies will not even consider issuing a fire policy on them.* And in all these places the only heating and cooking medium is the coal fire, the only illuminant candles and oil lamps. This is indeed the final touch of the primitive in the biggest city in the world, the governing centre of British imperialism, the masterwork of the British bourgeoisie, the "hub of the universe" for the gay world of the lords and ladies and all the fine gentlemen.

The Banister-street area is at last to be dealt with: but the Ministry of Health has so limited the scheme that the number of persons who can be re-housed under it has been reduced from 1,420 to 650. This will greatly hamper future schemes, and the Hackney Borough Council has passed a resolution expressing its "great regret" at the Ministry's decision. Dr. Dart himself writes, under date March 1st, 1933, to observe that "considerable difficulties have been experienced in this Borough owing to delay that has taken place in the Central Administration and the way in which our schemes have been mutilated." It is in face of facts like these that the Minister of Health now has the impudence to talk about a "massed attack on the slums."

This account of Hackney could easily be parallelled all over the East End, and in the working-class quarters of North London. Clustering round the northern railway termini are the infamous slums of Somers Town and the lower end of the Caledonian-road and its byways. North-west they stretch to Kentish Town, north-east through the network of miserable streets between the Caledonian-road and Upper-street, Islington (with its continuation northward in the Holloway-road) and right beyond to the Shoreditch border at Hoxton, notorious for its slums, poverty and crime. Dr. Clark Trotter, the Islington medical officer of health, reports as follows on the Queensland-road area, a group of dead-end streets just off the Holloway-road, jammed up against the Borough Council's refuse wharf and the embankment of the L.N.E.R. main line, and a stone's throw from the Arsenal football ground. These one, two and three room tenements house a population of 1,400, of whom one-third are children:

The houses are all aged, badly planned, poorly fitted up, many having long outlasted their term of useful service. In Queensland-road are a number of basement dwellings with dark and damp lower

* One recalls the frightful fire disaster in an exactly similar Birmingham slum street last Christmas, when six children of an unemployed ex-serviceman were burned to death.

rooms. The roofs call for constant attention and repair. . . . In a few, oil lamps are still used. . . . The staircases are generally dark, narrow and worn to a dangerous degree. Repairs are invariably done in the lowest, cheapest way possible, and are not lasting.[27]

Identical conditions are to be found right through the wide working-class belt of South London, all the way from Woolwich in the east to Battersea in the west, through Greenwich, Deptford, Bermondsey, Southwark, the north of Camberwell and Lambeth, and the north-east of Wandsworth. Greenwich has a thousand ancient "utterly worn-out" and low-lying houses, many of them back-to-back; they were "represented" for clearance as far back as 1919. In the same year closing orders were placed on nine tumbledown and dangerous houses in White Lion-court, Bermondsey; but six of these houses still stand to-day, and four of them are occupied. In Bermondsey, too, "a very large number of houses inhabited by more than one family have the water supply either on the ground floor or in the yard, and there are many houses without a direct supply from the rising main."

Insanitary holes of this order—or tenement blocks like Wolseley Buildings, Dockhead—are the homes of the thousands of workers who line up early each morning outside the Surrey Commercial Docks for the daily demoralising scramble for work. Wolseley Buildings need to be visited to be believed. The only comparison I would venture is with the stifling barracks which the industrial autocrats of Tsarist Russia flung up for the peasants whom hunger drove from the land to toil in their factories. There are 1,036 people packed into the 191 tenements of Wolseley Buildings, representing London's uttermost extremity in density of population—at the rate of 1,650 persons to the acre. The sanitary arrangements are disgraceful. Two families have to share one w.c., four families one tap and sink; there are neither sculleries nor baths. And "the question of proceeding with an improvement scheme for this area is in abeyance." Dr. Connan, the medical officer of health, sums up the Bermondsey position in these words: "most of the property in the borough is between 70 and 150 years old, and a goodly proportion is frankly worn out, irreparable and scarcely habitable. . . . The prime defect in most cases is dampness, followed closely by darkness and inadequate flow of air both inside and around the houses."[28]

So the damnable tale of the East End in the south could be continued. The relentless facts have recently been set forth by the Bishop of Southwark in his book *In the Heart of South London*, from which one quotation must suffice:

On the ground floor of a house in South London there lived two families. In the front room were the father and mother with six boys and girls; the eldest was ten and the youngest one. Two of these slept in their parents' bed, the other four as best they could on mattresses on the ground. The rest of this floor was occupied by a family of ten; the parents and two children slept in one room, three in the kitchen, and the other three in a small boxroom most of which was occupied by furniture and a perambulator. The whole house was in a bad state of repair and infested by rats. In the four rooms were four adults and fourteen children. Measles broke out among the children, one of them died from pneumonia following it; two were removed to the hospital suffering from the same complaint, and one of these also died. A crowning touch of horror was added to the tragedy when the undertaker entering the room with the coffin killed a rat which was trying to get at the dead body of the child. This is not a story of the Middle Ages or of some Asiatic village, but of South London in the year of Our Lord 1930. No doubt the incident is exceptional, but it ought to be impossible in a civilised land. Only in degree is it worse than other cases, for there are to-day tens of thousands of children living in crowded, dark, damp, badly ventilated, insanitary rooms.[29]

But our survey of the slums is not yet completed. Beside the East End and the solid working-class quarters of the north and south there are slum "outcrops" in the heart of the most luxurious bourgeois quarters. In Paddington, for example, a whole class chasm separates the grand houses that front on to Hyde Park, and the fearful slums of Clarendon-street and Amberley-road along the Grand Junction Canal—perhaps the worst streets in the whole of London, whose ground-rents swell the coffers of the church. The extremely well-to-do residential areas of the Hampstead slopes contrast with the crowded working-class areas of Kilburn and Kentish Town at the foot of the hill.* In the latter the density of population is six times as great as it is for the whole borough, and nearly one-fifth of the families in inspected tenements are overcrowded.

Marylebone is not composed exclusively of the wealthy mansions and flats of St. John's Wood, nor of the rich squares on the north side of Oxford-street. A few minutes away are crowded streets of low-standard tenements, of which there are 1,894 containing at least one more than the overcrowding standard of

* The celebrated case of No. 83, Palmerston-road, Kilburn, is worth mentioning. Because, *inter alia*, of its damp basement rooms, this house was ordered to be closed and demolished in 1909. Eight years later the closing order was quashed, as the basement rooms had been closed. But in 1928 these rooms were found to have been re-opened for habitation, in as bad a state as ever. The case went through every court, up to the House of Lords; and Dr. Scrase, the medical officer of health, comments simply that "the conditions which gave rise to all this litigation still persist" (*Hampstead Health Report*, 1930, pp. 112-113, 131-132).

two to a room; this was the estimate of the medical officer of health eight years ago, and there has been no measurable progress since in remedying these conditions.[30] This is what workers in Marylebone say of the way in which they are forced to live:

A working-man: Me and my wife and three children are all living in one room under terrible conditions. We have no place to do any washing, or to bath our children. The house is damp, which is the cause of my children's illness. The doctor has ordered my baby boy away to hospital.

A working-woman: I think it's not decent for us all in one room with two well-built girls and a boy 10 years sleeping beside them. My nerves are getting so bad with the worry of bringing them up decent. My doctor said I must get more rest, but it is impossible to rest at night.[31]

Most brutal of all are the contrasts in Westminster and Kensington, those governing class quarters *par excellence.* A brief walk, or a few moments on the 'bus, are enough to take one from the oligarchic splendour of Mayfair or Belgravia to the poverty and overcrowding of Pimlico or the Soho back-streets; from Eaton-square, Park-lane or South Audley-street, where the very houses seem bloated with self-complacent opulence, to the squalor of the dilapidated streets off the Vauxhall Bridge-road. Within a stone's throw of Buckingham Palace and White-hall one can find "husband, wife and five young children living in two rooms. Two children have died there. The rooms are infested with rats. A dog is kept in the room while the children sleep to protect them. Gas has to be burnt all day long, and the rooms are so small that the children have to sit on the bed to eat their meals."[32]

About housing in Kensington, the Royal Borough, a book could easily be written. To step from the south division of the borough to the north is to step from surfeit to bitter need, from magnificence to misery, so suddenly that it comes as a physical shock. There are 2,000 mews-dwellings in Kensington, many made intolerable by the vegetable refuse which the costermongers, who frequently inhabit them, leave in the yards. In South Kensington there has in recent years been a large increase in accommodation for the wealthy who may desire to live there. And in North Kensington, screened by the genteel frontages of such streets as Ladbroke Grove, what do we find? Mr. Howard Marshall shall answer:

It was just off Ladbroke Grove that I saw my first room there, a basement. The husband, ironically enough, was an unemployed builder, who, with his wife and five children, received 31s. 6d. transi-

L

tional benefit. Father, mother and son slept in one bed, the baby in a cot, two more children on a very small collapsible bed, and another boy on a chair with his feet on this bed. It was dark, frowsty and damp. 5,600 persons live in rooms entirely below the level of the pavement, and there are 13,000 inhabited basements in the borough. There are many of these basements in the Portobello-road. One I saw there took its only light and air from a grating in the pavement about a yard long and a foot across. The room was pitch dark; gas had to be burnt all day, and cost a shilling a day, and it was so damp that clothes in a chest of drawers were wringing wet. Incidentally, there were five families in this house—approximately thirty people— with one working water-closet. Sewage water comes into some of these cellars, forced back from the sewers, and it did not surprise me to learn that for every three cases of infantile rheumatism in the southern half of the borough there are forty-three cases in the north. Then, in addition to the dozens of structurally sound but overcrowded and ill-adapted houses and the basement dwellings, there are many families living in mews flats. There are dozens of them with four, five and six people sleeping in one bed. I went into one where mother, father and seven children occupied two small rooms over a garage. The rooms were about eight feet square, one of them lit only by a skylight—a draughty, totally unsuitable place for a family to occupy.

These are the conditions existing literally on the doorstep of Mr. Montagu Norman, Governor of the Bank of England, and the other personages of wealth and rank who have their mansions on that salubrious eminence, Campden-hill. And two years ago the Kensington Housing Association reported that "even when the various specially bad spots . . . have been cleared up there will still remain the major difficulties of the Kensington housing problem, viz., overcrowding and bad basements . . . The solution of the problem awaits the provision of fresh accommodation on a scale much larger than anything that is at present in sight."[33]

Our survey may fittingly conclude with a word or two about the general lack of domestic amenities in the slum and near-slum areas. Valuable light has been thrown on this by a house-to-house inspection in the St. George-the-Martyr Ward of Holborn, which Dr. Hutt, the medical officer of health for that borough, had made. Any visitor to central London may easily traverse the mean streets of this ward, which lie between Southampton-row and Lamb's Conduit-street, and lead off Theobald's-road. To one who has made even this cursory survey it will not be surprising to learn that only 290 of the 1,066 tenements here were classified as "good" for general sanitary condition. In half the houses the w.c. is outside in the yard or area. In only 14 per cent. of the tenements are the cooking arrangements satisfactory; the use of gas stoves, without flues, and usually disposed on the open landings, means that their fumes, and the reek of cooking, invade the whole house. The facilities for food storage are "most unsatisfactory"; in nearly a quarter of the tenements there is no food storage at all, and in the majority of the remainder the only storage is unventilated cupboards. For laundry purposes some 40 per cent. of the tenements have not even the use of a wash-house; for personal toilet most have only a bowl in the room, and baths were fitted in only twenty-seven of the thousand-odd tenements. St. George and his martyrdom are an ancient myth, but the martyrdom of the housewives in this London ward is a modern reality.[34]

LONDON HOUSING—THE GORDIAN KNOT

We have now seen how vast masses of workers are housed in London; and it is necessary to answer the question—*why* is housing so scandalously bad, *why* do the slums remain and even multiply? We shall only be able to do this by considering housing not as something static, but as part of a social process, as a product of the whole system of capitalist social relationships. Housing is a remarkable instance of the insoluble contradictions inherent in capitalist social development; and in London, where these contradictions have culminated in a Gordian knot defying all efforts to loosen it, the phenomenon appears in its clearest and most classic form.

London affords the supremely parasitic example of what the then Liberal Mr. Winston Churchill called in 1907 that "great monopoly so ancient that it has become almost venerable"— the monopoly in land, the "plunder system" (it is Mr. Churchill's phrase) of landownership. Great nobles like the Duke of Westminster, with his 600 acres in the heart of London, the Established Church, the Crown,* wealthy and close corporations like

* The Crown estate covers a wide area round Regents Park and the Marylebone-road. The estate authorities are responsible for the collection of refuse in the area, as a result (I presume) of some queer feudal survival of Crown rights. Dr. Porter, the St. Marylebone medical officer of health, makes the following pungent comment: "From the appearance particularly of the vehicles in use, the opinion one has formed is that the arrangements in operation at the moment are still those which might have been devised half a century or more ago. No attempt has been made to bring the methods into line with those which the Borough Council . . . is endeavouring to perfect in the health interests of the inhabitants" (*Report for* 1931, pp. 11-12). This is a biting contrast with the recent "loyal" excitement over the King's health, and the decision that he should not return from Sandringham to London in order to avoid the risk of contracting influenza.

the Corporation of the City of London and the Colleges of Oxford and Cambridge; these toil not, neither do they spin, but sit back and draw their tribute from soaring land values and rising rents. The exact extent of private monopoly in London land is not known. It has always been discreetly shrouded by a conspiracy of silence. The great survey of landholding made in the seventies significantly omitted London. And the London County Council, which has occasion to collect information on this topic, has always treated it as "confidential."

Prices of land for London sites range from £10,000 to £25,000 an acre (in the centre of the city up to literally millions an acre). For the nine-acre Foundling site in Bloomsbury £450,000 was demanded. In Greater London landowners, and speculators who borrowed money to buy land for appreciation, have raked in tens of millions of pounds; an estate agent familiar with the suburban building "boom" reckoned early in 1931 that no less than £120,000,000 had changed hands in land sales. The church drew nearly £380,000 from rents of houses and premises in London in 1930, and over £53,000 from the so-called London Bishopric Paddington Estate,* which contains some of London's vilest slums.[35]

It is hardly necessary to emphasise that a direct product of the land monopoly and of capitalism in the building industry has been the concentration on luxury building which has been typical of recent years in London. It is far more profitable to build a new Regent-street, to rush up huge new hotels, luxury flats (at rents up to £1,000 a year and more apiece), banks, stores, "super-cinemas," and so forth, than to provide houses for workers. With all the present talk about the slums the latest announcement by

* The Ecclesiastical Commissioners were greatly annoyed by revelations of the horrible conditions on this estate made by a local inquiry. In their report for 1930 they executed a series of angry manœuvres designed to "pass the buck" to the leaseholders. After which they complacently added that "ground rents continue to expand with building development, particularly around London, and there are increases from rents of London house property and in the receipts from the Paddington estate" (83rd *Report from the Ecclesiastical Commissioners*, pp. vii-ix). It was in reference to this Paddington scandal that the Bishop of London's Housing Committee declared that until such a "reproach" could "be rolled away your Committee believes that slum protest meetings under Church auspices are calculated to do more harm than good; they merely confirm the unfortunate tenants and their friends who have to live in such conditions that the Church is not in earnest, and nothing can be more utterly ruinous to her reputation" (*Fourth Annual Report*, p. 2). Needless to say, the "reproach" has not been "rolled away," and the church continues to "protest" against the slums.

the Building Industries National Council of work projected in London was simply this—"five new super-cinemas are shortly to be built, at a cost of approximately £750,000."[36]

The prohibitive level of land values in London results from the combination of the land monopoly and the fact that all available sites are built up, especially in the more central areas. This in itself is an insuperable bar to housing development; thus the Shoreditch Housing Association declare that "the crux of the difficulty" is that "land values in Shoreditch are so high that a cleared site at a price that can be contemplated for housing work is practically impossible to find."[37] But there are two special factors, inseparable from capitalist development, which have played a big part in sending land values soaring, and have in other ways contributed to the worsening of housing conditions.

The first of these is industrialisation. As industry grew, especially along the riverside, both north and south, it meant that whole streets of working-class houses were demolished to make factory sites. The population partly migrated and partly crowded worse than ever into the houses which remained—since most of them could not afford to live far away from their work. Both processes can be seen typically in Stepney, Shoreditch and Southwark. In the latter borough the development of industrialisation along its northern fringe—the riverside wharves, and the big printing and other works that dominate the neighbourhood—meant that in the seventy years up to 1931 the population in the parishes concerned, the famous old area of "the Borough," fell from 36,000 to 15,000. In the last thirty years the population of the whole borough fell from 206,000 to 173,000, and Dr. Stott, the medical officer of health, now reports that "there are 2,113 families housed in 1,531 decayed and dilapidated houses or dwellings, many of which are grossly overcrowded." Dr. Dart, the Hackney medical officer, reported in 1928 that in that overcrowded borough 435 houses had been converted into factories and workshops; the number has grown since.[38]

The second factor has been the invasion of what were once working-class areas, but which possess certain special amenities or attractions, by the bourgeoisie in person. Chelsea is the outstanding instance of this. Over the past thirty years and more, estate companies have bought up working-class property in Chelsea as the leases fell in, demolished it, and built fine mansions and expensive flats into which governing class tenants have flooded. To-day Chelsea has the highest percentage of "retired and unoccupied" persons of any London borough. The other side of the picture is that during this period some 20,000 working people and small traders were uprooted from their Chelsea homes; and the especially steep rise in land values has meant that the Ministry of Health has vetoed housing schemes submitted by the local authority for the amelioration of the wretched slums that continue to exist in the west of the borough, on the ground that the cost of the land was too high for working-class housing.[39]

The consequence of all this has been that population has been driven outward from the centre. In the last twenty years the population of the County of London was first stationary, and then fell; the population of Greater London has risen constantly. And this outward movement of working-class population has been reflected in an outward movement of overcrowding. The workers whom industrialisation drove out from the centre found industrialisation also in progress on the outskirts. Take West Ham; the eighteenth century village, with its 700 houses, has swollen into a big industrial town with 48,000 houses; within it lie the vast Victoria and Albert docks, the railway works of Stratford in the north, and the mass of chemical, soap, sugar, rubber and other factories of Canning Town and Silvertown along the riverside in the south. The housing shortage and overcrowding are acute. While in Greater London as a whole the index of persons overcrowded per thousand of the population rose in the ten years up to 1921 from 175 to 185, in West Ham it rose from 196 to 292.[40]

Capitalism can only reproduce its own social relationships; and since overcrowding and slums arise out of those social relationships (through the private appropriation of land, the resulting famine level of land values, high rents, and the workers' poverty) it is clear that capitalism cannot help but beget overcrowding and slums. A slum may be cleared in one spot; but the causes which produced that slum continue to operate and reproduce it elsewhere. Engels wrote in 1892 in his preface to the second edition of the *Condition of the Working Class in England in* 1844:

> Drainage has been introduced or improved, wide avenues have been opened out athwart many of the worst "slums" I had to describe. . . But what of that? Whole districts which in 1844 I could describe as almost idyllic, have now, with the growth of the towns, fallen into the same state of dilapidation, discomfort and misery. . . . The bourgeoisie have made further progress in the art of hiding the distress of the working class. . . . Police regulations have been plentiful as blackberries; but they can only hedge in the distress of the workers, they cannot remove it.

How many of the present working-class neighbourhoods of London are there that have not "gone down," as the saying is? It has happened in the outer eastern area, as in West Ham; it can be seen happening to-day in such areas as Westbourne Park, in the south-west of Paddington, where big old houses are being sub-divided into tenements, inhabited by poorly-paid hotel and domestic workers. The same thing has happened in Wandsworth.[41] No one who visited the recent Public Health Congress and Exhibition in London could forget the housing exhibit, which contained a scale model of a working-class house of the eighties, inhabited by one family and in a decent state, contrasted with the same house forty years later—inhabited by four families, and degenerated into a typical slum house.

It would be superfluous to spend time on demonstrating that working-class house property in general, and slum property in particular, is a highly profitable business proposition; but it is profitable mainly as a "going concern," not from the point of view of capital investment in constructing new houses. The older the property and the greater the degree to which repairs and maintenance can be pared down, the more profitable it becomes. It is in an attempt to "rationalise" this primitive process that capitalism has had to resort to municipal housing schemes. But these schemes are simply a form of monopoly, affording a profitable field for the gilt-edged investment of loan capital. The L.C.C. buildings and estates house a population of over 230,000—a large city in itself; and the net housing debt of the L.C.C. and the Metropolitan Boroughs exceeds £43,000,000, on which vast sum the annual interest and sinking fund charges are nearly £2,500,000. When to this figure is added the cost of the land for housing schemes* it is easy to see why the L.C.C.'s principle, that rents should be so fixed "as to ensure the undertakings being financially self-supported," inflicts such an unbearable burden upon the worker-tenants, and excludes so many who cannot afford to pay the rents demanded.

The line of the "National" Government now is to abandon housing to the profit-making efforts of the private builder, and to afford the great finance corporations which are called Building Societies outlets for their surplus capital in the profitable financing of houses to let; though, as the Bishop of London's Housing Committee remarks, "if schemes for housing the poor could be

---

* The net cost of the land alone for the Becontree estate was £295,000. The landowners pocketed this huge sum for land which, according to the assessment for local rating, was valued at £7,000. (House of Commons *Official Report*, May 4th, 1931, col. 50.)

self-supporting, builders, public ·or private, would quickly enough do all that is required. . . . There would be no housing problem." It is appropriate to quote here (from the *Star* of January 17, 1933) the following London example of what the control of working-class housing by a large-scale capitalist concern means in real life:

> Mr. H. L. Smith, an unemployed ex-service man, with his wife and three children, were evicted by bailiffs from a house in Arch-street, Southwark, to-day. The eviction order was obtained by the land-lords, the London Property Investment Trust, Ltd., Mr. Smith being £2 8s. in arrears with his rent. When bailiffs attempted to execute the order last Friday, 300 unemployed men went to Mr. Smith's assis-tance, and the order was extended. To-day Mr. Smith barricaded the windows of his flat with stout wooden laths. He joined the Army as a boy in 1900, and was a trumpeter in the Dragoon Guards. During the war he served in France, and in the East with the Royal Engineers, and was discharged in 1919 with a disability pension of 10s. 6d. a week. On this and the transitional benefit he, his wife, two girls, aged thirteen years and two years respectively, and a boy of five, have had to live. . . . It was not long before the bailiffs had fought a way in, and then an iron bedstead, two or three wooden chairs, a packing-case —all the Smiths' meagre furniture—was carried downstairs into the street. . . . There was a pitiful scene when Mrs. Smith, who was weeping, came out with the two-years-old child in her arms. "Cheer up, old girl!" neighbours cried after her as, accompanied by her husband, who was also in tears, and the other two children, she left her home. "I have no idea where we shall go," Mr. Smith told a reporter. "I have searched, and know how impossible it is to get alternative accommodation. What is going to happen to us?"

The London Property Investment Trust, which evicted this ex-serviceman, is one of a number of similar concerns owning working-class house property in London. It has an authorised capital of a quarter of a million in £5 shares; and after its A and B shares have received their regular dividends of 6 per cent. and 5 per cent. respectively, and 25 per cent. of the profits remaining has been allocated to reserve, the heads of the con-cern, who hold special "founders' shares," divide the surplus among them. The dividend on each founders' share rose steadily from £250 (on a £5 share, remember) in 1923 to no less than £710 in 1931. In nine years the "surplus," extracted from hundreds of families like the evicted Smiths, gave the holder of each founders' share a fabulous dividend exceeding 80,000 per cent!

A word needs to be said about the Housing Associations and Public Utility Housing Societies which have sprung up in considerable numbers in London during the past few years. The political aims of these bodies are discussed in a later chapter.

Here it will suffice to note their general charitable-religious flavour, on the one hand, and their inevitable character of merely rather more "refined" capitalist landlordism, on the other. Royalty, lords and ladies, generals and admirals, bishops and priests, big finance-capitalists, figure among the patrons and leaders of these organisations. Here are, with significant irony, some of the very biggest landowners in the country, Their Graces the Dukes of Sutherland (who owns 1,000,000 acres), Richmond & Gordon (286,000 acres), and Portland (183,000 acres). The Courtauld family, the colossal artificial silk monopolists, donate substantially to the Marylebone Housing Association. The St. Pancras House Improvement Society (capital over £162,000 and rent roll over £11,000) boasts of its patronage by such a White émigré as "Father Behr, the Russian protopriest."

There is at the same time a tendency for the municipalities to link up with these bodies. In Paddington the Borough Council has taken up £5,000 in shares in the Paddington Houses Association, and Lambeth Housing Ltd. has received loans of £7,300 from the L.C.C. This is a natural thing, for the Public Utility Societies are just like the municipalities in that they have, as their first charge, to earn interest on capital. Their rents are excessive, too, like those of the council houses and flats. After all, they have to pay their regular 2½ per cent. to 4 per cent. on loan and share capital, and they are always concerned to stress what a "safe" investment they offer.* The three-room flats of the Marylebone Housing Association rent for 13s. 6d. a week; they admit that many of their tenants are in "acute poverty" (the Kensington Housing Trust state that heavy unemployment is bringing "sickness and misery" to their tenants), and instance the case of a labourer earning 35s. a week with a wife and five children to support, but conclude that the rents are "such as they can afford to pay."(!) The four-room flats of Lambeth Housing, Ltd. rent for 17s. 6d. a week, and the Society boast that "in accepting only tenants with an assured income and satisfactory references" they are "protecting their interests as landlords." Such are the sweet uses of "charity" for the workers in the slums! And, to "protect their interests as landlords" these Societies, like any other landlord, proceed from time to time to take their tenants to court, and secure eviction orders (as the St. Pancras Society and the Kensington Trust have done).[42]

Finally, these Societies give an excellent example, in miniature, of the way in which the burden of capitalist tribute presses

* See p. 241, below.

down like an alp on the worker-tenant. The balance-sheet of the Lambeth Society shows that some 66 per cent. of its gross rental goes in repayment of loans and interest on capital, and the Shoreditch Society estimated that 60 per cent. of their gross rental would be absorbed by interest on loan capital and dividend on shares.[43]

And now—where does all this end? Whither have all these municipal and charitable efforts led, after a decade of talking and writing and pother? Here is a cry from the heart of a parson who has been in the forefront of these efforts in the East End of London, the Rev. R. A. Edwards, formerly Vicar of St. Faith's, Stepney. He asks:

> Why is it that so little has been done? Why is it that the whole horrible thing—these vile, leaking, verminous houses, these insane conditions of unspeakable overcrowding—still goes on? For it does go on. Here and there a Municipality puts up a tenement or a Public Utility Housing Trust reconditions a row of old houses or builds a block of flats, but neither seems to do more than touch the fringe of the slum areas that we know. Round London Housing Estates have sprung up, and our slum dwellers have looked at them with eager eyes, but rents and travelling expenses have been far outside their reach, and so they have remained in their slums. At the same time outwards and outwards has crept the City; land that we thought might have done so admirably for housing purposes has provided a site for offices and warehouses; while we have sometimes pessimistically told ourselves that the only slums that have come down have done so to make room for garages and cinemas. . . . Have the forces opposed to us, the criminally negligent landlords who do no repairs until they are summonsed, the speculative individuals and syndicates who buy up slum property, the hide-bound cherishers of the story of the man who having nowhere else to put it kept the coal in his bath, the people who detect the Red Hand of Bolshevism in the mildest suggestion of reform—have all these people been too strong for us, and successfully damped down the mines which we hoped our publicity would explode?[44]

The reverend gentleman is anxious to get a move on; but then he proceeds to outline the difficulties that lie in the way. "How," he demands, "should the compensation payable for a slum house that is to be demolished be assessed? How are you to bridge the gap between the *economic rent* of a new house and the sum which the rehoused tenant can actually pay? . . . *How is land for housing purposes to be secured* in 'built up areas' over which commercial undertakings are rapidly spreading and *where the value of land is rising every year?*" (My italics.) He has answered his own question why so little has been done. The acceptance of the existing social relationships, the existing property relationships, of capitalism means that the housing question remains a baffling and insoluble problem. The Gordian knot cannot be unloosened. It has to be cut; and the sword that will cut it is the sword of the social revolution.

A MOTHER WHO STARVED TO DEATH

In London, in the year 1933, a working-class housewife and mother of a family starved to death. The family, it is significant to note, were living on the new Downham estate of the London County Council. They had been among the "lucky" ones who had escaped from the slums. Here is a newspaper report of the inquest:

How an unemployed man's wife literally starved herself to death for her children was told at an inquest on Mrs. Minnie Annie Weaving, aged 37, of Elmscott-road, Downham, S.E. George Henry Weaving, the husband, said his wife had not seen a doctor since July, when she had twins. They had seven children living. On Monday she complained of pain, but refused to see a doctor. On Wednesday she said she would get up to bath the twins, and he went to get a doctor. On his return he found his wife dead and the children crying around her. Major Whitehouse (the coroner): "Did she have enough to eat?"— "That is the trouble with us all. I am out of work." Mr. Weaving said he was drawing the dole, 35s. 3d. a week, and was getting 5s. from the Relieving Officer. His little girl was earning 8s. a week. He had been taken to court for arrears of rent, and had to pay two weeks in one. He was now paying three weeks in two. *Major Whitehouse: "I should call it starving to have to feed nine people on £2 8s. a week and pay the rent."* Dr. Arthur Davies, pathologist, of Harley-street, W., said Mrs. Weaving's body was much wasted. Death was due to pneumonia. He added: *"I have no doubt that had she had sufficient food this attack would not have proved fatal. It appears that she deliberately stinted herself and gave such food as came into the house to the children, and so sacrificed her life."*[45]

This is an extreme case; but to those who may strive to extract comfort from that fact we may reply in the words of Engels, who, after recording a number of cases of a similar kind in the forties, wrote: "I am far from asserting that *all* London working-people live in such want as the foregoing . . . I know very well that ten are somewhat better off, where one is so totally trodden under foot by society; but I assert that thousands of industrious and worthy people—far worthier and more to be respected than all the rich of London—do find themselves in a condition unworthy of human beings; and that every proletarian, everyone without exception, is exposed to a similar fate without any fault of his own and in spite of every possible effort."[46] Here is another example of a mother's sacrifice.*   A Marylebone woman (by a curious coincidence she is thirty-seven, the same age as Mrs. Weaving) has a large family and a husband unemployed. She was married at sixteen, and her eldest son is twenty years old, while her youngest child is three months.   To keep the home together she works at the hard and poorly-paid job of office-cleaning, going out at 6 a.m. every morning.   The benevolent writer who recounts her case says that "it is monstrous that she should be working so hard," and that she "miraculously keeps her rent paid and her family fed and clothed."   Mrs. Weaving, of Downham, also performed miracles. [47]

The foregoing cases are instances of the devastating impoverishment which unemployment has brought to London workers.   The nature of London industry has always meant that the average percentage of unemployment is less than in the areas of the basic industries.   This is the case to-day.   But at the same time unemployment in London has shot upwards dizzily since the onset of the crisis.   In the London division of the Ministry of Labour there were 142,000 registered unemployed at the end of 1929, and 297,000 at the end of 1932; in the south-eastern division, which includes a number of London's satellite towns and areas, the corresponding figures were 70,000 and 149,000.†   The latest Poor Law returns show that there are in addition 109,500 persons in London receiving outdoor relief.   From the first operation of the Means Test up to September 1932 there were 162,000 applications made by London unemployed workers for transitional benefit, of which no less than half were either refused payments altogether or were only granted benefit at reduced rates; in the same period there were 321,000 renewal applications and revision cases, and more than one-third of these were similarly treated.   The manner in which this forces the poor to keep the poor may be deduced from an official enquiry made in London in 1931 into cases which had been disallowed un-

---

* An enquiry by the Deptford medical officers into the gross under-nourishment among the workers there stresses that the mothers are the hardest hit.   "The signs of malnutrition are insidious.   There is a loss of vitality, with mental depression, apathy, anæmia, decay of the teeth with inflammation of the gums, and an unhealthy appearance of the skin, with spots or rashes, and a tendency for cracks, sores and wounds to remain unhealed . . . chronic colds, and a liability to catch any infection, usually described in medical certificates as 'general debility.' Amongst the mothers included in the list, a large proportion . . . showed these signs" (*Manchester Guardian*, February 20th, 1933).

† In January 1933 the figures shot up further still, to 340,000 (London) and 172,000 (South-Eastern).

employment benefit; the enquiry revealed that a majority of the
cases were being supported either wholly or in part by relatives.
Even the *New Survey of London Life and Labour* cannot deny the
evident fact that this "must doubtless in many cases have
involved hardship and sometimes even poverty to those who contributed."[48]

It will have been remarked that the Weaving family were not
saved from awful tragedy because the father was in receipt of
both full unemployment benefit and relief. But this position is
a most exceptional one. Out of 190,000 unemployed workers on
the register in the London County Council area there are only
2,300 who receive relief in addition to benefit, no matter how
acute their need may be. In one case a man with a wife and two
children, drawing the full benefit of 27s. 3d., had a rent of 11s. 6d.
to pay (not at all an unusual figure) and what was left had to
feed and maintain four people. He went to the relieving officer,
and was eventually grudgingly granted 8s. relief and told he must
not be seen again. In Shoreditch a family of eleven (parents and
nine children) have a net income of 21s. 6d. after paying 15s.
rent, and a family of four (parents and two children) have a
net income of 9s. 4d.; the observer who describes these cases
comments that they "can be multiplied over and over again."
And if conditions like this are the lot of families who receive
both full benefit and relief, the conditions of those cut off, or on
reduced benefit, under the Means Test, can be imagined.[49]

A word may be interpolated here about the so-called "industrial colony" at Belmont. This notorious establishment is a
thinly-disguised prison, where some 800 London unemployed
workers are herded, having been separated from their families,
and "set on work." They do typical prison tasks, under jail-
like supervision, and in return receive a few pence a week, in
coupons exchangeable only at the canteen on the premises.
This may be reduced as a punishment for lateness at work.
Belmont is a name that stinks in the nostrils of every working-
man in the metropolis. No wonder—when one hears of such
outrages as the case of a man recently sent to Belmont one week
after his wife had been confined.

The *New Survey* takes the year 1929 as its central point; it
reviews conditions, that is to say, before the London workers
felt the blows of the crisis in vastly increased unemployment and
and impoverishment; and this the authors admit. The striking
thing is that, even under the conditions of 1929, poverty is shown
to be enormously widespread. On the "very low and bare . . .
minimum standard of subsistence" of Charles Booth's poverty

line there were over 250,000 people in East London in 1929—or
one in ten of the population—below that line. If the Survey's
two classes P and U* are taken together as representing the
poverty groups, then no less than half the inhabitants of East
London fell below the poverty line in 1929, compared with
three-quarters in the 'nineties. The highest percentages of
poverty recorded in the eastern area of the *New Survey*, on the
basis of Booth's poverty line, and giving first the percentage of
families in poverty, then (in parentheses) the percentage of
population, were—Poplar 19.5 (24.1), Stepney 19.3 (15.5),
Bermondsey 14.7 (17.5), Bethnal Green 14.6 (17.8), Shoreditch 13.8 (18.0), West Ham 13.6 (14.5), Deptford 12.4 (15.6).
The average for the whole area was 12 per cent. in both categories.[50]

An additional sidelight is thrown on Deptford poverty by the
fact, recorded by the medical officer of health, that in 1931 out
of 11,311 applications for milk at the child welfare centres,
10,565 were in respect of families whose weekly income, after
deduction of rent, amounted to less than 7s. 6d. per head. Dr.
Borland, in Bethnal Green, reported in 1928 that child welfare
centre enquiries tended to show that the majority of families
were below the "living wage" level of £4 a week for a family of
five; two years later he wrote, "I am afraid that the general
level of wages is much lower now than it was then." His colleague Dr. Mackay, reporting on the Bethnal Green clinic for
delicate children, says that "the family income as stated by the
mothers of many children attending this clinic was often so low
that one marvelled how they were able to carry on at all."[51]

A purely quantitative and static comparison of poverty at
widely separated periods, as attempted by the *New Survey*, fails
in two vital respects; the first objective and the second subjective. First, it leaves out of account the development, both actual
and potential, of the productive forces; and this has been colossal
between the 'nineties and the present day. Second, it omits any
consideration of changed outlook, and higher material and
cultural demands, on the part of the working class. Dr. Harry
Roberts, an experienced medical practitioner and social worker
in the East End, commented on this latter point in the *New
Statesman and Nation* of December 17, 1932. He observed that
"members of the cultivated classes are accustomed to measure
the condition of working people—when they bother their heads

* P is the poverty group, taken as those with an income of less than
£2 a week. U is the unskilled labourers' group, taken as those with an
income of from £2 to £3 a week.

about it at all—by a standard very different from that which they apply to their own. The people of the East End are no longer prepared to discuss their problems on this basis." After a remark on the "light-heartedness" he found in the East End when he first went there twenty-five years ago, he says that to-day "new standards of cleanliness, of wholesomeness and of decency prevail; but the light-heartedness is less noticeable, and everywhere one sees the marks of anxiety, of disappointment." "I believe (he adds) that there has never—certainly not within my experience—been so much misery as there is in East London at the present time." This further observation of Dr. Roberts is very pertinent:

> Every day I come across middle-aged men, healthy and competent, driven almost crazy by a persistent unemployment of which they have had no previous experience; a state which they had been taught, and had believed, to be the fruit of sickness, incompetence, idleness or dishonesty. It is poor compensation to such men to learn that "the average London workman can now buy one-third more of the means of subsistence than he could forty years ago, in return for daily labour of an hour's less duration."*

What is the fate in London to-day of those two most helpless categories of the proletariat, the aged and the homeless? Even the *New Survey* has to admit that the old age pension "is just sufficient to keep above the poverty line an old couple of pensioners living together, but not enough to prevent a recipient living alone from falling into poverty"—to say nothing of the loneliness and general hardship of old age for the working man or woman. As for the homeless their numbers are higher now than at any time since the end of the war. The lodging-house and casual ward† population is increasing; the official census showed a total of 20,000 in 1931, and unofficial estimates suggest that the figure in the winter months is twice as high. It is significant that in 1931 there were nearly nine times the number sleeping in free shelters that there were in 1920. And a repulsive aspect of increasing poverty is seen in the fact that 119 children were found in lodging-houses at the census of the homeless in February, 1930, compared with an average of seventy-five in recent previous years. [52] The London doss-house in 1933 stands in the most glaring contrast to the glittering luxury hotels of the West End. The authors of the *New Survey*, sitting in academic ease in their Aldwych offices, evoke a rosy picture of the great "improvements" in the

---

* The quotation is the central contention of the *New Survey of London Life and Labour*. † See p. 196, below.

common lodging-house. They rhapsodise over the "cheery coke fire" of the common kitchen and, telling us that there are "none but the simplest regulations," they conclude that the "outstanding attractions of lodging-house life are freedom from responsibility and freedom from inquisition." One wonders why Sir H. Llewellyn Smith and Professor Bowley do not immediately take up their residence in such an Arcadia; and one draws one's own conclusions from the fact that they both prefer to continue dwelling in the comfort of The Grove, Highgate, and Park-avenue, Harpenden, respectively. A writer with a more intimate experience of doss-house life, Mr. Eric Blair, has recently penned a bitter exposure of the "horrible fetid dens" of overcrowded dormitories, the filthy and verminous beds, the lack of all privacy, the dirty kitchens swarming with cockroaches and beetles. He declares that the L.C.C. regulations are a mockery so far as ameliorating conditions is concerned, that they neglect such an elementary provision as the enforcement of cubicles in the dormitories; he adds that the regulations are all of the *verboten* type, and "can only be defended on the theory that a man poor enough to live in a common lodging-house thereby forfeits some of his rights as a citizen." In the "model" Rowton House and Salvation Army establishments the discipline is such that "to stay in them is rather like being in jail"; so that the choice lies "between an easy-going pigsty and a hygienic prison." [53]

The lot of those who find themselves left helpless and alone in London, through no fault of their own, is bitter. Here is one case, reported in the *Evening Standard* of January 31, 1933:

> So shocked was the South London Coroner by a woman's story of how she and her little daughter lived on 10s. or 12s. a week that he made her a grant of £5 from his relief fund. Then he ordered a taxi-cab to take her home. The coroner, Mr. Douglas Cowburn, was holding an inquest on the child, Margaret Turner, aged 3½, of Stonhouse-street, Clapham, S.W. Mrs. Doris Turner said she left her daughter in bed on Friday. She had just lit a fire in the room. Later she heard the child scream and found her in flames. Her husband, she said, had left her and she lived on a few shillings her mother sent her. She paid 7s. a week rent. "This is a shocking case," said the coroner, "How any woman could live on a miserable pittance like this with a little baby to keep passes my comprehension."*

* This case irresistibly recalls the passage in which Engels refers to the inevitable neglect of the children in workers' homes, and to the consequent frequency of deaths from burns and scalds, notably in London. He adds: "These unhappy children, perishing in this terrible way, are victims of our social disorder and of the property-holding classes interested in maintaining and prolonging this disorder" (Engels, op. cit., pp. 108-109). Once more 1933 shows itself as barbarous as 1844!

A final sidelight on London poverty is cast by the increase in the number of stalls in the street markets, selling goods of low price and equally low quality. There are at least 50 per cent. more stalls now than there were in the 'nineties, and there is a most marked increase in clothing and especially old clothes stalls. The *New Survey* records these facts with much pained surprise, and its authors are at a loss to explain them, because they do not fit their thesis that "poverty has largely decreased." It does not strike them that here is a refutation of their thesis. Significant, too, is the position in regard to the furnishing of the workers' homes. The greater part of the furniture sold in London is on the hire-purchase system. And the Hackney Furnishing Company, which had a mainly working-class clientele, and which has just gone into liquidation, has stated that its hire-purchase contracts which were cancelled in 1932 amounted to £145,000, compared with £75,000 in the previous year. Of that £145,000 worth of furniture 15 per cent. was repossessed within six months of the contracts being entered into. The Company reports that from 1929 onwards there were increasing demands for lengthened credit; their cash trade fell from 10 per cent. to 3 per cent. of turnover, and there was a new rate of slowness in payments on hire-purchase accounts.[54]

The Social Causes of Mortality and Disease

In the review that we have now made of housing and poverty in London, the predominant influence of these two factors on the health of the mass of the population has already become apparent. The general proposition that high rates of mortality and morbidity are the result of social causes, of the social disorder of the capitalist system, has indeed been demonstrated in earlier chapters. But it will be worth while to elaborate this proposition once more in concrete application to conditions in the metropolis, for the results are extremely revealing.

The connection between the influenza epidemic* of 1932–33 and the lowered vitality and morale due to a lowered standard of living has been brought out by the *British Medical Journal* itself. It is stressed by the officials of the big Friendly Societies, who are being overwhelmed by claims for sick benefit. And the toll that impoverishment and worsened industrial conditions take of the nervous and mental condition of the people is shown by

* Deaths in the County of London in 1931 exceeded those of 1930 by 3,296. The increase is officially stated to be almost entirely due to influenza.

M

the rise in the out-patients at the Maudsley, London's greatest mental hospital, from 1,608 in 1930 to 1,993 in 1931.[55]

A comment, which applies to all working-class areas in London, is made by Dr. Borland, of Bethnal Green. He refers to the unemployment and short-time that are rampant among the workers in that borough, and says:

> The reduced earnings in these families, taken together with the fact that one-fifth of the natural breadwinners are out of work and their dependents living on the meagre allowances provided by unemployment insurance or public assistance, make it not surprising that the health records for the year should show a serious deterioration. . . . The increased mortality is due to general social causes, unemployment and low wages resulting in a reduced family income available for necessary nourishment, clothing and shelter. . . . Grants of milk to necessitous mothers and children have substantially increased during the year, but such assistance only goes a very small way to remedy the lowered vitality which follows prolonged poverty.[56]

Tuberculosis has a notably heavy incidence among the workers in certain London trades, of which clothing is the outstanding example. Thus in Stepney, workers in the various sections of the clothing industry (tailoring, dressmaking, furriery, etc.) form easily the largest industrial group among both the notifications of, and deaths from, tuberculosis each year. Some reflection of the increased employment of girls in unhealthy offices and shops in London may be seen in the remarkable rise in the phthisis death-rate in the past twenty years among young women of 15–25 years old. While the death-rate in all other age-groups has sharply decreased over this period, in the age-groups 15–20 and 20–25 it has risen by 23 per cent. and 30 per cent. respectively.[57]

A tubercular case in Battersea was found "living in one room on her own, her only income being her National Health Insurance benefit of 7s. 6d. a week. Her parents were dead, and her sister was married and had seven children, and although she gave the patient a little help at times she was not able to do much." In Finsbury, West Ham, Holborn and Greenwich the conditions of overcrowding and lack of any facilities for domestic hygiene are specially stressed as both nullifying the measures taken for the treatment of tuberculosis, and actively assisting to spread the infection. The conditions, indeed, are appalling. Rare is the working-class sufferer from the fearful scourge of tuberculosis who is able to have both a separate bed *and* room. In Greenwich, 85 out of 174 patients shared a bed; out of 49 households in Finsbury where there were tuberculosis cases, and only one bed available, a total of 54 persons were bed-fellows for tubercular patients. The bedroom conditions in Finsbury were also frequently bad; the rooms were dark and ventilation remarkable by its absence. In 69 cases the kitchen was being used as both living- and sleeping-room. Out of a total of 145 Finsbury tuberculosis cases there were 22 in one-room tenements, and in the same number of tenements there was only one cupboard for storing both food and coal!

The worker who has contracted tuberculosis as a result of the conditions imposed upon him by capitalist society, finds the hand of that society turned against him.* Dr. Lennane, in Battersea, records the case of a married man with two dependent children who "was recommended for sanatorium treatment but was very worried, as he was afraid he would lose his post." Dr. Thomas, in Finsbury, remarks that attempts to adapt employment and secure the necessary rest for tubercular patients are "usually impracticable" under present circumstances. He describes the "very common and distressing" process of the tubercular worker finding it impossible to sell his labour in competition with strong, healthy adults, and so slipping down "step by step from one grade of employment to another grade lower and less profitable." In contrast, as the doctor pointedly reminds us, "the rich consumptive can look after himself."[58]

Poverty and overcrowding play the main part in causing acute rheumatism among children, which in its turn is responsible for what is rightly termed the "appalling death-rate" due to heart disease among adults, averaging 15,000-25,000 annually in England and Wales. Rheumatism is characterised as "essentially a disease of faulty social environment, for it is practically entirely confined to the children of the poor, and does not appear in them if they are taken out of their homes and educated in residential poor law schools"; and the conclusion of Dr. Alison Glover, one of the main authorities, is that "the incidence of acute rheumatism increases directly with poverty, malnutrition, overcrowding and bad housing."

These conclusions are grimly borne out in London. Out of 79 cases in Holborn, only six had a separate room; there were 34 who shared a bed, seven of them with more than one person, and seven poor little sufferers were compelled to have their beds in the living-room; five of the cases were in one-room tenements, and in eight homes there "is a history of chronic poverty." Investigations at two London County Council rheumatism centres showed that 62 per cent. of the children shared a bed

* Other references to this point will be found in Chapter II, p. 80 above.

with one or more others, rendering it impossible for the little patients to secure the rest that is absolutely essential. At the same time hospital accommodation lags behind requirements. The children's diet was found to be insufficient at the Hammersmith and Marylebone centres. In 19 out of 38 new cases in Paddington in 1931 the home circumstances were found to be "poor" or "very poor"; in 12 cases there was overcrowding, and 7 cases were living in basements. Kensington has 90 per cent. of its acute rheumatism notifications from its northern division, grouped principally in the slum areas which we have earlier described; in 54 out of 78 cases reported on the home circumstances were "reduced or very poor."[59]

In general it is upon the health and lives of the mothers and children in London, as in every working-class area in the country, that the blows of the present social disorder fall most brutally. Dr. Borland writes, in words that every London medical officer of health might well echo:

> The domestic conditions and physical environment in Bethnal Green are definitely inimical to healthy child life, and maternity is a function which is conducted under considerable difficulties and a good deal of added risk. Poverty too often means a restricted or unsuitable dietary, insufficient or wrong clothing, inadequate housing accommodation and other handicaps. Lavatory basins and bathrooms with a regular supply of hot water are unknown in the borough. Cleanliness is a continual struggle with very adverse circumstances.

He refers to the influence of attempted abortion upon maternal mortality and morbidity, remarking that the majority of the women concerned are married, and that the sexual morality of Bethnal Green is conspicuously good, "when compared with that of more prosperous boroughs in other parts of London." He therefore concludes "that the attempts to secure abortion are mainly due to economic pressure, particularly at a time of prevalent unemployment and low wages." In Battersea the maternal mortality rate jumped sharply in 1931 to over 6 per 1,000 births, more than twice the rate for the previous five years; while in the borough maternity hospital the rate for a decade has averaged only 1.4. The Finsbury medical officer of health emphasises, in sardonic contrast to the conditions prevailing in his borough, the supreme importance of the mother being well fed and housed at all times.[60]

Ante-natal care has been developed in London in recent years; but overcrowding and poverty have grown worse. What radical change can ante-natal care bring when, as in Holborn, the home conditions of a number of mothers

showed that out of sixteen confinements in one-room tenements
only two had separate beds, and that mothers were often unable
to go into hospital because they could not arrange to have their
other children looked after, "or had to remain at home in order
to contrive ways and means of living on the very small family
income"? Dr. Thompson, of Lambeth, pointedly observes that
ante-natal care is not enough, that overcrowding must be
attended to, that, in short, "the principal aim should be directed
to improving the environment." Dr. Borland, of Bethnal Green,
reports that "of 50 cases where stillbirths occurred half the
families were overcrowded. In one case there were seven persons
living in a single room. The prospects of a satisfactory live birth,
to say nothing of the child's after life, in such conditions can
surely be appreciated by the most limited imagination."[61]

But here is another side to the medal. The following paragraph
appeared in the gossip columns of the *Daily Telegraph* on December 5, 1932—the self-same day on which, in a leading article
entitled "Costly School Medical Services," that journal demanded that these services "be carried on with greater
economy":

> Little Lady Jane Douglas is highly delighted at being promoted to a
> real bedroom of her own, opening off the night nursery, at the new
> Cheyne Walk house to which her mother, Lady Queensberry, has
> moved. *The nurseries . . . occupy a whole floor. . . .* The day nursery
> has pale pink walls and gay green furniture, while the night nursery
> is done in two tones of a darker, more restful green. A great joy must
> be a large play-house, with a real front door, complete with knocker,
> and a silver horseshoe suspended above it. Lady Queensberry's own
> bedroom is also in cool pastel shades of pink and green, with a quilted
> pink satin "petticoat" to the dressing-table, and green padded
> bedstead.

In the Cheyne ward of Chelsea, where Lady Jane Douglas has a
whole floor for her nurseries, the infantile mortality rate is only
23 per 1,000 births; in the adjoining Church ward, with its
working-class population housed in gloomy tenements and poky
old houses, the rate is 70.

The infantile mortality figures in London give the same general
picture that we have observed elsewhere; the working-class
areas are above the general average, and the worsening of
conditions consequent on the crisis is reflected in a tendency to
a rise in the rate between 1930 and 1931. In the County of
London as a whole the infantile mortality rate rose in these two
years from 59 to 65. Here are the boroughs which were above
the average in one or other of these years—for the most part in

both—and the boroughs similarly below the average, arranged
in descending order of their rate for 1931:

INFANTILE MORTALITY RATES IN METROPOLITAN BOROUGHS

(a) *Above Average*

	1930	1931		1930	1931
Bethnal Green	60	88	Fulham	57	68
Paddington	78	87	Hammersmith	64	68
Stepney	76	78	St. Pancras	61	67
Poplar	55	77	St. Marylebone	62	66
Kensington	69	76	Finsbury	64	66
Shoreditch	65	75	Islington	69	63
Westminster	61	74	Bermondsey	64	57
Holborn	89	74	Deptford	61	53

(b) *Below Average*

	1930	1931		1930	1931
Greenwich	48	65	Woolwich	42	59
Wandsworth	54	62	Battersea	55	57
Hampstead	58	61	Camberwell	52	56
Southwark	57	61	Stoke Newington	55	54
Lambeth	57	60	Lewisham	43	50
Hackney	50	60	Chelsea	40	42

Several points emerge from this table. The obvious one is the
correlation of the worst housing conditions and the worst poverty,
as described in previous sections of this chapter, and the highest
infantile mortality rates. It will be noted also that there are
some very steep rises in these boroughs (Bethnal Green and
Poplar, for instance), and likewise in some of the below-average
boroughs (Greenwich and Woolwich). But why do some
working-class boroughs appear in the below-average list? The
answer is that they frequently include middle-class residential
areas, with a low rate of infantile mortality, which bring down
the average rate for the borough.

The separate statistics for the districts and wards in 1931 make
the position clear. Thus in Southwark, where the borough
average is 61, in Christchurch and St. Saviour's—the old, overcrowded area near the river—it is 72 and 76 respectively. In
Battersea, with an average of 57, the middle-class neighbourhoods of the south-western division have a rate of only 46,
whereas in the working-class eastern division it is 66. The low
average of Hackney is accounted for by middle-class areas like
Stamford Hill, where the rate is only 41; but the slum areas of
West Hackney and Homerton have rates of 90 and 76. In
Lambeth the exclusively residential district of Norwood has a

rate of 53, but the working-class area in the centre of the borough has a rate of 76. Hampstead shows a sharp contrast between the rates of 33 and 29 in the residential Town and Central wards, and of 77 and 112 in the working-class Kilburn and Priory wards. St. Pancras wards show similar contrasts—for example between rates of 43 in ward No. 1 (Highgate, etc.) and of 139 and 91 in wards Nos. 7 and 8 (Tottenham Court-road and King's Cross). Paddington, with its rate of 87, is the second worst borough in London; but the position is far worse in its slum areas. In Church ward, which includes the notorious Clarendon-street, the rate is 116; and in the four worst slum areas in the borough taken together the rate is 102.

A detailed study by North Kensington medical practitioners in 1930 has set forth the direct connection of social conditions and infantile mortality. They found a difference of over 20 per 1,000 births in the average infantile mortality rates of the working-class and slum north and the bourgeois south; between individual wards the difference exceeded 50. These skilled investigators found that in nearly 40 per cent. of the cases they examined the family income was "unsatisfactory," and they concluded that in these cases "illness and death were probably due, not to any one adverse factor, but to the effects of several unsuitable environmental factors. These unsuitable conditions are mainly due in the first place to poverty, which must be the real cause behind a number of these deaths." Dr. Oates, of Paddington, confesses the bankruptcy of purely medical measures operating under capitalist social conditions when he says that the high infantile mortality rate in his borough is "due to causes which are largely social and do not admit of an immediate remedy." And in Greater London working-class areas, where the rate is generally less than the London average, it is significant to note that the neo-natal mortality rate (that is, the rate of deaths under one month old), which is principally due to prematurity and congenital debility, remains unchanged. West Ham presents these phenomena typically; and Dr. Collins, its medical officer of health, comments that "economic social conditions must be considered in addition to the health of the expectant mother, if the number of infant deaths from prematurity is to be further materially reduced."[62]

And what chance has a London worker's child of a healthy upbringing when it is past the age of one year? Dr. Mason and Dr. Mackay, in Bethnal Green, point to the serious effects of lack of sleep among young children, which they ascribe to over-crowding and to the inability of the parents to go out unless they drag the children with them; and Dr. Mason refers to the lack of outdoor life, due to the impossibility of the mother constantly dragging a pram, and one or two children as well, up three or four flights of stairs every time she goes out. Dr. Borland notes that more than half the Bethnal Green school children medically inspected required treatment; and they are below the London average for nutrition (the percentage classified "good" is 11.8, compared with the London average of 20.6), state of teeth and vision, though equal to it for cleanliness. He says:

> There can be no doubt this is mainly due to economic causes, which are certainly responsible for the fact that only 22.5 per cent. of Bethnal Green children are well clothed and shod, compared with 60.8 per cent. throughout London. The irony of this situation is that the clothing and boot and shoe trades are two important local industries in which there is much unemployment.[83]

The quantity, and even more the quality, of food consumed, is vital to health. How are the London workers faring? Mrs. Irene Barclay, an experienced London estate manager, draws the following picture which, she observes, is "literally true of only too many homes to-day," where unemployment benefit has been exhausted and everything pawnable has gone; "the food provided by the Public Assistance Committee includes some meat and groceries and bread. It does not include fresh milk or eggs, fruit or vegetables. The children have had only tinned milk, and no food which is rich in vitamins, for months. Some of them are suffering from rickets or rheumatism. Nearly all of them when they catch cold develop bronchitis, and many pneumonia. All of them are an easy prey to whooping-cough, measles or diphtheria." A special local inquiry has shown that "the average resident in Bethnal Green gets less than half the national ration of milk, less than a third of butter and only a little more than half of margarine"*; on this basis a Bethnal Green worker's family, of five persons, would consume only 7¾ pints of milk a week, 0.8 pounds of margarine, and 0.6 pounds of butter. Dr. Borland remarks that "having regard to the relatively high cost

---

* The actual figures of estimated consumption per head per annum are interesting. Giving first the figures for Great Britain, and then (in parentheses) for Bethnal Green, they are as follows: Milk 22.6 gallons (10.1 gallons), Butter 21.5 lbs. (6.26 lbs.), Margarine 13 lbs. (8.3 lbs.). Dr. Borland stresses that "unless vitamins are specially added it [margarine] is not really a substitute for butter"; while Dr. Hutt urges that "until this is done the menace to health arising from the continual and ever-increasing substitution of butter by margarine will remain serious" (*Holborn Health Report*, 1931, p. 28).

of the other vitamin-containing foods like greengrocery and fruit, butter is an essential article of working-class diet, and the low consumption of this valuable food is a disquieting feature of this inquiry. The consumption of milk is also seriously low, compared with the requirements of the child population."[64]

Not only are masses of London workers quite unable to purchase the supply of milk that they and their families need, but the quality of the milk that they do get is often most doubtful. The present legal standards for milk are not definite quality standards, and are no guard against poor quality milk, as Mr. Douglas Henville, the Stepney Borough analyst, has demonstrated in the course of a detailed technical criticism. Mr. Henville points out that small percentages of water may quite legally be added to high-grade milks, "and considerable profit may be made by this system of 'toning' down the composition of milk." The markedly low percentage of solids-not-fat in Stepney milk "is due to judicious watering of the milk supplies before the milk is passed on to the consumer."[65] So much for the protection afforded the workers by the much-vaunted "pure food" legislation of Britain!

Then there is the grave question of tuberculosis in cattle, the extreme seriousness of which we have examined in Chapter II. Dr. Annis, the Greenwich medical officer of health, points out that no less than 33 per cent. of the cows slaughtered in London are tubercular, and that 31.5 per cent. of tuberculosis in children under 15 years of age is due to tubercular milk. He adds this revealing observation, upon which I only need to comment by italicising one portion of it:

It certainly seems very strange that nothing more radical is attempted. Large amounts of money are spent on the slaughtering of cattle, both healthy and otherwise, in connection with outbreaks or suspected outbreaks of foot and mouth disease, which is a disease affecting particularly the property of the farmers, *whereas nothing whatever of this practical nature is done to deal with tubercular cattle, which is a condition affecting the lives and not so much the property of the people.*[66]

Growing impoverishment means that workers in London have to stint themselves on meat. In Bethnal Green "still fewer animals were slaughtered [in 1931] than in the previous year. The meat inspector attributes this to the continued high prices of live cattle and the diminished purchasing power of the people. Where a silverside was formerly cut into two or three pieces, it is now cut into seven or eight pieces." At the same time active adulteration is highest in the working-class quarters of the East End; in Bethnal Green and Poplar it exceeds 7 per cent. of the samples

analysed, compared with 2.9 per cent. for the whole of London—
and the Poplar figure now is three times what it was ten years
ago. The Poplar analyst reports this outrageous case: "a sample
of 'strawberry jam' was purchased which was labelled 'of the
finest quality.' On examination it was found to have been made
from preserved pulp, and contained sulphur dioxide.   The
manufacturer . . . promised to alter the wording of future
labels"!* In Marylebone—and Stepney reports similarly—the
analysis of cream consistently shows that while loose cream has
an average fat content of 50 per cent., tinned cream has less than
30 per cent. That is indeed an abominable swindle practised on
workers who scrape up their pence to buy a tin of cream for an
invalid member of the family, under the natural impression that
it is as rich as dairy cream.[67]

RATIONALISATION ON THE JOB

Large numbers of small enterprises remain a characteristic of
London industry; but the concentration of capital has also
proceeded apace.   There are 34 very large establishments
(employing more than 2,000 workers each), and half the total
number of workers are employed by one-twentieth the total
number of employers. The outstanding very large factories and
works are in general and electrical engineering, printing, food
and tobacco, building, gas, water and electricity supply, transport, hotels and shops. This fits in with the sketch of London
industry given at the opening of this chapter; and if the 300-odd
establishments employing from 500–2,000 workers are examined,
the other traditional London industries like clothing and furniture
will be found well represented.[68]

The intensification of labour by the various methods of rationalisation, mechanisation and piece-work, has advanced rapidly
during the past decade in London. The old type of craftsman,
who was a very special figure in the industry of the metropolis
a generation ago, has virtually been wiped out. These processes,

---

* Mr. Henville, the Stepney analyst, has subjected the recently
introduced standards of the Jam Section of the Food Manufacturers'
Federation to a very damaging criticism. He observes that they do not
define the composition of jam, and do not preclude the use of "approved"
colouring matter or glucose; that even "first quality" jam "need not be
made from fresh fruit and refined cane sugar with a high proportion of
fresh fruit"; and that in two-fruit jams "the cheaper fruit is in equal
proportion when mentioned last and in a proportion of 3 to 1 when
mentioned first." "This (he adds pointedly) would not be obvious to
the purchaser of the jam" (*Stepney Health Report*, 1931, pp. 82-83).

and the parallel growth in woman, boy and girl labour,* have been particularly marked in the recent industrialisation of Greater London. Some idea of what this growth of the labour of women and girls has meant is conveyed by the fact that in the industries mainly concerned—for instance, engineering—the average weekly earnings of females are only half the earnings of males.

As for wages in general, it is true that the "London rate" has always ranged higher than the provincial rates for the same class of labour, though this is offset by the higher cost of living (and especially rents). But it is interesting to note that a calculation made by the *New Survey* for its eastern area shows that one-half of the full-time weekly earnings are below 61s. 10d., one-quarter below 53s. 7d. and one-tenth below 43s. 6d.[69] These figures are averages which take into account both time and piece earnings. They naturally do not reflect the inroads of short time, which is severe in industries like clothing, to give one example only. While general figures of this kind bear little relation to the reality in different industries, it is significant that they should show such a large proportion of workers receiving an income which makes a decent standard of life impossible.

It will be convenient to begin our survey of industrial conditions in London with engineering, remembering that this industry, in all its infinite variations, has been to the fore in the industrialisation of the Greater London area during the past decade. In London engineering the proportion of women and girls employed has risen in forty years from 1 in 50 to 1 in 5; and the *New Survey* remarks that in the past ten years there has been "a marked fall in the proportion of men employed." Between 1923 and 1930 the percentage of women and girls employed in general engineering in London rose from 7.4 to 10.7; in the manufacture of electric cables, lamps and batteries it rose from 29.6 to 36.2; and in electrical engineering it rose from 14.2 to 21. Even these figures by no means fully reflect the real increase in female labour, for the incidence of unemployment is more than twice as heavy among men engineers as it is among women.[70]

Through the introduction of automatic and semi-automatic machinery of all kinds—such as capstan and turret lathes, pressing, stamping and planing machines—the old cleavage between the craftsman and the labourer has been broken down. The skilled turner has been largely transformed into a semi-skilled so-called "process worker"; and the skilled fitter finds

* The general aspects of this question are discussed in Chapter **VI**.

himself similarly displaced by a semi-skilled assembler, eternally performing the same monotonous operation as the conveyor moves endlessly and tirelessly on. Engineers' hours in London are 47 a week, but with overtime (for which the rates were cut in 1931) the average week worked is over 50 hours. Forty years ago piece-work, always firmly opposed by the engineers, was rarely found in London, and then "not usually in the best class of shops"; but to-day half the workers in the federated shops are paid on one or other of the many piece-work systems. A worker at one of the largest telephone and electrical apparatus works in Greater London describes the nagging inquisition and sharp practice of the piece-work system operating there. His average wage is not more than £2 10s. a week; and when he has paid 15s. rent and 5s. in fares, there is 30s. left to keep himself, his wife and three children. He remarks that the shilling lunch in the works canteen is not for him, and he has to "make do" with bread and cheese.[71]

Female labour is an even more striking feature of the clothing industry, accounting for two-thirds of the total labour-force in the industry in Greater London; while in the ready-made tailoring factories five-sixths of the workers are women and girls. Short time and heavy seasonal fluctuations are characteristic. The Trade Board minimum wages are fixed at the low level of 28s. a week for adult women and 46s. a week for adult men. Workers on piece-work complain that they have to spend much unpaid time waiting for jobs to turn up; they may have to hang about all day in this way, to be told at the last minute that they must work on after the usual finishing time, or on Saturday afternoon—without overtime pay.[72]

It is in the "new" light industries of the London region, where women and girls form the majority of the workers, that there has been some introduction of the notorious Bedaux system, the last work in "scientific" speed-up and inhuman intensification of labour. This is particularly the case in the food industries. In a chocolate factory operating this system a woman packer, whose output considerably exceeded the norm fixed by the Bedaux experts, would only earn 6s. 9¼d. for a nine-hour day. In a biscuit factory girls, who were labelling 1,125 tins a day, were punished by a severe caution for one mistake, suspended for a day for two mistakes (with further suspensions for each mistake up to five), and dismissed after the sixth mistake. Girls so dismissed were told at the Labour Exchange that "inability to keep up the pace" constituted "misconduct," and so had to wait six weeks, according to rule, for their unemployment benefit.[73]

The intensification of labour brought by mechanisation and piece-work is far from being confined to those industries in London where female labour is characteristic. Let us see what it has meant in the exclusively male industries of transport and building. On the London docks the tonnage handled nearly doubled between 1921 and 1930, while the average number of dockers employed fell from 34,000 to 26,000. The great majority of dockers are now paid on piece-rates; on one wharf the numbers so paid increased in the past seven years from 20 per cent. to 90 per cent. of the total employed there. And this increased exploitation has been super-imposed on an existing system of exploitation which has always been marked by its own peculiar and oppressive forms, of which the most notorious is casualisation.

The evil wrought by casualisation of dock labour has been denounced these many years, and the Shaw inquiry in 1920 demanded that the detestable system "be torn up by the roots." But it flourishes to-day in London more than ever. Registration has done nothing to stop it (the numbers on the register have incidentally been cut in ten years from 61,000 to 36,000). The *New Survey*, which is concerned to sing hosannas over the "improvement" of dockers' conditions, and to proclaim that the dockers' trade "is becoming one to which fathers are glad to bring their sons"(!) is forced to recognise the "ominous" sign that "a new fringe of under-employed casuals is beginning to form outside the scope of the register." The fact is that the majority of dockers are casuals, and are under-employed. Examination of a typical sample of men on one London wharf showed that only one-quarter worked five days a week or more, and 41 per cent. worked less than two days a week.

Casualisation's evils have been greatly accentuated by the big increase in total unemployment among dockers caused by the crisis. In December, 1932, more than one-third of insured dock and riverside workers were registered as unemployed; the monthly returns of the Ministry of Labour for London (which are only partial) show a 20 per cent. reduction in the numbers employed between the end of 1929 and the end of 1932. Never have there been such crowds of tens of thousands of hungry men lining up twice every day at the two hundred calling-on places for dock labour in the Port of London, forced to struggle and scramble for perhaps half a day's work. A man who gets half a day (wages 5s. 7d., less insurance) may get nothing more that week, or for weeks after. But day after day he has to go through the same disheartening, debasing line-up, with its foul flavour of the slave market.

A casual docker who gets a day or so's work a week will have an average weekly income of £2, including both wages and unemployment benefit.* The *New Survey* remarks that "there is probably no industry in London where anomalies and inequalities of pay and opportunity exhibit themselves so glaringly as in dock labour." In the sample of dockers to which reference has already been made, it was found that the median earnings of the fortunate "preference" men did not exceed £3 a week; while 43 per cent. of all the men in the sample earned under 30s. a week. These meagre sums are subject to the cut of 10d. a day imposed in January, 1932, plus the wiping out of a whole series of customary extra payments—for work during the dinner and tea hours, for late working, and so forth. But many of the large wharf and lighterage concerns do well for themselves, despite the crisis; like Hay's Wharf, which made a profit of over £230,000 in 1931.[74]

Railwaymen are not casual workers, but mechanisation has taken heavy toll of them in London. In traffic handling especially, the introduction of mobile cranes, motor trucks, containers, automatic control of the big hydraulic lifts, has rendered many men "redundant" and liable to de-grading and/or transfer, or to dismissal. Since August 1930 nearly one-tenth of the adult staff of 5,000 in the goods department of the L.M.S. Railway, London area, have been dismissed. Boys are dismissed, on the ground of lack of work, on attaining adult age. Last summer the Southern Railway dismissed hundreds of young employees. Miscellaneous staff engaged on maintenance duties have been heavily reduced. Supervisory positions have been abolished on the retirement of their present holders, thus blocking lower graded men's hopes of promotion. On the Underground men have been displaced by the substitution of escalators for lifts, by the introduction of automatic doors on trains, by devices for the automatic issue of tickets.[75]

And what are the living conditions of the hard-driven railwaymen who are still employed? A grim picture was given by a railwayman's wife at Crewe, who was interviewed by a special correspondent of the *Sunday Express* (December 4th, 1932), in connection with the companies' demand for a wage cut of 2s. in the £. The correspondent remarked that he found many similar cases in London, with the exception that their rents were usually higher. This particular railwayman earned 44s. a week,

* The Gregory Commission proposes severe cuts in this type of benefit: see p. 187 below.

and this was his wife's weekly budget for themselves and their
four children:

First of all, 2s. has to go to insurance and clubs. My mate goes without
everything, but he must have a shilling or so for the week. On Fridays,
I put 38s. on one side, and this is what I do with it:

		s.	d.
Rent ..	..	8	2
Milk, 1 qrt. a day ..	..	4	1
Coal, 3 bags in winter	..	6	6
Margarine, 2½ lbs. ..	..	1	9½
Sugar, 4 lbs. ..	..		11
Tea, ¾ lb. ..	..		11
Flour, 3 lbs. ..	..		8½
Potatoes ..	..	1	3
Meat, 6d. worth a day	..	3	6
Bread, 2 loaves a day	..	3	6
Bacon, 1 lb. ..	..		8
Eggs, 6 a week	..	1	0
Lard, ½ lb. ..	..		4
Currants, ¼ lb.	..		4
Soap, 1 lb. ..	..		6½
Matches, 3 boxes	..		3
Soda ..	..		2
Blacking ..	..		3
Tinned fruit, for Sunday	..		6
Onions ..	..		3½
Carrots ..	..		2
Doctor's weekly bill ..	..		6
Total ..	..	36	4

You see, I have 1s. 8d. left—on paper. As a matter of fact, to-day is
pay-day, come and look what I've really got! One halfpenny and
half a loaf! That's what I've got left! I have not put down a crowd
of things that cost some hard-earned pennies. Pepper and salt, wool
to darn with. Have you ever seen a pair of children's stockings that
have been what I call darned? There is more darning than sock! . . .
How do you think I can get boots and clothes on what is left out of
that 1s. 8d.—which is actually ½d. this week? If my man did not
mend the boots, God knows what we would have to go without!
Would you like to find clothes for six people out of that two shillings?
I go down to the market and I buy scraps and make them into something which the kiddies can wear. . . . Cut four shillings from my
miserable thirty-eight bob to keep six people? As it is, life is not
worth living. No butter, no cakes, no jam. I never go to a picture,
nor do the kiddies. I never have a glass of beer. My husband has
bread-and-milk for breakfast. The bacon is for the kiddies. That
they should have something we have to go without. We would do
anything for them, but is it necessary?

No wonder that Lord Beaverbrook's correspondent spoke of
this brave woman's "face taut with anger!" He noted also that

there were cases far worse than this one, where out of a wage
of 44s. rent of 15s. a week had to be paid. Such a one is that of
a London railwayman living on the Dagenham estate of the
L.C.C., who says "three years ago I came to stay on this estate.
My wages then were £3 10s. To-day they are £2 5s. Yet I still
pay 14s. a week rent. This leaves £1 11s. to feed my wife, four
kids and myself." Here is another London railwayman, living
in St. Pancras, who earns 48s. a week and, while he pays the
relatively low rent of 7s. 6d. for two rooms, has himself, his wife,
and eight children (ages ranging from 14 years to one year) to
keep; and this says nothing of the nature of these two rooms
and their overcrowded condition.[76]

Speeding-up has been sensationally applied in the case of the
London bus service,* evoking an equally sensational reaction in
the dispute of 1932, the establishment of the busmen's rank-and-
file movement, and the strike of January 1933. Workers on the
motor-coach lines that ply from London work scandalously long
hours, in some cases up to 80 a week, with no overtime pay. It
has been stated that on the coaches of a large concern operating
in the eastern section of the Greater London area, drivers work
73 hours one week and 60 the next; and the proprietor has been
fined more than once on charges brought under the Road
Traffic Act, for working drivers in excess of the legal limit of
hours. Lorry drivers are exploited even worse. Cases of men
driving for 15 and even up to 29 hours are frequently before the
courts; and men have constantly been dismissed for protesting
against hours of 16 to 20 a day, and for refusing to break the
law by exceeding the speed limit.[77]

In the building trades the use of machinery and the development of new processes, such as steel erection, has reduced the
time in which jobs can be completed; and the pronounced
casual and seasonal character of building work has therefore been
heightened. Work has also been speeded-up through the "time
and progress schedule," by which every operation is allotted a
time in which it must be completed. The heavy seasonal unemployment in the London building trades is witnessed in the
fact that even during the years of the "boom," up to 1930, there
were 30 per cent. of the painters workless throughout the winter
months. Now one-third of the 180,000 building workers in
London are unemployed. While piece-work is strongly opposed
by the men, it is operated on house-building jobs in a number of
outlying suburbs by means of a contract system; a bricklayer or

* The details are given in the two pamphlets of the busmen's rank-
and-file movement, *The London Busmen's Case* and *Speed*.

a carpenter agrees to do a certain job for so much, and takes his own assistants, often just lads, as and when required. On such jobs well under the agreed rates are paid, and week-end overtime is worked for no extra pay. Complaints of unsafe conditions on scaffolding, of bad sanitary and messing arrangements, are widespread.[78]

The miscellaneous host of other London industries can only be referred to in the most summary fashion. In furniture-making the development of the big mass-production factory has only served to make conditions worse in the mass of small shops in the East End; so that even the *New Survey* cannot help concluding that "so far as concerns the lower section of the industry, Charles Booth's classification of the Furniture Trades among trades connected with poverty has not altogether lost its validity." Similarly they note the continuance of sweated conditions in the boot and shoe industry. A distributive trade of recent growth is that of the ice-cream tricyclist. For a seven-day week of 80 hours or more the payment for this work is £1 a week, plus commission, which means a total wage of 25s. to 30s.; this is liable to stoppages for replacement of equipment, and in addition there are a whole series of tyrannical regulations (no smoking on the round, no excessive bell-ringing, though the bell has to be rung to attract custom), the breach of which involves instant dismissal. Married women still do home-work to help out with the family income; an investigation showed that the highest they earned in the tailoring trade was but little over £1 a week. And a contemporary observer records finding a Shoreditch woman "in her only room—with five children there—machining the sort of caps that are given out on gala nights at big hotels. For this work she was paid at the rate of 5d. a gross, and a gross took her six hours to make."[79]

PUTTING BACK THE CLOCK OF CULTURE

In the built-up conditions, the bad housing and overcrowding, which capitalist anarchy and profit-seeking have brought to London, what on earth are the chances of healthy recreation and cultural development, even when abstraction is made of the impoverishment of the mass of the working class? Parks and open spaces are grossly inadequate. A population of nearly one million in the central areas has only 400 acres of open spaces, and the majority of these are patches less than an acre in extent. In the Outer Ring the open spaces have been overwhelmed by the growth of population. The parasitic claims of rent, interest

N

and profit demanded that land be built up at all costs, for there is no money to be got from leaving open spaces when land values are soaring.

The children in the central working-class quarters, as Dr. Thomas of Finsbury remarks, "have nowhere to play except in the dangerous open streets," where "they may be seen skipping, spinning tops, playing at soldiers, playing cricket with heaped coats for wickets and a tied-up cap or newspaper for a ball, swinging and climbing over hand-trucks, baiting dogs or teasing cats." He reproduces the following "Finsbury street cameo," which is a bitter commentary on the "civilisation" of capitalist society in the wealthiest city in the world:

> Some children were sprawling in the dirt on their bellies on the pavement with their heads just beyond the kerb, after a heavy shower, watching "ships"—ships that pass in the gutter, stray pieces of vegetable debris, derelict bits of paper—carried off by the downpour. The score was made by the child who first saw the "ship," and was thereby entitled to be its captain and to convoy it safely with its fingers beyond the posts of observation.
> "Thet's moine."
> "No, it ain't."
> "Yuss, it is, I seen it fust."
> "There's another—that's moine."
> "No, it ain't."
> "Yuss, it is, I seen it fust."
> "I'm captin 'f that one."
> "No, you ain't, that one ain't got no bleed'n' captin—'e's only got a mite, see!"
> The pity of it all! The glorified ecstasy of being captain of a castaway gobbet of vegetable refuse on a gutter sea.

The provision of sports grounds is not merely scandalously below the need, but is far worse to-day than it was a score of years ago. The total number of public sports pitches available in London in 1929 was forty-two below the total for 1912, despite a vastly increased pressure of demand. Only three-fifths of the football pitches applied for could be supplied. Anyone who has had experience of workers' sports clubs in London knows that many have been forced to disband because of the impossibility of obtaining playing facilities—having to turn up at grounds not knowing till they arrive whether a pitch will be available for them or not.[80]

An important contributory factor to the discomfort of London life is the extreme pollution of the atmosphere, which has actually grown worse in the past five years, so futile are the measures—merely tinkering with the smoke abatement problem—that have been adopted. In the congested central working-class quarters the situation is most acute; here the amount of solid matter deposited from the air aggregates 11 cwt. per acre, compared with 8 cwt. per acre in the Outer Ring. In the past decade there has been no improvement worth recording. How this intensifies the misery and toil of life, especially for the harassed working-class housewife, it is unnecessary to demonstrate.[81]

The London workers are not behind their brothers in the other industrial centres in the urge for culture; though the many cultural advantages of the metropolis lie beyond their reach under the present social order. The number of borrowers from public libraries in London is more than four times the figure of thirty years ago, but since the war there has been virtually no increase in the public library system, which both quantitatively and qualitatively lags behind the needs of the masses. Some light on the cultural standards and demands of workers, many of whom hail from London, is thrown by the statement of Mr. Knowles, the organising secretary of the Seafarers' Education Service, that "during the past ten years or so the literary taste of merchantmen at sea has improved out of all recognition and these men are, literally, hungry for books"—mainly for books by modern authors of the type of Anatole France, Arnold Bennett, H. G. Wells, Lytton Strachey, Rupert Brooke and H. M. Tomlinson.[82]

London affords excellent examples of the perversion of powerful cultural instruments by the bourgeoisie to its own class ends. Here the cinema, as everywhere, has undergone a meteoric expansion while the number of theatres and music-halls has declined. And the whole purpose of the cinema under capitalism is expressed in the cynical comment of the *New Survey* on the report that unemployed men were seen visiting cinemas—"there is no reason to regard the time or money as necessarily wasted or ill-spent. With all their defects the cinemas at least serve to divert the thoughts for a time from dark forebodings. As one of the London unemployed observed: 'They make you think for a little while that life is all right.' "[83]

The Working Class on the Move

The working class of London, in resisting the social degradation and industrial exploitation which have been exposed in this chapter, are fighting the bourgeoisie in its own citadel. For it is natural that in the capital the influence of the governing class over all sections of the population, including the working class, should be at its strongest. Present conditions, both social and ideological, intertwine with past tradition to make the task of building a revolutionary movement in London one requiring the greatest skill in approach. The miasma of capitalist influence hangs heavy over London, confusing and poisoning men's minds. And London is also the main centre of the reformist leadership of the Labour movement. Here are the headquarters of the Labour Party and the Trades Union Congress General Council, and of the principal national Trade Unions. It is characteristic that the leader of the London Labour Party is Herbert Morrison, the reactionary, one of whose main claims to fame is as organiser of campaigns against the Communists.

But it would be surprising indeed if London, where the contradictions and class contrasts of capitalist society have always appeared in their most brutal form, were not a cockpit of determined struggle between the two opposing classes. The London workers have in fact written, and are writing, some of the most inspiring pages in the history of the class struggle in this country. Any detailed survey is out of the question here: we may, however, recall such epoch-making events as the development of the "New Unionism" after the great dock strike of 1889, bringing that "revival of the East End of London" which Engels hailed in 1892 as "one of the greatest and most fruitful facts of this *fin de siècle*." The big upsurge of the 'eighties, and the beginnings of the revolutionary Socialist movement in this country, were first and foremost London phenomena.*

As these pages go to press the unconquerable spirit of the London working class, and the rapidly rising tide of revolt amongst them, has been made clear for all to see in the immense demonstration of February 5 this year. That demonstration was remarkable for two things: one, that 200,000 workers, employed and unemployed alike, came on to the streets, demonstrating their hatred of the "National" Government, at the first call of those leaders who have been so prone to cover up their own cowardly passivity and surrender to the enemy by slanders about the "apathy" of the workers; the other, that the General Council's attempted ban† on the participation of revolutionary organisa-

---

* See Ralph Fox: *The Class Struggle in Britain*, Part I, ch. IV, especially pp. 73-82.

† This ban, proclaimed and re-proclaimed with all the stage thunder at the command of Transport House, aroused the most tremendous resentment throughout the London labour movement. It was beyond question the vilest piece of provocation from start to finish, and showed the General Council leaders lined up with the police. Only a week before the demonstration the General Council issued a statement that the *Daily Herald* suppressed, in order not to expose its authors still

tions in the demonstration collapsed, like a sand castle overwhelmed by the incoming tide, before the unanimous will of the workers for unity in action.

London to-day is the centre of some of the most outstanding developments in the working-class movement. Out of the bus dispute of last year arose the London busmen's rank-and-file movement, whose campaign was successful in winning a partial victory for the men when the Union leaders were recommending complete defeat. The movement has since gathered strength, which it displayed with startling effect last January, when half the bus fleet came out on strike following a lightning strike at the Forest Gate garage against the operation of the new speeded-up schedules: two tram depots also struck in sympathy. The strike lasted a week, and succeeded in securing an understanding that the grievances would receive immediate attention. The rank-and-file movement led this strike in the teeth of the L.G.O.C. and the officials of the Transport and General Workers' Union alike; the complete unity of these two bodies was witnessed by the simultaneous statements issued by the Union Executive, "insisting" that the men return to work, and by Lord Ashfield, for the company, declaring that "on this issue the company must take the same view as the T. & G.W.U."

Out of the bitterly-fought lightermen's strike last year, a hitherto isolated key section of water transport workers were brought into touch with the militants. This, coupled with the steadily growing ferment among the dockers, has laid the basis for the Port Workers' Unity Movement, which has already gained considerable strength along London's riverside. The railwaymen are astir against the menace of the companies' pooling scheme and wage-cut demands; rank-and-file "vigilance committees" are springing up and developing into a Railwaymen's Vigilance Movement, whose first national all-grades conference was called on the initiative of the London Vigilance Committee. This conference met in Stratford on January 22 last, and was attended by 147 delegates, of whom 56 were from the provinces and the remainder from London railmen's union

further. It said, according to the text published in the *Daily Telegraph* of January 31, 1933: "we have received evidence that the Reds are desirous of making the occasion their own. *They will be disagreeably, if not painfully, surprised.* . . . The authorities whose duty it is to keep order on the march will see to it that their banners are conspicuously absent" (my italics). But the banners of the "Reds" streamed in the wind beside those of Trade Union branches, Co-Operative Guilds, and every other section of the movement, as the masses marched to Hyde Park on that historic Sunday.

branches and depot committees.   Similar rank-and-file movements, in varying stages of development, exist among other
sections of workers in London—the engineers, the builders,
woodworkers and furnishing trade workers, printers and clothing
workers, the last-named having a revolutionary union, the
United Clothing Workers' Trade Union.

Much might be added.   There is the significant movement
against rent exactions, and of resistance to evictions, which has
found expression in the growth of Tenants' Defence Leagues.
Among Co-Operators in London, and particularly the most
active Co-Operators, the members of the women's and men's
guilds, there is a deep urge for a forward movement.   This is seen
in the growing discontent with the Co-Operative Party's func-
tioning as a mere appendage of the Labour Party.   It is seen
also in the signal triumph of the militants in the South Suburban
Co-Operative Society, who have carried through that Society
proposals for a change in price policy which mark a complete
break with the high-price line hitherto followed by the Co-
Operative leaders.   The present ferment in the Independent
Labour Party has been most sharply expressed in the resolution
adopted by the London and Home Counties divisional conference
of that Party on February 12, demanding that the I.L.P. terminate its affiliation with the Labour and Socialist International
and ascertain in what way it may assist in the work of the
Communist International.

CHAPTER V

UNEMPLOYMENT AND THE "ECONOMY" ONSLAUGHT

In the preceding chapters we have seen something of the deadly effects of unemployment in the lives of the working class in the principal industrial areas of the country. Well over 3,000,000 men, women and young people, or a quarter of the whole working class, are denied work by capitalist society. In a region such as South Wales even the official figures show that nearly 40 per cent. of all workers are unemployed. The state of impoverishment in a Welsh town is illuminated by a report in the Newport evening newspaper of the queue of workless ex-servicemen (heroes yesterday, starved to-day) who, "pinched of face, haggard looking," attend the British Legion office to receive, after searching inquisition, a "benevolent" grant of a food voucher. "Men whose ages ranged from 32 to 60 lined up in the queue, just as their wives had lined up with ration cards fifteen years before. The hand that had held the rifle received the food chit." These cases are cited:

> He had been a private in the South Wales Borderers. He was forty-eight, married, with four children. He would have a shot at any sort of work, but cannot get it. He gets 31s. unemployment benefit, and the rent runs away with 12s. weekly. He is losing heart because his children are suffering. . . . One of the men helped has to support a wife and ten children on £1 19s. 3d. dole. He pays 5s. rent for what serves as a home. . . . A veteran of sixty-five, who has been out of work for three years, has to pay 6s. rent out of 14s. 8d. pension he gets weekly.[1]

It is well known that the official monthly statistics of unemployment do not reveal its full extent. These figures give the total number of unemployed workers who are registered at the Labour Exchanges. They exclude the greater part of those workers in uninsured occupations who are unemployed. They exclude those unemployed workers cut off the register by recent changes in the Unemployment Insurance Acts; the number of these so cut off was last estimated by the Ministry of Labour at 170,000. They do not show the decline in the numbers registered due to many who have been refused benefit ceasing to register; some idea of the discrepancy here, even with allowance for the duplication of individual cases, is conveyed by the fact that while, last January, there were nearly 300,000 of the registered unemployed returned as not in receipt of either benefit or transitional payments under the Means Test, the number of cases disallowed benefit from February 1932 to January 1933 exceeded 450,000.

Of the registered unemployed in January over 1,100,000 were on the Means Test; and of over 800,000 cases which came up before the Public Assistance Committees in December–January over 300,000 were only granted benefit at rates below ordinary unemployment insurance benefit, while 48,000 were refused any payment at all. In the first nine months of 1932 the latter two categories accounted for 50 per cent. of all Means Test cases. The corollary of all this is seen in the heavy increase in the numbers receiving poor relief. During 1932 there was a steady increase each month; and this January, at 850,000, the figure for a selected number of large towns showed an increase of 26 per cent. over January 1932. For Scotland the increase was 37 per cent. At the beginning of 1933 there were 509 persons per 10,000 of the population in receipt of poor relief, compared with 404 a year previously. Thus the average increase per 10,000 of the population was 105, but in such important centres as Cardiff, Southampton, Liverpool, Glasgow, Norwich and Sheffield the increase ranged from 235 to 642 per 10,000.

The degree of pauperisation of this vast mass of unemployed can be gathered from the statement of the Socialist Medical Association that unemployment benefit or poor relief "are entirely insufficient to keep their recipients in physiological health." The Association points out that:

> Dr. G. P. Crowden, writing in the *Lancet* in April 1932, on "The Minimum Cost of Physiological Adequate Diets for Working-class Families," regards 7s. a week as the minimum cost of the food necessary for a labouring man. Mr. Caradog Jones, as the result of a Social Survey carried out under the auspices of the University of Liverpool, puts it at 6s. 3d. The members of the Advisory Committee on Nutrition of the Ministry of Health, in a report on the Diet in Poor Law Children's Homes (1932), state that the food that they recommend for such children will cost 4s. 6½d. per week provided that all provisions are bought at contract prices. Now it must be evident that if the above statements are correct a good many families have not at the present time sufficient coming in week by week, after the rent is paid, to provide themselves with a sufficiency of food, even if we assume that nothing is being spent on cleansing, warming, lighting, clothing and other necessities.[2]

These conclusions are powerfully reinforced by a detailed inquiry that has just been concluded by Dr. Keith, the medical officer of health of the Metropolitan Borough of Deptford, assisted by his colleagues Drs. Donnelly and Hill. As a result of this inquiry the Public Health Committee of the borough state that "it is clear that in the case of families in receipt of public assistance the amount of relief afforded cannot assure the recipients the minimum varied diet recommended by the Ministry of Health in their publications relating to nutrition and diet in Poor Law homes." Dr. Hill found a large proportion of families with a net income of only 5s. per head per week, and comments that "it is not possible to buy sufficient food of the right kind at this low price."

In the effort to lift themselves out of this all-devouring morass of pauperism, of semi-starvation, the unemployed workers struggle desperately for work. Never has the competition between worker and worker been so acute. It is only necessary for a few jobs to be publicly advertised for hundreds, even thousands, to attend in the forlorn hope of securing one. On every occasion of this kind heartrending scenes can be witnessed. I have space for only one typical example. The *Manchester Evening News* published the following report on July 15th, 1932:

> Two thousand people assembled in pouring rain outside the Broadway Theatre, Eccles Cross, to-day—to apply for thirty-five jobs. Two men had walked from Oldham [a distance of twelve miles] and after being interviewed were faced with the prospect of another long walk home in the rain. This morning was the time appointed for interviews for the jobs. Applicants came early. Half a dozen men waited all night. Some women turned up at a quarter to six. Then the crowd began to gather in earnest. The rain drenched the overcoatless and ran in streams from umbrellas, but not one would give up his or her position and, soaked to the skin, they awaited the call, "first applicants, please." When the door was opened the crowd stormed the building.

No wonder that with some desperation turns to despair, and that it is officially estimated that every day there are two suicides due to unemployment. Any reader of newspapers will be familiar with cases like that of Henry Fuller, of Islington, who gassed himself because after two years constant striving he had been unable to find work (after being in regular work for thirty-eight years), or of Arthur Taylor, a Birmingham engineer, who drowned himself after his benefit had been cut under the Means Test.[3] The verdict is always the same—"suicide while temporarily insane"—when it ought to be one of social murder.

Does history record a more damnable situation than this? British capitalist society condemns millions of working people, the most skilled in the world (as it is never tired of boasting), to be divorced from production and to live in the direst want. It follows this up by a grand assault on the already wretched standard of living which it accords to the unemployed. The "insurance against revolution"—for which the workers have to pay—is cut to the bone: contributions have been raised and benefits lowered; administration has been tightened up to the harshest possible point; women factory workers, for example, have their benefit disallowed if they refuse to go into domestic service in places many miles from their homes. Of the infamous Means Test, with its fifty-point questionnaire designed to drag out every fact about a worker's individual and family life and position, it is not necessary to speak again in detail. Through its agency the unemployed are robbed of half-a-million a week, or nearly £30,000,000 a year.[4] In Co. Durham, Rotherham and Swansea the Public Assistance Committees have been superseded because their administration of the Test was insufficiently severe, and their places taken by Government commissioners, at salaries of £14 a week (the first commissioner in Durham receiving £23 a week) plus allowances up to an extra £5 a week, and travelling expenses. It is characteristic that as one of the commissioners an individual was chosen who learnt the technique of oppression in the thorough-paced imperialist school of high position in the Egyptian and Sudan civil service.*

The whole line of the bourgeoisie is quite openly and brutally to drive the unemployed into pauperism, and to treat them as paupers. Transitional payments under the Means Test are officially described as poor relief and not unemployment benefit; and every unemployed worker who has received twenty-six weeks' continuous benefit automatically goes under the Means Test, even though he may have been an unbroken subscriber to unemployment insurance for a score of years and be far from having exhausted his claim to benefit, from a strictly insurance point of view. The unemployed have to face the dragooning process of test and task work—providing the local authorities with cheap labour, to undercut the employed—or have their relief stopped. They have to endure the petty tyrannies of the relieving officers, and frequently can only extract relief when they are supported by a demonstration to the relieving office.

Mr. MacDonald has voiced the point-blank refusal of the governing class to countenance large-scale public works that might assist in relieving unemployment. Instead he has the

*The name of another Durham Means Test commissioner, Mr. Kenneth G. Holland, has been mentioned in the Westminster County Court as a debtor for £105, arising out of betting transactions with West End bookmakers. The debts are alleged to have been occurred in 1926. (*Daily Herald*, February 28, 1933.)

cynical audacity to emit vague generalities about the need for stimulating industry; which is the thing above all others that capitalism is totally unable to do. And so we have this preposterous paradox: in the most industrialised country in the world, with huge factories idle, the unemployed workers are offered "charity" work at petty handicrafts; local "employment" campaigns are run—to encourage the middle-class to have their houses and shops painted, their carpets beaten, their gardens tidied, and new wireless sets installed.

But this is not all. The Government, which can provide no work for the workless, establishes centres to train the younger men in various trades—when in many skilled trades young fellows who have completed their apprenticeship tramp from works to works only too anxious to get the chance of being taken on as labourers. The Government, which is robbing the unemployed of tens of millions of pounds, grants £10,000 to the National Council of Social Service as the recognised central body for "charitably" doping the unemployed with recreation centres, games, gymnasia, wireless talks, and what not. Under Quaker influence a committee functions to provide the unemployed (at a price) with seeds and tools to cultivate allotments; that hoary device to distract attention from the class struggle is furbished up anew in order, as its promoters smugly say, to give the workless "occupation for the body, interest for the mind, and to prove that they are willing and able to do good service for the community." Under the much-advertised patronage of the Queen wealthy ladies have combined in a kind of glorified Dorcas organisation called the League of Personal Service. The traditional coals and blankets policy of the bourgeoisie, formerly reserved for the lumpen-proletariat, is what is now offered to the working class as a whole. Finally, Government centres are being established for the physical training of the unemployed, with a true military smack about it; in London the instructor is described as "lately of the Royal Air Force," and the Labour correspondent of *The Times*, in the course of a lyrical description of a visit to the London centre, declares that for the first time he heard "hearty cheers" for a Ministry of Labour official.

All this impudent display of mock solicitude for the unemployed is very far from marking any change of heart among the capitalist class. In the King's speech on November 22nd last their Government declared that "any provision for unemployed persons should not only afford material assistance, but should also be designed to maintain their morale and their fitness to resume work when opportunities can be found." In other words, the bourgeoisie is at last seriously alarmed at the results of its own handiwork: it fears that the mass unemployment its system has created will deprive it, on the one hand, of a labour force in a fit condition to produce surplus-value, and on the other hand, is causing many to lose their "morale," that is, to become imbued with a revolutionary outlook.

"Bread and circuses" is the classical formula for successfully continuing the oppression of the plebs in order to maintain the patricians in power. It has been slightly modified by the rulers of Britain to-day; feeling that man does not live by bread alone, they are keeping the ration down to the lowest possible level, and concentrating on the "social service" circuses. But these "circuses," as we shall see later, have aims other than distraction: and charity-mongering is in any case only the smoke-screen. Behind it a tremendous onslaught has been launched on the unemployed in particular and the working class in general, an onslaught on the whole system of public services now existing.

The strategy and objectives of the offensive are laid down in the reports, presented towards the end of last year, of the Committee on Local Expenditure presided over by Sir William Ray, and the Royal Commission on Unemployment Insurance, whose chairman was Judge Holman Gregory, and which was appointed by the Labour Government. In spirit these two reports, which express perfectly the whole outlook of the bourgeoisie to-day, put the clock back a century. The *New Statesman and Nation* wrote in its issue of December 3rd, 1932:

> The Ray Report is but one chapter in a serial story of crime and disaster which is being published in parts under the ægis of a temporarily triumphant Conservative reaction. It is, however, a specially significant and sensational chapter, because of the clarity with which its recommendations foreshadow the subsequent development of the plot. If this Committee, purporting to be representative of the collective opinion of the local authorities, is allowed to have its way . . . our local institutions will revert, if not to the status, at any rate to the state of mind, of a century ago. There is much in the Ray Report, as well as in the phrases of the Royal Commission on Unemployment Insurance, irresistibly to remind the reader of the mentality of the famous Poor Law reforms of 1834.

To appreciate that quotation one needs to recall that the new Poor Law of 1834 was, in Engels' words, "the most open declaration of war of the bourgeoisie upon the proletariat," carried through "with the most revolting cruelty," of which he cites many hideous examples. "So frankly, so boldly had the conception never yet been formulated (Engels concludes) that the non-possessing class exists solely for the purpose of being exploited, and of starving when the property-holders can no longer make use of it."

The Gregory Commission, in its majority report,[5] proposes to split the unemployed by instituting a "dual system," as outlined to them by the National Confederation of Employers' Organisations. Unemployed insurance is only to apply to the occasionally unemployed. And even for them the insurance scheme is to be intolerably tightened up. Thus the period of benefit, already cut to twenty-six weeks, is to be halved. That is to say, an unemployed worker who has thirty contributions in the previous two years will come under the Means Test after three months, instead of after six months, as at present. If he has more than thirty contributions he will be entitled to draw further benefit, after the expiry of the thirteen weeks, at the rate of one week for each ten contributions paid in the previous five years; but the maximum period of benefit is thirty-nine weeks, after which he goes on to relief.

The Commission heard evidence that the present rates of benefit, following the 10 per cent. "economy" cut, are grossly inadequate; "the 10 per cent. margin, small though it may seem to be, makes all the difference between the subsistence level and acute poverty," one witness told them, and the Committee of the Clergy of Newcastle declares that "benefit is now failing to maintain families adequately even at a bare maintenance level." But Judge Gregory and his colleagues propose to cut benefits still further, by sums ranging from 3d. to 1s. a week, the blow being aimed most heavily at single and young people.

Further, a Means Test is to be introduced even into the insurance scheme; an "earnings test" is to be applied in the case of all short-time and subsidiary earnings, and deductions made from benefit to the extent of 50 per cent. of the total of such earnings over £1.* An additional thrust is aimed at casual workers (especially dockers) by the proposal that a condition for benefit should be availability for a *full* day's work. The proviso by which married women are allowed benefit, if their husbands are incapacitated or are not themselves drawing benefit, is to be

* The effect of this proposal may be judged from the following example: a docker, with a wife and two children, who earns £2 at special rates for a day and a night's work, would at present draw 18s. 2d. benefit for the remaining four days of the week when he was unemployed. Under the new "earnings test" he would draw only 8s. 2d.; if he happened to have subsidiary earnings of, say, 15s. a week as a Trade Union branch official, he would draw only 8d. (*The Royal Commission's Final Attack on the Unemployed:* National Unemployed Workers' Movement, p. 7.)

rescinded. Unemployment insurance is not to be extended to agriculture and the other excluded occupations. The autocratic power of disallowing benefit is to be restored to the Insurance Officers. And the Commission even anticipate the complete and dictatorial abolition of the insurance scheme; they say that if the annual review of the finances "showed growing financial instability without prospect of reasonably early recovery, it might be necessary, by a series of emergency measures, to establish simply a system of unemployment relief with a test of needs."

Now for the other side of the "dual system." The vast mass of the permanently unemployed—the "superfluous scrap" as Mr. MacDonald callously called them, estimating their number at 2,000,000—are to be placed outside the insurance scheme altogether, and treated on a relief basis. To administer relief the Commission suggests the establishment of a new piece of bureaucratic machinery in the shape of local "Unemployment Assistance Committees," centrally controlled by the Minister of Labour and a specially-appointed statutory commission. It is coolly admitted that the plan is to forge the most ruthless and tyrannical instrument possible to enforce pauperism on the majority of the unemployed. The Commission do not conceal the fact that they are devising, to this end, a form of extra-parliamentary dictatorship. The aim of the statutory commission, they explain, is to take the relief scheme out of politics (as the phrase goes), since both Government and Parliament are susceptible to "electoral pressure." Central control, it is pointed out, will stop local authorities using "discretion" too far (i.e., giving way to mass pressure). At the same time, the local authorities will be made to feel "responsible," will have an inducement themselves to tighten up administration, since the relief scheme is to be financed by a special 4d. rate, plus an Exchequer grant where this is insufficient.

The proposed Committees would grant relief after applying a Means Test—and what a Means Test! For the whips of the present infamous test the Commission plans to substitute scorpions. They suggest in place of the present family Means Test, with whose unbearable inflictions we are already familiar, the far worse inflictions of a household Means Test. The income, not merely of father, mother and children, but of other relatives living in the same house, and indeed anybody who can by any distorted bureaucratic fiction be construed as a member of the household, is to be taken into the reckoning.

If the Committee refuses for any reason whatever to make a cash payment the unemployed worker will then be flung to the tender mercies of the Poor Law, which will also deal with those who "might require treatment of a deterrent or disciplinary nature." Actually the proposed new relief machinery simply means an extension of the Poor Law. The operation of the new scheme would in fact involve the employment of the evisting Public Assistance Committee officials, the Relieving Officers, with their whole detestable Poor Law tradition and, as one witness said to the Commission, their "frankly deterrent" outlook.

In the true spirit of 1834 the Commission lay it down that "the amount of relief should as a rule fall so definitely below the prevailing level of wages as to avoid the danger that applicants might consider themselves to be in a better position when receiving relief than when earning wages."* They add that relief should also be generally less than the already cut rates of unemployment benefit, which they have proposed to cut still further.

But the accents of 1834 echo most brazenly in those sections of the Commission's report where the true meaning and perspective of all the "social service," "voluntary labour," "occupational" hullabaloo is revealed. Our forefathers, in their hatred and fury against the workhouses of the new Poor Law, dubbed them "the Bastilles." The Gregory Commission shows that the aim of the bourgeoisie to-day is to turn the whole of Britain into a monstrous Bastille, where the two millions of "superfluous scrap" will be condemned to relentless regimentation, to forced labour, in return for the mouldy crumbs of relief. A condition of the receipt of relief is to be that the unemployed must register at the Labour Exchange and express their "willingness to accept such employment, training *or occupation*, as the Exchange deems suitable." Thus the pretence that the "occupation" to be provided by the "social service" schemes is to be voluntary is abandoned. The Commission explicitly state that they "see no objection in principle to the application of compulsion if opportunities exist for the provision of occupations for able-bodied unemployed workers after the resources of commercial employment and voluntary service are exhausted." They go further and, in referring to the "voluntary" schemes, say that "it may be that occasionally it would be possible to require the unemployed to avail themselves of the opportunities so provided as a condition for the receipt of unemployment payments."

. * An analogous viewpoint was expressed by Mrs. Sidney Webb, who treated the Commission to a disquisition, which their Report quotes with much approval, on the horrors that would ensue if unemployment benefit were to approach the level of wages (*Minutes of Evidence*, para. 14, p. 1321).

The Commission press for a "more comprehensive policy," jointly developed by the central Government, the local authorities, and the voluntary charitymongers, in providing occupation centres for the unemployed, particularly the young unemployed. They make no bones about the fact that such centres will not aim at teaching a trade, but are to provide the modern "socially useful" (!) form of task-work, carried on under rigorous supervision so that there shall, as they say, be no "easy-going" atmosphere. The power to enforce task-work, not hitherto existing in Scotland, they recommend should be extended to that country. As a final sample of the Commission's serf labour objective we may cite the following: after remarking that the wages cost on relief works is too high, they propose that work should be allocated, in such schemes, to the unemployed "not on the basis of proportioning their pay to the duration of their work, but on the basis of assigning to them periods of work corresponding to the amount of payment made to them."

The Ray report also deals with unemployment. It echoes many of the sentiments of the Gregory Commission, but goes farther in suggesting that relief should be taken entirely out of the hands of the local authorities and should be administered by official nominees. They wish to see a ruthless inquisition operating by means of a large staff for investigation, which "ought to include home visiting and the verification of the wages of all members of an applicant's household." They consider that the statutory provision, whereby the first 7s. 6d. of Health Insurance benefit and the first 5s. of Friendly Society benefit is not taken into account in assessing relief, should be repealed. Disability pensions and school meals for children should likewise be taken into account. Present special scales for the sick and infirm are "unnecessarily high," since supplementary relief can always be granted on the certificate of a district medical officer; and a dozen lines further on they proclaim that there should be "closer control over relief granted on the certificates of district medical officers"! Task-work as a condition for out-relief should be insisted on, and the practice of driving the able-bodied into the workhouse should be "revived and extended." Casuals should be kept in the workhouse for two days and put on task, and they should not automatically be given the full prescribed ration, as at present, but doled out bread "according to their wants."[6]

The Ray report, in compiling its catalogue of "economy" cuts totalling £40,000,000, does not limit itself to joining hands with the Gregory Commission in the vicious onslaught on the unemployed described in the preceding paragraph. It proposes reductions in the salaries and wages of local government employees and in the expenditure on roads and bridges. In every sphere its motto is: "Make the people pay," and the spirit of the Means Test dominates its every page. It requires that in Poor Law hospitals all patients should be made to pay "as far as their means permit," and that a Means Test should be applied to the parents of children in Poor Law homes; a "substantial proportion of the cost" should be recovered from the parents in the case of day nurseries, whose scope should be severely limited; there should be strict control to see that all milk at infant welfare centres is paid for, "in all but the most necessitous cases"; the charges for public baths and washhouses should be "reviewed"; the fees for evening schools and all technical education are to be increased, on a Means Test basis; students at higher educational institutions should be accorded loans, not grants; the costs of school medical treatment and school meals should be recovered from the parents.

The principal attack of the report is directed against the services of housing, health and education; and here its "t"s are crossed and its "i"s dotted by the parallel report of the 1922 Economy Committee, the unofficial committee of Tory backbenchers, who aim at a total slash of a hundred millions. It is noteworthy that these latter gentlemen proclaim that their proposed economies "are less than the necessities of the case required," and "are based on general considerations of economic policy rather than merely on the nature of the present emergency."[7]

With the scandalous housing conditions in every working-class area we are already acquainted. On the very day that the Ray report was presented the Bishop of Winchester, in the housing debate in the House of Lords, repeated the commonplace that "tens of thousands of our fellow-countrymen are living under conditions of squalor, misery and wretchedness." At Christmas the whole country was horrified by the burning to death of six little children of an unemployed and crippled ex-serviceman in a "back-to-back" slum house in Birmingham, which was bound to be a death trap in case of fire, and where nine persons slept in the one bedroom. The Building Industries National Council states that the Government's "economy" campaign has already meant the holding up of £30,000,000 worth of housing and public building schemes, which would have given employment for a year to 167,000 workless builders and, through the fillip to ancillary trades, to 340,000 workers in all.[8] Yet the Ray report proposes the immediate abolition of the housing subsidy, the sale

o

of Council houses, an investigation with a view to an increase of Council house rents (already notoriously far too high), the substantial reduction even of the slum clearance subsidy, and the leaving of the field entirely free for the speculative builder and private landlord to do their profiteering damnedest.*

It is in the spirit of the Ray report that the Government are now framing their housing policy, as exemplified in their new Housing Bill, aptly dubbed the "Anti-Housing Bill." This measure reduces the number of houses for slum clearance to the preposterous figure of 12,000 a year. Sir E. D. Simon, in the *New Statesman and Nation* for January 28, 1933, gives a typical concrete example of what this means: the need for new houses in Manchester to clear that city's slums is of the order of 90,000; the Government would tackle this at the rate of 300 a year—or two to three centuries for the whole number!

In the field of public health the past year has seen a ruthless pressing of the Government's attack. A dastardly blow was dealt at those least of all able to bear it with the reduction of women's National Health Insurance sickness and disablement benefit, the reduction being heaviest for married women; and arrears due to unemployment are now to be excused only by one-half instead of wholly. It was pointed out in the House of Commons that the incidence of sickness among married working women is especially heavy because of motherhood. An inquiry by the cotton trade unions showed that out of 5,724 weeks' sickness of a group of their married women members 3,625 weeks were due to childbirth. Maternity benefits have been annulled and, without eight health insurance stamps in two consecutive half-year periods, unemployed workers are not to be permitted to requalify for free health benefits. The Minister explained that, while cash payments to unemployed are to cease, he proposed that there should be one more year (1933) of free medical benefits, "because they are necessary to maintain the health, *and in*

* An interesting comment in advance on the idea behind all this was made a couple of years ago by Dr. Scrase, the Hampstead medical officer of health. He said: "The alternative to the provision of housing accommodation by the State for lower paid workers is the provision of that accommodation by private enterprise; but private enterprise will only operate where profits are to be made, and to enable such workers to rent the accommodation necessary for their family needs would demand all-round increases of wages. Since this is presumably out of the question and an industrial impossibility at present, the State must step in if the existing minimum standards of housing that are compatible with decency and sanitation are to be upheld, and these standards are such that a lowering of them is not feasible." (*Hampstead Health Report*, 1930, pp. 109–110).

that way the employability, of the man" (my italics). Which is a candid statement of the bourgeois attitude to the workers' health —it is regarded simply as a means of ensuring the extraction of surplus-value.[9]

Any reader of the reports of the local medical officers of health will know that essential expansion of the public health service is already checked on all sides. Inadequate hospital accommodation means sometimes that surgical cases requiring in-patient treatment may have to wait for as long as a year (Wigan), or the almost total lack of isolation facilities "in many instances has been responsible for the fatalities resulting from infectious disease" (Monmouthshire).[10] Hard facts like these mean nothing to the Ray Committee, which opines that the development of the health services has been "too rapid" (!), and that a miserable million should be saved at the expense of salaries and staffs, of hospitals and maternity centres, and of the tuberculosis and mental deficiency services.

Hospitals, the Committee declare, should be built and maintained cheaper (that is to say, nastier). A "saving" could be effected on the number of tuberculosis cases sent to sanatoria by "more conservative diagnosis"; in other words, let workers rot with consumption so long as they do it quietly at home and don't cause the public health department any expense. Even such essential amenities as public baths and parks are "unnecessarily costly" in equipment, or have "costly schemes of lay-out," which should be banned. The standards of construction for mental hospitals are "too elaborate and expensive"; the Committee not only wish to see mental defectives worse housed, but set to do work which should provide a "proper financial return." Recalling the infamy of the early capitalists in this country, who, in taking children from the poorhouses to slave in their factories, specified that they would take one idiot child for every twenty sound children, the Ray Committee proposes that "for higher grade mental defectives the greatest possible use should be made of the system of securing for such persons employment, in domestic service or otherwise, with suitable employers who are prepared to act as guardians."*[11]

The Ray report likewise desires to put the school medical

* A typical piece of reactionary obscurantism is the Ray report's recommendation that the annual reports of the medical officers of health should be skinned down to the "essential minimum," omitting many statistics, and refraining from "recommending policy" (p. 101)— in order to save a few pounds on the printing bill. The intention is clearly to suppress the facts, very disagreeable for capitalism, which these reports reveal.

service, which all told costs well under five millions a year, under the axe. School medical officers report, as at Norwich, that "economy" has already stopped the provision of an urgently needed ear clinic and extra dental assistance and equipment, and has meant the indefinite postponement of the opening of a nursery school; or, as at Shipley, that open-air school plans have been postponed, though "in an industrial area such as Shipley an open-air school is a necessity." But Sir William Ray and his colleagues are indifferent to all this. Instead they propose to "save"—and what a monstrous saving!—at the expense of the unfortunate abnormal children, by cutting down the provision of special schools; they urge severe limitation of school medical research.[12]

On education the Government has already launched a devastating attack. While many schools are in a most unsatisfactory hygienic condition,* school building has been drastically reduced and a circular has been issued by the Board of Education enjoining measures of economy in school construction, such as the diminution of space, the lowering of standards of finish, and the decrease of school amenities. While the large size of classes is a long-standing scandal (there are on the average only three teachers to every hundred children, and there are 58,000 classes with over forty children apiece), the Board has still further reduced the number of entrants into teachers' training colleges. The Ray report wishes to increase the size of classes even more, reducing the number of teachers by more than seven thousand.

The Hadow reorganisation scheme has been in effect abandoned; what is left of it has been distorted into a rationalisation plan of closing down and regrading of schools, which in many places inflicts great hardships on children who may have to travel long distances to school; this has given rise to much ferment, culminating in school strikes at Birmingham, East Ham and Whitley Bay. The Ray report desires to see the process of closing down of all schools below a certain size made universal; with an unctuous rubbing of hands they opine that schools "could be closed, at the expense it is true of causing a certain amount of inconvenience to the scholars, but to the great benefit of public funds."[13]

The Government has not limited its attack to elementary education: indeed, its attack on secondary education, through the now notorious Circular 1421, has created the biggest sensation and evoked the most stormy protests throughout the educational world. That circular, it will be recalled, prescribes a

* See, for example, pp. 43, 88, above, and 222, below.

general raising of secondary school fees, abolishes the few free
secondary schools that exist, and institutes a means test for free
places in secondary schools; free places embrace over 40 per cent.
of all secondary school children.* An income limit of only £3
to £4 a week is suggested for parents with one child, plus 10s.
for each extra child; this is less than half the income limit for
free places which has hitherto existed in the County of London.

The Association of Education Committees has objected to these
proposals, which every professional organisation of teachers has
denounced in unmeasured terms. It is pointed out that parents
with incomes of from £3 to £6 a week will find it impossible
to give their children a secondary education.[14] Since only about
half the children in free places come from working-class homes,
it will be seen that this is in particular a blow at the black-coats
and the small middle-class. "The plain fact remains (says one
educationist) that £400,000 is to be collected from parents of the
lower middle-class if they happen to have clever children."[15]
The Government has thus kicked a whole series of rungs out of
the boasted "educational ladder"—which, even under present
conditions, is a mockery. An inquiry that has just been made by
the University of Liverpool points out that:

> The "educational ladder" is not so broad as is commonly supposed,
> nor is it so easily climbed. A child requires unusual ability and will
> power to study for examinations under the cramped conditions which
> prevail in many working-class homes. . . . Comparatively few chil-
> dren from the very poorest homes are found occupying free places. . . .
> The proportion of scholarship winners steadily decreases as over-
> crowding increases.[16]

The inquiry notes that even free places are out of the question for
many working-class children, because of the need for them to
contribute to the family income at the earliest possible moment.
And of those who do get free places the majority get no further
training, but go into minor clerical or distributive jobs.

The Ray report proposes to carry this attack further by abandoning the traditional principle of free elementary education
and instituting fees for selective central schools. There will be
exceptionally heavy pressure on these higher elementary schools
with the operation of Circular 1421. But the parents who fall
back on the central schools as the only alternative to the

---

* The only doubts raised among the bourgeoisie by this plan are
counter-revolutionary doubts: as *The Times* (September 19th, 1932)
wrote editorially: "Some will regret the change on the ground that
cheap and efficient secondary education is one of the mainstays of
national stability."

secondary education which they cannot afford will, if the
Ray Committee has its way, find that they have to pay there
too.

Prolonged mass unemployment, coupled with the ruthless
assault on the standard of living of the unemployed, has had its
inevitable effect in a startling increase in the numbers of the
lumpen-proletariat, of the workers who are driven down and
down, through the whole gamut of misery and degradation, into
the ranks of the "submerged tenth." The doss houses and casual
wards are full as never before. At the end of last March the
number of cases accorded the jail-like relief of the casual wards
was the highest for the past twenty-eight years. And it is the
youth who suffer most disastrously. The London *Evening Standard*
reported the following on January 3rd, 1933:

> The number of tramps has risen from a few thousand before the war
> to more than 200,000 in 1932. The old professional class of tramp is
> steadily disappearing. His place is taken by the young member of a
> working family who sets out to walk to a big town, is disappointed
> at not finding work and falls into a life of vagrancy. Three-quarters
> of the present number of tramps, it is stated, is made up of boys
> between fifteen and sixteen years of age.

The overcrowding of casual wards means the daily turning
away of youngsters who may have a dreary tramp of eighteen
miles before them to the next town, with no guarantee that the
casual ward there will take them in.

To make an elaborate demonstration that this increased poverty
and vagrancy accounts for the increase in crime is not necessary.
The annual statements of the Home Office on the criminal
statistics show this clearly. Even a policeman may remark, as the
chief constable of Leeds has done, that the upward tendency of
the crime figures has "become apparent immediately upon the
reduction in Poor Law relief and unemployment benefit."[17]
The existing system of property relations produces crime as
surely as night follows day; and it is natural that the increase in
crime is notably in crimes against property—burglary, house-
breaking, banditry, robbery with violence, smash-and-grab raids.
The present crime "wave" is an unmistakable sign of social
break-up and decline.

That capitalism manufactures criminals is seen most glaringly
in the case of the youth. The 1929 criminal statistics showed
that convictions of those under sixteen years of age were 46 per
cent. more than in 1907, and of those from sixteen to twenty years
of age 18 per cent. more. A Manchester official investigation into
the juvenile offenders who appeared before the courts during the

first six months of last year shows that half of them lived in working-class areas. In 25 per cent. of the cases where theft was the offence, the family income averaged not more than 5s. per member, and in a further 21 per cent. of cases between 5s. and 8s.—"well on the starvation border-line," as the *Manchester Guardian* commented. The investigators declared that "the expediting of slum clearance, the provision of more playing-fields, and a return to industrial prosperity, would probably do much to reduce the volume of juvenile crime." The Manchester investigation confirms a recent Home Office report on the same subject; but though the facts are so damningly clear, the reaction of the capitalist State machine is simply to intensify repression. The Home Office tells us that there has been a "change of policy," meaning that, "faced with an even greater increase in crime than in preceding years, the courts continued to use the Probation of Offenders Act very freely, but also passed more sentences of imprisonment and penal servitude and passed longer sentences."[18]

But for every unemployed worker whom capitalist society drives to crime, hundreds and thousands are revolting against that social order, and its "National" Government, which condemns them to such unbearable misery and want. The past year saw the struggle of the unemployed at the highest point it has yet attained, exceeding even that of the great demonstrations in the autumn of 1931, when the "economy" cuts were in their initial stages. It is a historic thing in England when workers on a mass demonstration, charged by police on foot, mounted and on motor-cycles, do not give way, but fight back stubbornly with whatever weapons come to hand—sticks, stones and bars torn from railings. The demonstrations in Birkenhead, Liverpool, West Ham and a dozen other towns, the Belfast uprising, and the unprecedented Hunger March demonstrations in London in October, were real street battles. The unexampled support won by last year's Hunger March, and the general sensation it created, testified to the growing spirit of revolt amongst unemployed and employed alike. The demonstrations and prolonged fighting with the police in St. George's Circus, Hyde Park, and Parliament Square, and the demonstration in Trafalgar Square that was accompanied by the biggest mobilisation of Metropolitan police ever recorded, marked a new advance in the class struggle in Britain.

The old law-abiding traditions have received a stunning blow. How "un-English"—in the bourgeois sense of servile acceptance by the workers of oppression—is the picture of the Birkenhead

fighting conveyed by the report in *The Times* of September 19th
last:

> During what amounted to a series of pitched battles between the
> mob and the police nine officers and seven other persons were taken
> to hospital. . . . The police tried to break up the mob, but were
> met with a rain of bottles, bricks, stones, lumps of lead, hammer-heads
> and other missiles. . . . Wherever the police were seen sweeping up a
> street the rioters disappeared into houses, from the windows of which
> women threw all kinds of missiles. . . . In one street the manhole
> cover of a sewer was lifted and a wire rope was stretched across the
> street. A number of police fell over this. . . . One of the motor-
> omnibuses conveying police reinforcements had all its windows
> broken.

The result of their "rioting" (in working-class language their
fearless demonstration) was that the Birkenhead unemployed
secured an immediate increase in the relief scales to unemployment benefit level. This striking fact, with its obvious moral, has
not been lost on the leaders of the Labour Party and the Trades
Union Congress, faced with the problem of retaining their hold
on the unemployed and keeping them from revolutionary
influences.*

* In this connection Sir Stafford Cripps, the deputy leader of the
Labour Party, gave a classical demonstration of the fundamental unity
of the reformist leaders with the bourgeoisie. Speaking in the House of
Commons on September 19th, 1932, he said: "Members of the Labour
Party who had been working in Bristol had been doing their utmost to
try to get the unemployed away from the evil influences of the Communists. It was a tremendous task. What were they to say to the
unemployed of Bristol who pointed to Birkenhead . . . ? Was anybody
going to convince an unemployed man, who was told by a Communist
that the way in which he could force relief out of a local authority was
by rioting, that these concessions had not been given as the result of
force? If only the Prime Minister would give some expression of his
intentions, it would assist those people who were trying to preserve law
and order in the country." Mr. MacDonald answered that he "would
respond most readily. He recognised fully that Sir Stafford Cripps and
his immediate associates held precisely the same views as he did on the
question."
With this may be associated the attitude of the Labour Party leaders
to the Means Test. After the development of the general movement
against the Means Test they have purported to oppose it. But Mr.
Lansbury, the leader of the Labour Party, said in the House of Commons on November 13th, 1931 (amid objections and interruptions from
other Labour members) that "if a person has gone out of ordinary
benefit and has means of his own to maintain himself, I am not prepared to pay him State money." Mr. Greenwood, the Labour Government's Minister of Health, told the House of Commons on September
14th, 1931, in a significantly evasive speech, that he was not opposed to a
"national scheme" for a Means Test, but objected to it being administered under the Poor Law. This acceptance of a Means Test *in principle*

It is from this last point of view that one needs to appraise the action of the General Council of the Trades Union Congress in refusing to be associated with the National Council of Social Service, and in shelving its own proposed charity schemes for the unemployed by way of flag days and old clothes collections. The General Council has also for some time past been striving to divide the organised forces of the unemployed, to split the rapidly growing revolutionary National Unemployed Workers' Movement. Under its ægis, and led by the Trades Councils, local Unemployed Associations have been established in a number of places. These bodies have as their main function the provision of recreation and sports for the unemployed, plus the work of defending individual cases at Courts of Referees and the like. Their whole line is to steer the unemployed away from mass action. But it is significant that Bristol, the birthplace of the reformist Unemployed Association which the General Council took as its model, has been the scene of repeated stormy demonstrations of the unemployed during the past year and of violent conflicts with the police.

is repeated in the Minority Report signed by the two Labour members of the Royal Commission on Unemployment Insurance; they restate the Labour Party's policy that a form of Means Test is unobjectionable if it is administered by the Labour Exchanges (Report, pp. 430-439). Such is the "opposition" of the Labour Party to the Means Test!

CHAPTER VI

"WOMEN AND CHILDREN FIRST!"

ENGELS has a moving passage describing the effect of the widespread introduction of the labour of women and children in the early days of capitalism in England. He quotes a letter written to the Tory democrat, Richard Oastler, by a Leeds worker in the 'forties. The letter tells of Joe, a worker on tramp, who came to St. Helens, in Lancashire, and sought out an old friend, Jack; to his astonishment Joe found Jack sitting at home in a wretched damp cellar by the fireside, mending his wife's stockings. He said:

"Jack, what the devil art thou doing? Where is the missus? Why, is that thy work?" And poor Jack was ashamed, and said: "No, I know this is not my work, but my poor missus is i'th'factory; she has to leave at half-past five and works till eight at night, and then she is so knocked up that she cannot do aught when she gets home, so I have to do everything for her what I can, for I have no work, nor had any for more nor three years, and I shall never have any more work while I live"; and then he wept a big tear. Jack again said: "There is work enough for women folks and childer hereabouts, but none for men; thou mayest sooner find a hundred pound on the road than work for men . . ."; and he cried bitterly, and said: "It has not always been so . . . thou knowest when I got married I had work plenty . . . and we had a good furnished house, and Mary need not go to work. I could work for the two of us; but now the world is upside down. . . ." Now when Joe heard this he told me that he had cursed and damned the factories, and the masters, and the Government, with all the curses that he had learned while he was in the factory from a child.[1]

"This condition," added Engels bitterly, "which degrades, in the most shameful way, both sexes, and, through them, Humanity, is the last result of our much-praised civilisation, the final achievement of all the efforts and struggles of hundreds of generations to improve their own situation and that of their posterity." To-day, nearly a century after, this condition is being repeated on an ever-widening scale. Here are three casual instances from the Midlands:

There are many families here [at Bilston, in the Black Country] where the girl is the only one working. Sometimes a boy as well; often just the girl. They swarm into the factories and workshops at Birmingham in the early morning. They earn about 13s. a week. Since the Means Test came in they've had a wretched existence. Before that they got a shilling or two pocket-money. Now their money is counted in the family income, and the unemployment allowance is reduced accordingly. Every penny they earn has to go towards food for their parents and the rest of the family, as well as meeting their own needs.

There is at least one important works here [it is a Black Country steel worker speaking] which employs girls of fifteen at 12s. 9d. a week. As soon as they are sixteen they are sacked and younger girls are taken on. . . . The employers get all they can out of the girls for two years. Then they become too costly, so they scrap them. They can do it more easily than scrapping machines. They have to buy the new machines, but the new girls are waiting on the doorstep.

The family [in Birmingham] is on the Means Test. Rather, *two* families are on the Means Test. In one: man, wife, daughter of eighteen and son of sixteen. The daughter alone is working. In the other: older son, wife and two young children. The wife is working *overtime* as a polisher for 25s. a week. "Seems as though it's only the women and girls can get jobs these days," says the middle-aged man.[2]

The parallel is exact almost to the very words used by the unemployed men—at ninety years' interval.

1844: "There is work enough for women folks and childer hereabouts, but none for men."

1932: "Seems as though it's only the women and girls can get jobs these days."

Here, indeed, is "the last result of our much-praised civilisation!"

What we are witnessing is a two-sided process. The drive of the capitalist employer for cheap labour is one side: the other is the general growth of impoverishment, the effect of mass unemployment, which compels women to seek work for wages in order to sustain the family. The first is as old as capitalism itself. The second is peculiarly a product of the post-war decline and depression in Britain, aggravated by the last three years of crisis. It is evident that these two sides are intimately connected and react one upon the other, that they are but two sides of one process, and that the depression and the crisis in their turn have greatly intensified the first side, the natural drive for cheap labour. We have already had something to say of this process in our survey of the different areas. In South Wales, a typical area of heavy industry and predominantly male labour, we have examined the social effect of chronic unemployment in the basic industry, as seen in the increased employment of women and young people in the abnormally swollen distributive and similar trades. In the wide region of the metropolis we have seen how the industrialisation of recent years, the development of the "new" light industries, has been accomplished mainly on the basis of the application of the labour of women, boys and girls to modern, highly mechanised and rationalised plants, with the most up-to-date and ruthless methods of speeding-up. These two instances present another double process, which has been summarised in these words: "Increased mechanisation has facilitated the entry of women into industries [while] certain industries, such as the catering or distributive trades, where employment of women and girls is customary, have expanded relatively to other industries."[3] All the available information shows that these processes are not confined to particular areas, but are typical for the whole country.

The most elementary statistical index in this connection is that showing the proportion of insured females to insured males. For the United Kingdom as a whole this proportion rises from 348 insured females for every thousand insured males in 1923 to 384 in 1930, an increase of 10 per cent. In South Wales, during this same period, the proportion of insured females to insured males increased by over 20 per cent. The same tendency is to be noticed from a comparison of the total numbers of insured persons. Thus, during the five-year period 1926-30 the number of insured men remained stationary (increasing by only three-quarters of 1 per cent.), while the number of insured women increased by 9 per cent., the number of insured boys by 5 per cent., and the number of insured girls by over 11 per cent. The absolute increase in the number of insured women was 230,000, practically four times the absolute increase in the number of insured men. The fact that the proportionate increase in the number of women insured is practically as great for the five years ending in 1930 as it is for the eight years ending in 1930 suggests that the growth of female labour has been gathering speed as the years go by and depression and crisis intensify. This is confirmed in the case of the main industrial area of Scotland, the south-west, where the number of insured women increased by over 12 per cent. between 1923 and 1930; during this period the average yearly increase in the number of women insured amounted to only one-half of 1 per cent. of the total female population, but in 1930 this figure more than doubled, rising to 1.3 per cent. The *Industrial Survey* of the region comments:

> The bulk of the increase is no doubt due to a reduction in the family income, which has caused some additional women and girls to seek work in an insured occupation. This tendency will no doubt continue during the period of depression.[4]

So far we have considered only the figures of the numbers of insured persons; these figures, while revealing the general tendency clearly enough, greatly under-estimate the actual extent of female and juvenile labour in industry to-day—for the reason that they leave out of account unemployment and its relative incidence among men, women, boys and girls respectively. Thus in the engineering trades in London the proportion of women and girls employed rose between 1923 and 1930 from one-sixth to one-fifth; but the incidence of unemployment among men is more than twice as high as it is among women.[5] In the same period in South Wales the number of males in employment fell by more than one-quarter, while the number of females in employment rose by one-twelfth. On the north-east coast "employment of insured women and girls increased absolutely and, of course, relatively, to men and boys. By 1929 the number in employment was 12 per cent. greater than in 1924, and that level was maintained during the general depression of the next two years."[6] Our analysis up to this point may be effectively summed up in two tables. The first shows the striking increase in women in certain industries in the decade up to 1921; and from all that has been said it is obvious that the industry figures of the 1931 census, when they are made available, will show an infinitely more startling discrepancy between the increase in male and female labour in the decade up to 1931. The second illustrates the greater severity of unemployment among men, in roughly the same industrial categories as the first table, during recent years:

INCREASE IN NUMBERS EMPLOYED IN CERTAIN INDUSTRIES (1911-1921)

	Males per cent.	Females per cent.
Chemicals	15	87
Engineering (incl. ironfounding and ship-building)	34	436
Vehicles	74	192
Electrical Apparatus and Installation ..	86	247

PERCENTAGES UNEMPLOYED IN CERTAIN INDUSTRIES IN LAST FIVE YEARS*

	1928	1929	1930	1931	1932
Chemicals:					
Males	6.3	7.2	16.3	20.4	20.1
Females	2.9	2.9	7.0	9.6	5.7
General Engineering:					
Males	10.7	10.5	20.6	30.2	30.9
Females	4.8	4.4	11.0	19.8	12.4
Motor Vehicles, Cycles & Aircraft:					
Males	9.7	9.6	17.0	24.7	21.3
Females	7.3	6.9	11.4	17.6	8.8
Electrical Engineering:					
Males	5.4	4.1	9.4	16.0	18.9
Females	4.3	4.1	9.0	13.4	6.8

* The period taken is the end of September in each case.

No argument is needed from these figures to show how, with the deepening of the crisis, the percentage of women unemployed has fallen relatively to that of men; or, in other words, as this chapter has been concerned to demonstrate, that capitalism is turning more and more to the cheaper labour of women. "Seems as though it's only the women and girls can get jobs these days" —as in capitalism's youth a hundred years ago, so now in its vicious dotage. The point should also be noted that in these statistics the category "males" includes both men and boys, while the category "females" includes both women and girls.

The point is of importance in this way: our analysis has generally demonstrated that the labour of women and girls is being employed at a far greater rate than the labour of men and boys; it has also generally demonstrated that the labour of adult women is being employed at a greater rate than the labour of adult men. But the tendency is not quite as simple as that. It embraces within itself another, and in some respects, opposite tendency; that is, for juvenile labour (of both sexes) to increase at a greater rate than adult labour (of both sexes). Recall the figures given earlier in this chapter on the percentage increase in the numbers of insured men, women, boys and girls for the five-year period 1926-30. These figures can be combined to show, first, that the labour of women and girls together is increasing more rapidly than the labour of men and boys together; they can also be combined to show that the labour of boys and girls together is increasing more rapidly than the labour of men and women together. And of especial significance is the fact that the highest percentage increase of all is recorded for girl labour. The point may be expressed another way; the percentage of adult to juvenile entrants to insured occupations shows a sharp decline. In Great Britain in 1923-24 the percentage of men to boy entrants was seventy-six and of women to girl entrants seventy-two; in 1930-31 it had dropped to twenty-nine and thirty-five respectively. The *Industrial Survey of South Wales* remarks, with characteristically genteel moderation:

> That boys and girls are able to find employment more easily than men and women is probably true all over the country. It means that in many trades "blind alley" occupations still exist; and in some instances it indicates a substitution, during times of bad trade, of juvenile for adult labour.[7]

To the "blind alley" job we shall return. It is now necessary to give a short supplementary review of the conditions in those industries where the labour of women and girls has extended so rapidly. A recent comment on the position in the bakery trade—

that "the increasing substitution of elaborate plant for the older hand processes is tending to the replacement of skilled workers by young unskilled girl labour"—can be applied generally. We have seen something of its meaning in the clothing trades, where, in London, five-sixths of the factory workers are women and girls, and the old skilled craft of tailoring has almost disappeared. "Elaborate plant," of course, may displace women as well as men, but to nothing like the same extent. Take the bakery trade again; in the main urban centre of South Wales, the Cardiff-Barry region, the number of insured males in this trade declined between 1923 and 1930 over six times as much as the number of insured females. The same thing appears in the mass of minor trades making articles for personal use other than prime necessities; exit the craftsman and his careful handwork; enter the machine and its girl operator—at half the craftsman's wages. This is the case in the manufacture of fancy leather goods, predominantly a London trade, whose rationalisation and mechanisation is a post-war product. An experienced worker in the trade writes that "where formerly in a shop of 100 workers seventy were men and thirty were girls, the position is now entirely reversed," and he significantly adds that girls "will not demur at being offered thirty shillings a week for work which was formerly priced at double that amount."[8] What a tale of old standards ground into dust, of unbearably speeded toil, of heightened exploitation lies behind these bald figures! And this applies not only to miscellaneous small trades, but to big industries dominated by some of the most powerful of all the monopolies in the country.

The chemical and allied industries (including soap, fats, etc.) are the province of the tremendous trusts of Imperial Chemical Industries Limited and the Unilever group, who count their capital in scores and hundreds of millions sterling, and whose yearly profits each run into seven figures. We have already seen how the number of women in the chemical industry increased nearly six times more rapidly than the number of men in the decade up to 1921; for the nine-year period ending in 1931 the number of women in the whole group of these industries rose from 53,000 to 59,000, while the number of men fell from 163,000 to 155,000. And the largely increased unemployment which the crisis has brought in chemicals is nearly four times more severe among men than among women. A revealing light is shed on this process when we turn to the figures of average wages paid in the chemical industries; in 1928, when they reached their highest point, chemical wages averaged 61s. 8d. for men and

25s. 4d. for women. Heavy cuts have since been imposed; but the striking thing is the enormous difference between the two levels. The decline of £3 a week labour and the increase of 25s. a week labour; fewer men employed, and more women and girls; there, in briefest fashion, we have the outline of monopoly capitalism at work; there is expressed the increased exploitation which swells the bank balances of my Lords Melchett and Leverhulme and their clique of relatives, associates and hangers-on.

Now let us examine the position in the distributive and catering trades, where the employment of women and young people has always been predominant, and whose parasitic development during a period of decline of basic industry has been frequently noted. The old Napoleonic jibe about the nation of shopkeepers might be more accurately rendered to-day as "a nation of shop assistants." And it is in the distributive trades that large numbers, perhaps even the majority, of the women and girls who have been driven to take a job by family impoverishment, have found employment. Of the 1¾ million workers returned as employed in the distributive trades in 1930 there were 700,000 women; and if shop assistants alone are taken, women form a majority.

There is to-day "an increasing substitution of women for men in shops."[9] This growing army of women and girls in shops works for wretched wages under conditions and for hours that are abominable—that, indeed, recall in many respects the factory conditions of a century ago. Vivid and grim confirmation of this is afforded in the Report, presented in 1931, of the Select Committee of the House of Commons on Shop Assistants. The Committee states that in a large number of distributive trades the majority of the assistants work from forty-eight to sixty hours a week, and considerable numbers over sixty hours a week (on Merseyside, for example, over 15 per cent. of the shop assistants fall in the latter category). They observe that, even if only 5 per cent. of the total number of shop assistants all over the country were working such shockingly long hours, the number involved would be between 50,000 and 100,000, "many of them women and children."[10] In Glasgow three-quarters of the shop assistants work over sixty hours a week. Cooked food and fried fish shops in popular resorts such as Southend and Great Yarmouth work their employees any hours from sixty-five to eighty, and even ninety-one, with the scandalous figure of ninety-six at the height of the season—or a six-day week of sixteen hours a day. Ice-cream and confectionery shops are particularly bad; one young woman in an establishment of this type in South Shields worked seventy-three hours a week exclusive of meals;

"she was very rarely able to leave the shop until midnight, and spoke of the dark and lonely walk home when the train service has ceased. She left because her health began to be impaired by the strain."[11]

This is the state of affairs to-day, when the scandals of long hours in shops have been notorious for generations. It was in 1890 that Dr. Richardson, an eminent medical authority, delivered an address before the Royal Sanitary Institute on this very subject. He pointed to the injurious effect of long hours of shop labour on lads and young women, adding that "to the female the mischief is of the kind calculated to extend to the offspring she may bear. . . . In my opinion eight hours daily is the maximum time during which labour ought to be carried on in shops."[12] And in 1932 labour of twelve hours and more a day is still general.

What kind of "life" does this shop slavery mean for hundred of thousands of women and girls? Miss C., a shop assistant who worked 66½ hours a week, excluding meal times, gave evidence before the Select Committee; she said: "Such a life is terribly monotonous. I find no pleasure in life when working like that."[13] And there are others working twenty and thirty hours a week more than Miss C.! Mind-destroying monotony, physically exhausting toil, the removal of every possibility of healthy recreation and cultural satisfaction (shop assistants can hardly ever attend evening classes), the reduction of human existence to a drab and endless sequence of daily drudgery—this is what a committee of the House of Commons shows shop "life" to be to-day.

> The girls in small shops, we were told, are very tired after their day's work, and are disinclined to take part in social or club life in the evenings. One shop assistant, who looked fairly strong, said that after long hours in a confectioner's shop she was so tired that she had supper and went straight to bed.[14]*

Not only are the hours for women shop assistants outrageous; the conditions under which they have to toil during these long hours are no whit better. There are frequently no arrangements whatever for meals (which have to be taken crouching behind the counter, with constant interruption from customers) or else the arrangements are grossly inadequate and unhygienic; there is poor natural lighting; notably in food shops there is no

---

* This paragraph was omitted from the Committee's report, but is printed in the proceedings. The omission, which was carried by four votes to three, was moved by none other than Sir Gervais Rentoul, subsequently chairman of the notorious Tory economy committee.

P

heating and the bored and numb girl cashier, aged fifteen, will be lucky if she has a tepid "hot"-water bottle for warmth; sanitary provision is inferior to that in factories (70 per cent. of the shops in the City of London have no hot-water supply), and the lavatories (which are often not separately provided for men and women) are described as being sometimes in "a beastly state"; often there is no lavatory at all; though an Act of 1899 requires that seats shall be provided in shops for female employees this is rarely observed, since employers think it is more "business-like" for women to stand for eight and twelve hours a day, and do not hesitate unscrupulously to take advantage of the fear, as the Committee says, of "young, tired and nervous girls" for their jobs to enforce this barbarism upon them. In consequence the health of women shop assistants is particularly affected:

> Not only do they suffer from flat feet, varicose veins and inflamed toe joints, but also from anæmia, nervous strain and from every form of dyspepsia. They suffer from menstrual troubles, and frequently from uterine displacements, which lead to much backache and malaise.[15]

To which we may add that even the inconsiderable legal regulation of conditions of shop employment that exists is rendered farcical by the fact that there are no powers of entry to shop premises for inspection comparable to the powers conferred by the Factory Acts.

In the hotels, restaurants and tea-shops women and girls are exploited as much as, if not more than, they are in shops. There is the same increase in female labour. Between 1923 and 1930 the numbers employed in hotel and restaurant services increased by nearly one hundred thousand to over 350,000; and of this increase over 70 per cent. was an increase in the number of women and girls. Taking the catering trades as a whole the proportion of women to men to-day is roughly as two to one. The lower wage-level of women is indicated by such facts as the far higher proportion of women living-in; for instance, in the larger hotels over 80 per cent. of the women and girls live-in, compared with less than 15 per cent. of the men and boys. In the larger hotels, too, over one-third of all employees work sixty hours a week or more. In boarding-houses and unlicensed hotels, where the employees are overwhelmingly female, over one-half work these intolerable hours. Cheap and overworked female labour is the foundation of the bloated prosperity of the largest hotels. Only recently the Piccadilly Hotel, to take a random instance, reported a dividend of 120 per cent.—in the depth of the crisis.

Monopoly is widespread in the other main section of the

catering trade, the unlicensed restaurants and tea-shops. It is enough to quote the name of Lyons. Women and girls form the great majority of the workers in this section; and in recent years their wages are moving down and their hours moving up. An inquiry of the Ministry of Labour showed that between 1925 and 1929 there was a notable decrease in the number of these workers employed for forty-eight hours a week and less, and an equally notable increase in the number employed for fifty-four hours a week and more; among women the percentage employed for over sixty hours a week in some cases doubled during this period. It is noteworthy that this worsening of conditions applied with especial force to waitresses, and particularly to waitresses between the ages of eighteen and twenty; these are precisely the categories where the girl who is driven to augment the family income by unemployment and increasing poverty finds a job. As to lowered wages, the Ministry of Labour figures, which certainly underestimate the situation, show that during the period in question there was an increase of 10 per cent. in the numbers of those workers (principally women and girls) who receive less than 30s. a week "total remuneration"—this last being an artificial figure, including cash wage plus the employer's liberal estimate for tips and allowances in kind.[16]

We can now return to the "blind alley" job and the question of juvenile labour. This directly connects with the distributive trades, for these trades are the main employers of boy and girl labour, accounting for over one-third of the total number of insured boys and girls. To-day boys and girls between sixteen and eighteen years old form one-eighth of the insured workers in the distributive trades, and boys and girls between fourteen and sixteen number at least as many. In these trades the legal limit of hours for juveniles is seventy-four; and so it is possible for abominable sweating of mere children to take place in a perfectly legal manner. The Select Committee of the House of Commons, to which reference has already been made, gives a whole catalogue of examples of this quite legal overworking which, it says, are "typical of many others":

A girl of fourteen employed at Blackpool as a waitress and kitchen-maid. Daily hours 9 a.m. to 10 p.m. Weekly total sixty-nine hours, including meals.

A girl of fourteen employed at Newcastle by a confectioner and tobacconist. Daily hours 9 a.m. to 9 p.m. and 10 p.m. on Saturday. Half-day Monday. Weekly total sixty-five and a half hours.

A van-boy of fourteen in the wholesale hardware trade. Daily hours 8 a.m. to 8 p.m. "His parents took him away as a result of a trip to

Yorkshire, when he was on the van from 8 a.m. on one day to 11 a.m. on the next."

A baker's van-boy of seventeen.   Daily hours 8.30 a.m. to 9 p.m. Wednesdays to 3 p.m.   No pay for overtime.   "He rarely had his mid-day meal before 3.15 p.m., and eventually had to give up the work, as his health suffered."[17]

The Committee stresses that these are "legal" hours, and that cases of illegal working of children for eighty or ninety hours a week occur.   They were told by the Association of Juvenile Employment and Welfare Officers that "there are many boys, not long out of school, whose working week is nearly twice as long in actual hours as, for example, the normal working week of the joiner."[18]   If meal hours are included no less than 85 per cent. of all juveniles employed work more than forty-eight hours a week, according to a recent Ministry of Labour statement.[19]   The Bishop of Southwark wrote in 1930:

> We congratulate ourselves on various Factory Acts which have limited undue hours.   But not all boys are in protected trades.   There are many who work as long as their masters require or their physical strength will allow. . . .   Three years ago Sir Wyndham Deedes made an enquiry as to the hours of boys and girls who had left a group of schools in Bethnal Green; out of 200 boys of sixteen years of age ninety-four were working from 54-58 hours a week, forty-nine from 58-74! . . . These long and late hours exhaust a growing lad and make it im-possible for him either to continue his education or to obtain healthy recreation.   They would not be tolerated in any organised trade, and years ago the State should have made illegal this shameful exploitation of boy labour.[20]

Long hours and unhealthy shop conditions take their toll of the very lives of the young shop workers.   Mortality among shop assistants between the ages of sixteen and twenty is noticeably higher than the average mortality for the trade.   The Select Committee reported that there was:

> A considerable amount of unnecessary ill-health and lowered vitality, leading to a depressed standard of physical well-being. . . .   A welfare worker said that she did not think it could be necessary to ruin children's health, by making them work overtime, in the way she had seen it done year after year.   The same witness spoke of the poor health and depressed outlook on life of workers employed for years in basements, and the long hours of overtime worked by them. She also said that it was her experience that after a "rush season," when much overtime was worked, the assistants were worn out and had no interest in anything, and the whole department would succumb to an epidemic of influenza.[21]

Here is another authoritative witness, Mr. R. J. Patten, the president of the National Federation of Class Teachers, reported in his address to the thirty-ninth annual conference of that body:

Referring to the Children's and Young Person's Act, Mr. Patten said that a great amount of illegal employment of school children was taking place in many parts of the country without interference by local authorities. Recent inquiry revealed cases of boys working up to four hours each evening, up to fifteen hours on Saturdays, and up to ten hours on Sundays. Disgraceful wages were paid, and in one instance a lad worked twenty-seven hours for 2s. 6d.

It was a subject for great regret that that opportunity was not taken to bring under the operation of the Act the large field of adolescent labour which was at present not under legal control—those occupations in which were engaged lads and girls too old to be protected by regulations which applied to school children and which did not come within the scope of the Factory Acts. Authentic cases had come to light of outrageously excessive hours, ranging up to seventy or more per week, worked—often for a mere pittance—by van boys, cinema attendants, boys and girls employed in hotels and restaurants, boys engaged on milk rounds and others, involving a total of nearly a half-million people. [22]

Youngsters are taken into a shop or a factory when they leave school at the age of fourteen. They are sweated mercilessly, under the conditions that have been described, for a few years. Then they are flung on to the street to make room for more youngsters. So the cycle goes on, its revolutions speeded-up in the present crisis by the tireless drive of the employers for cheaper and cheaper labour. The extent of "blind alley" employment has been indicated by a special inquiry of the Ministry of Labour into the records of the boys and girls between the ages of fourteen and eighteen on the unemployment registers in February 1932. The inquiry brings out forcefully the sinister effect of the sixteenth birthday, when juveniles come within the scope of unemployment insurance. One-fifth of the jobs lost had been lost because the unfortunate holders of them were "too old at sixteen"— as many as those recorded lost through trade depression. The Ministry says "of those aged sixteen years . . . only 32 per cent. of the boys and 28 per cent. of the girls had claims to benefit. Of those aged seventeen nearly all were insured, and the proportions of claims to benefit were 86 per cent. for boys and 80 per cent. for girls." [23] Could there be a more lurid reflection of the present existence and extension of the "blind alley" than these figures, which illustrate the large-scale dismissal of young workers directly they reach insurable age?

British capitalism built itself up on the factory slavery of women and little children. To-day, after a century and more of "progress" and "culture," it is coming back to the point at which it started. And this sweating of young people is vehemently defended. Hear a fine old crusted specimen of the real English gentleman, Lord Banbury, on the subject. Speaking in the

House of Lords on June 13th last, the noble and aged Baron opposed a clause in the Children's and Young Person's Bill which sought to give local authorities the power of regulating the hours of work of young persons under eighteen. This would be "the worst thing their lordships could do," since,

> in the obituary of the late Lord Inchcape it was said that at the age of sixteen he worked ten hours and longer with results they all knew. What was wanted was that boys and girls should work hard in order to restore the prosperity which we had lost because of the desire for a good time.

Any comment would be inadequate.

CHAPTER VII

THE TOILERS OF THE COUNTRYSIDE

It is just over a century ago that the starving and desperate agricultural labourers in the eastern counties rose in insurrection and were crushed by military force with unexampled ferocity. The misery of the years that followed found lurid expression in the wave of rural incendiarism—the movement named after the mythical "Captain Swing." And what have a hundred years of capitalist "progress" meant for the mass of the toilers of the English countryside? To answer this question requires some analysis of the class forces in the countryside and a brief survey of the development of capitalism in agriculture.

Modern capitalist agriculture really begins in Britain with the long and ruthless process of expropriation of the small peasant farmers, the sturdy yeomen. This was an essential feature of the primitive accumulation of capital, unforgettably described by Marx, which was the prerequisite for the development of capitalism in general, and capitalist industry in particular. This process was completed in the latter part of the eighteenth and the early part of the nineteenth centuries, the period of the sweeping enclosures of common land and the ending of mediæval methods in English agriculture. Farming lost its traditional aspect; it became a highly speculative business, in which the capitalist farmer, who got a much bigger yield from his improved tillage, was able to secure big profits by holding his stocks for prices to rise. Aided by the Corn Laws and the famine prices obtaining during the Napoleonic Wars, the big farmers waxed rich and the landlords especially made fabulous fortunes from soaring rents. The war boom ended with peace—that black "peace" of acute hunger and misery throughout England; but the "landed interest" were strengthened in their monopoly position and the monopoly profits they could reap out of the starvation of the masses by the new Corn Law of 1815. This was a position which was opposed to the interests of the industrial capitalists, and in 1846 they secured the repeal of the Corn Laws. But the "cheap food" victory did not prevent capitalist agriculture entering into its "golden age." This period, extending from the 'fifties to the 'seventies, corresponded with the enormous upward sweep of capitalist industry and the extension of the home market.

But as the industrial monopoly of the "workshop of the world" was ended by the development of capitalist industry in other countries, so English capitalist agriculture was brought low by the competition of foreign agriculture. English corn could not compete with the corn raised on the big virgin farms of the Middle West (where there was no hampering burden of landlordism to check the exploitation of the soil on the largest and most advanced scale) or the nobles' estates in the rich black earth regions of Russia (with serf labour or, after 1861, the cheap labour of the "emancipated" peasantry). In the 'seventies corn prices crashed and there began the great agricultural depression which lasted unbroken until the end of the century. From the turn of the century up to the imperialist war there was a slow change, and prices began to rise again, though the movement was a slow one and not of great account. There was a tendency for capital to concentrate, and the size of holdings increased. At the same time there had taken place the great change over from corn growing to live stock raising and dairy farming, from arable farming to pasture. The world war brought an artificial and temporary boom in agriculture; corn growing again became profitable; land that had not been under the plough for a couple of generations was turned over once again. The farmers' average profit doubled; and the landlords prospered exceedingly. The landlords, indeed, were able to reap a harvest more golden by far than that of the farmers by forcing their tenants to buy their farms when land was at its very top price. After the war prices crashed once more; there were three years of acute depression, succeeded by a period of relative stabilisation up to the world economic crisis (particularly in its agrarian aspect), as a result of which English capitalist agriculture is to-day at its lowest ebb.

Broadly speaking we may say that in relation to the productive possibilities English capitalist agriculture has been in a state of stagnation since the 'seventies. The development of capitalism destroyed the old balance between industry and agriculture, and made complete the differentiation between town and country. Capital could get a higher rate of profit in industry, or in exploiting agrarian countries (the Argentine, Australia or New Zealand, for instance) whose products competed with those of English agriculture. And the large-scale development of capitalism in agriculture—on the American model, for example—was prevented in England by the existence of landlordism, with its roots deep in the feudal past.

To-day the position of the class forces can be summarised as follows: first the landlords (their monopoly grip on the land is well illustrated by the fact that half the agricultural land in England and Wales is owned by just over 2,000 people); then the quarter of a million of employing farmers; and finally the 600,000 labourers, the agricultural proletariat (there were, incidentally, well over 1,000,000 of them sixty years ago). An index of the small and inefficient scale of capitalism in English agriculture is to be seen not only in the large number of farmers, but in the fact that the farm-holdings of more than 300 acres account for little more than 3 per cent. of the total farmed area. Anarchy of production, lack of plan and waste—those characteristics of all capitalist production—are grotesquely emphasised in agriculture, which is technically the most backward industry in the country. It is only necessary to cite such notorious facts as the complete lack of business methods among the farmers; the failure to keep any accounts; the enormous variation in the returns from farms of the same size and in the same region.

The ramshackle structure of farming in this country has received staggering blows from the world crisis. "The story of declining crop acreages and disappointing yields in England and Wales which were a feature of 1930 must, unfortunately, be repeated for the year 1931," says the Ministry of Agriculture. The arable area in 1931 was the lowest ever recorded; and while the number of live stock increased the output of meat was considerably over a million hundredweight below the average of the previous five years; the total value of produce sold showed a decline of some 9 per cent., of which the major part was accounted for by the continued fall in wholesale meat prices.

This is a cursory outline of the impasse to which capitalism has brought agriculture. And what has been the fate of the man who is the foundation of it all—the agricultural labourer? The landlord has drawn his rents. The big farmer has made his handsome profits. But the toilers of the countryside to-day are the lowest-paid workers in Britain; they live under conditions of backwardness that are frequently appalling; and they are "kept in their place" by a system of intimidation that would be impossible in the big towns.

A legal minimum wage is fixed for agricultural workers by the Act of 1919, as revived in an emasculated form in 1924. The minimum varies from county to county, with a rough average of a trifle over 30s. a week—miserable sum! As in all industries, the crisis has brought a relentless drive against wages; during 1930 and 1931 sixteen county wage committees reduced their minima, and in no fewer than eight counties the rate is now less than 30s. At the same time hours have been increased; for instance, from fifty to fifty-three a week in Norfolk. At the turn of the year it was stated that 200,000 agricultural workers had suffered, or were threatened with, wage-cuts. The aim of the capitalist farmers, who are crying to high heaven for Government aid to "save" agriculture from "collapse," was illustrated in the demand for a reduction of the minimum to 23s. 6d. put forward by the farmers' representatives on the Cambridgeshire and Isle of Ely wage committee last September; this figure, be it noted, is precisely threepence more than a married man, with no children, receives in unemployment insurance benefit from the Labour Exchange—at the present cut rates. And recollect that for the agricultural labourer there is no unemployment insurance.

An idea of what standard of life these wages mean is conveyed in a calculation made by the *Land Worker*, the organ of the National Union of Agricultural Workers. It is recalled that in 1913 Mr. Seebohm Rowntree estimated the subsistence level for a labourer's family to be represented by an income of 20s. 6d. a week. That income is to-day equivalent to 32s. 6d. (which is the Kent county minimum wage). And Mr. Rowntree declared that the subsistence level of his estimate meant "no butcher's meat, only a little bacon, scarcely any tea, no butter or eggs—a diet more austere than that provided in any workhouse in England or Wales."[1] If this is the position on the basis of the Kent county minimum what will it be in counties on a 30s. minimum or, worse still, on a 28s. minimum, like the great agricultural county of Suffolk? While the agricultural labourer and his family may have some advantage over the industrial worker in the towns in getting vegetables and fruit from their plot of garden, this is offset by the fact that the cost of living is on the whole higher in the countryside than in the town; it is the general experience that many foodstuffs, and most definitely clothes, household goods, and so forth, are dearer in the villages.

Budgets of agricultural workers and their families reflect their low standard of life. Thus a family of four (two children) in Lincolnshire, where the father earns 32s. a week, less the loss during wet weather, have bread and bacon bulking large in their budget; the only fats they consume are a half-pound each of butter, margarine and lard. After rent, insurance, heating, lighting (paraffin) and the other household "overheads" are met, they have a balance of 1s. 4d. left for clothes, boots, and "luxuries." A family of seven in Dorset (five children, the eldest ten), have a wage of 36s. to share. Bread is the largest single item in the budget, which is on the same lines as the Lincolnshire one, and they have a weekly balance of sevenpence for clothes and anything else they need. The woman writes: "When the children are ill, we are down to dry bread and potatoes. My husband can't afford to have a cigarette or a drink."[2]

Even the miserable minima mentioned do not exactly indicate the actual wages of the agricultural workers; for it is notorious that there is widespread and illegal evasion of the obligation to pay these rates. Just how widespread this evasion is nobody knows. The difficulties of inspection are manifold; and the fear of victimisation often renders it impossible to discover cases of evasion. It is significant, therefore, that a series of chance inspections revealed that the high proportion of one-third of the workers on the farms inspected were paid less than the legal minimum wage; recoveries of wages legally due rose from £298 in 1926 to £5,713 in 1931, which is as much an indication of an increased tendency to illegal underpayment as it is of increased vigilance in inspection. In recent years six additional wage inspectors were appointed by the Ministry of Agriculture for the specific purpose of checking these evasions. From the autumn of 1929 to the summer of 1931 these inspectors visited over 3,000 farms and found that over one-quarter of the workers were underpaid. But as one of the "economy" measures these inspectors' services were dispensed with. In this way the "National" Government saved the enormous sum of £5,000 a year, and struck a cowardly blow at the agricultural labourers' wages—no doubt in the interests of "saving" agriculture.

Rural housing remains an abomination. To the casual visitor the little old cottages nestling among the trees look "so picturesque": the bourgeois week-ender may buy a couple, knock them into one, spend a few hundred pounds on completely modernising the result, and be eminently satisfied with his agreeable and tranquil *pied à terre* in the country; but to the farm-worker and his family there is no comfort or pleasure in living in these decrepit dens, with their poky rooms, low ceilings, damp walls and often total lack of any conveniences in lighting, heating or sanitation. This is how a Yorkshire farm-worker's wife describes her home, where four people live:

We have one small bedroom which holds a double bed, a child's cot, and a few chairs and dressing-table. In some parts of it it is too low for us to stand up straight. No door to the room, and only nine steps up to it. Then we have a small kitchen holding a table, a couch, baby's pram, and a few chairs. No room to turn round. The floor is no better than a pigsty, chopped and hacked up. We have a small pantry where snails and wood lice continually visit us because it is damp and cold, and daylight all through the ceiling. The house is too low. It is dark now at four o'clock. Our outbuilding consists of a small lavatory, the seat broken all to pieces and no roof—not a tile on one half of it. When it is a wet day we have to take an umbrella with us. . . . Then we have a small outhouse for coals. We have to do our washing and everything in the one living-room.[3]

The amenities of home life are at their lowest in the smiling countryside of England; and substantially there has been nothing done to improve the housing conditions of the agricultural workers. Under the various post-war Housing Acts it is true that a number of houses have been built in rural districts; but of what earthly use to a man earning 30s. a week is a house rented at 7s. 6d. to 8s., with rates on top of that? These were the cheapest rents for houses built under the main post-war Acts; and, briefly, the position is that not more than 5,000 new houses have, during the whole period from the end of the war to the present day, actually been provided for agricultural workers. In addition, less than 5,000 dilapidated cottages have been "improved" by their landlords under the grants made by the Housing (Rural Workers) Act of 1926. And already before the war, a score of years ago, it was estimated that the need for new cottages in the countryside exceeded one hundred thousand.

Not only are the ill-paid agricultural workers, their wives and children, crowded and cramped in ancient and miserable cottages; where new ones are being built the "economy" hounds of the "National" Government are insisting on a scandalous lowering of the standards—lower and smaller rooms, narrower staircases, no parlour. Mr. Robertson Scott, the chairman of the Chipping Norton Rural District Council, in Oxfordshire, puts the position movingly:

> Unfortunately—under, as he personally believed, a mistaken sense of economy—the Ministry was pressing them to build smaller and smaller cottages, in which there was no refuge for the drying of the washing on a wet evening, no quiet place for school children to do their lessons, no spare room in sickness, no room which marked by its treasured contents a gradual rise in civilisation.[4]

Alderman Hewitt, of the Norfolk County Council, says that "where the cottages are being built the rural slums still remain. There are still not enough houses to go round. Couples that have been courting for nine years can find nowhere to go. I know of cases where twenty applicants wait for a claim on a cottage in which old people live."[5]

Sanitary conditions in the villages are shocking. Such an elementary need of civilisation as an ordinary piped water-supply is unknown in over two-thirds of the rural parishes in England and Wales. Pure water in plentiful supply is denied to the mass of the village toilers in this most "advanced, civilised, cultured" country of England in the year of grace 1933. The village house-wife cannot just turn on the tap in her scullery; she has to trudge to the common pump, perhaps quite a distance away, and bring the water back in pailfuls. Sometimes surface-catchments of rain water have to be relied on.

What the water supply of thousands upon thousands of villages is like may be seen from reports of the Ministry of Agriculture in connection with the grants it has made in aid of rural water supply schemes. Here is the official description of the state of affairs in two villages for which schemes were endorsed:

(a) The present water supply is entirely from rain-water caught from roofs and collected in ponds. The supply is totally inadequate and of questionable purity. In the drought of 1929 there was the greatest difficulty of getting water at all, and the farmers had to sell off most of their stock. For the remainder, water had to be carted two to three miles. (b) The existing supply is primitive. A few wells exist, the water in which is sometimes unfit for drinking.[6]

But while under this system of Ministry grants some 1,450 schemes have been endorsed, the small extent of the schemes, in relation to the countryside as a whole, is seen from the fact that six counties cover more than a half, and ten counties more than two-thirds, of the total number of schemes. And, as a finish-ing touch, the "economy" ramp stopped the approval of any new schemes during the past year. "Primitive" supplies, "sometimes unfit for drinking," continue to slake the thirst of the English village.

Housing in the countryside is not only grossly inadequate in quantity and scandalous in quality; the notorious "tied" cottage system still flourishes. This iniquitous system, which gives land-owners and farmers the absolutely unrestricted right of arbitrary and summary eviction of their labourers living in tied cottages, is simply a relic of feudalism. It stinks of serfdom. And between fifty and sixty per cent. of the agricultural workers of this coun-try to-day are living in tied cottages. The worker who lives in a tied cottage is not a tenant (though he pays rent) and has none of the usual legal rights of tenancy; the decisive clause in tied-cottage agreements reads: "It is expressly agreed . . . . that no tenancy is created by this agreement, but that the cottage is occupied solely by virtue of the employee's employment and any time this shall cease the employee undertakes to give vacant possession of the said cottage."

This servile system is a tremendous engine in the hands of capitalism in the countryside for maintaining its class power.

In the 'seventies the then Duke of Marlborough bluntly supported
the tied cottage system as a way "to keep the labourers in check."
The Liberal Committee which conducted the land enquiry of
1913 commented forcibly on the manner in which the system was
used ruthlessly to evict men "for political reasons, or for joining
the union, or because a daughter has got into trouble or a son
got drunk." Here are a selection of cases which show the operation of the tied cottage system to-day: they have been compiled
from an exhaustive enquiry made in 1931 by the National Union
of Agricultural Workers among its members, and are at once
fully authenticated and representative:[7]

DEVON.—A union man was called by the Ministry of Agriculture to
give evidence in respect to under-payment of wages to the employees
on the farm. The employer was ordered by the magistrates to pay the
arrears. Immediately upon returning to the farm our member was
given notice to terminate his employment and give up possession of
his cottage. He was unable to obtain another house.

CAMBRIDGESHIRE.—This member, whenever the weather was wet,
although he was willing to work, was refused employment. The
employer refused to pay for the time lost in wet weather, although
he was legally bound to do so, under the Wage Board orders. Because
the member objected to underpayment, he was dismissed from his
employment and ordered to leave his house. He removed his furniture
to a dilapidated barn, and resided in the barn until he could get
other accommodation. The employer had another house empty for
over six months.

NORTHUMBERLAND.—After this member had been working for his
landlord for a time, the landlord desired our member's wife to do the
washing at the farm. She did this for a time but found that, with her
own household duties, which had been increased by an addition to
the family, she could not continue to do the work. The landlord
thereupon informed our member that unless his wife could continue
to do the washing he would have to get another man whose wife was
willing to do it.

NORFOLK.—Two members had been employed on the same farm for
fifty years, occupying a cottage belonging to their employer. The
employer died and his son took over the farm. Our two members
were dismissed, it being pointed out that they were too old to carry
on with the work. Being unable to leave their cottage, application to
the court was made and they were ordered to give up possession within
three weeks of a cottage which they had lived in for fifty years.

LINCOLNSHIRE.—A member was not being paid according to the Wage
Board orders. Upon application being made for arrears by this union
he received notice to leave his employment and his cottage. The
member was taken ill and application was made by the landlord to
the court for an order. This was granted. The man was unable to
remove, and his goods were placed on the roadside and were there for
four days and four nights. Owing to public indignation in the locality
the employer allowed our member to put his furniture back into the

cottage. The landlord after a short period again ordered our member to leave the house. He was still unable to do so, and the landlord again applied to the court for an order. This application was dismissed. The landlord then took the matter into his own hands and ejected the member on to the roadside. We at once commenced proceedings against the landlord for trespass, but after the matter had been adjourned on a number of occasions, the judge . . . gave a verdict for the farmer. Whilst the man's furniture was on the roadside the police prosecuted him for obstruction. We defended him and were successful in the defence we put forward in his behalf. Finally our member went into the workhouse, and near enough the whole of the furniture was destroyed.

This is the true face of the idyllic English countryside! And nothing is done under capitalism to change it. The inter-departmental committee on tied cottages recently issued its report. This committee was appointed by the late Labour Government (the Agricultural Workers' Union enquiry, cited above, was submitted as evidence to it) and after being in labour for the best part of two years it failed to produce any agreed report; instead it resulted in three contradictory documents which have helped in shelving the whole business, as the Government which appointed this ridiculous body intended they should do. The farmers and landlords' representatives of course plumped for tied cottages. But the representatives of the Labour Party, Mr. W. R. Smith, Mr. George Dallas and Miss E. Picton-Turbervill, reported that the tied-cottage system should be abolished *except* in the case of stockmen—who account for perhaps half of the agricultural workers living in tied cottages. The Smith-Dallas report thus coolly takes away with one hand what it gives with the other; it is a mockery and a swindle. On this report and its authors the view of the Agricultural Workers' Union was thus expressed:

> While they acknowledge that the case for the abolition of the tied cottage has been made out, their remedies cannot possibly ensure that abolition. . . . The farmers' convenience will still be considered, and the sufferings of the worker's family still ignored. Frankly, we do not see how men acquainted with the real position of the workers could have supposed that these suggestions would end this tyranny of the countryside. . . . The reader gets the impression that the people who drew up this report got tired of it, and wanted to see the back of it, as no action was likely to be taken on it.[6]

It is not surprising that this "immense disappointment" should lead Mr. W. Holmes, the union's general secretary, to express some scepticism about the Labour Party's agricultural policy for a third Labour Government, and to say "what guarantee have we, for instance, that land nationalisation will have better treat-

ment than our tied cottage policy has had? . . . Have we to go
to the farm workers and tell them they must expect nothing even
from a Labour Government . . . Must we say that no policy or
promise is safe?" What is surprising is that Mr. Holmes and his
friends continue to support the Labour Party in a policy which,
on their own showing, is a capitalist policy and is therefore quite
unable to solve the problems of agriculture, as of capitalist
society in general, in this country. [9]

The squalor that we have observed in the cottages that house
the workers of the countryside is to be seen also in the schools.
Capitalism and landlordism not only condemn the vast mass of
the rural working population to live in gloomy hovels; they condemn the children to be educated in buildings that have been
scorchingly described by Miss Marjorie Wise in her recent work
on *English Village Schools*. Miss Wise tells, for instance, of a school
"which the adults of the village used as a hall in the summer.
But they refused to use it in winter, even for meetings lasting an
hour, as it was too freezing cold. Yet the children are expected
to sit in it for five hours daily"; or a school where "under the
windows are the lavatories. The infants are in a little room
twelve feet square and twenty feet high . . . like a lift shaft.
Hardly any light. Never any sun"; or a school where the windows cannot be opened and "the stench is too horrible," while
there is no water and only pail lavatories; or this, where out of
five teachers "four of them until recently had to teach their
classes all in one room, fifty children to a class. The room is
dark, bare and ugly." Miss Wise estimates that three-quarters of
the rural schools approximate to the worst types described, and
only one-tenth can be considered good.

It is now time to consider the position of the small farmer.
The small-holder proper has a bitter struggle. He has to toil all
hours on his small patch of land, with the help of his family too,
and at the end of it his standard of living will scarcely differ
from that of the agricultural labourer. At the present time it is
officially claimed that the quarter of a million small-holders are
standing the crisis better than the larger farmers; but the small-
holder has nowhere near the personal and domestic standard of
life of the big farmer; and it is admitted that small-holders to-day
are producing less and less for the market and are living on their
own produce—which means, in brief, that they are having to do
without more and more manufactured products; that their
standard of life is becoming more and more primitive. Now that
the usual crisis "back to the land" chatter is fashionable it is
worth noting that small-holdings have been declining for many

years; and that for every two small-holdings created three have
been absorbed in larger farms. In every respect small-holdings
are socially reactionary. A correspondent of *The Times* (October
22, 1930) summed up the matter neatly when he wrote that "the
success of the small-holder is to be found in the readiness of the
small-holder or the members of his family to do more work for
less money than the agricultural labourer." From such "success"
—read, from such brutalising and thankless toil—Good Lord,
deliver us!

The position of the small employing farmers to-day is frequently
little better than that of the small-holders. A recent astute
observer has described how wide areas of land in England's
granary, the eastern counties, are literally going to ruin. And
small-holder and small employing farmer alike suffer from the
feudal exaction of tithe—the impost levied by the State Church
on the tillage of the soil.

Tithe is such a characteristic English institution, it is so typical
of the clogging mass of parasitic feudal relics in English property
relationships, that it is worth some remark. The total sum
involved exceeds £3,000,000 a year, the assessments varying
greatly. And it is significant that the past year has witnessed a
whole series of stormy outbreaks among the farmers against the
payment of tithe. In village after village tithe collection has been
violently obstructed. Tithe collectors have been assaulted and
flung into the horse-pond. Distraints for tithe and forced sales
have been defeated by the solidarity of the farmers, who have
attended the sales in force, bid derisory sums for the goods and
stock sold, and then handed them back to the owner. Last
December some sensation was caused by the motor-lorry raid of
fifty police (some "disguised as farm labourers") on a number
of farms in Kent, to distrain for tithe. The observer quoted
above describes the burden of tithe in these words:

> To-day the cornlands of England are full of small farms whose owners
> cannot by reason of their losses take advantage of the guaranteed
> wheat prices. . . . It is on the lands of these men, who are their own
> landlords, that the burden of tithe falls heaviest. A couple of hundred
> acre farm may show no more than a gross profit of a pound an acre,
> many cannot show as much, and there may be a tithe charge of
> seventy pounds on that. . . . This is not a hypothetical case. "This
> may be a just charge," said one of the countless farmers who have
> been summoned, "say it is, if you like. But it is a fact that I couldn't
> pay it if I would. In 1931 my land didn't yield the tithe."[10]

When we turn to sum up the condition of the toilers of the countryside to-day, it is necessary to recall our sketch of the development
of capitalism in agriculture; to remember that the position to-day

has its roots in past history, described by the Hammonds in the *Village Labourer* in these words: "The labourers, stripped of their ancient rights and their ancient possessions, refused a minimum wage and allotments, were given instead a universal system of pauperism. This was the basis on which the governing class rebuilt the English village." The degradation of the eighteen-thirties finds its echo in the nineteen-thirties, as our survey has sufficiently shown. It is worth noting that the countryside cannot hold the youth. Agriculture is, more than any other, an old man's industry. It has the lowest proportion of workers between the ages of twenty and forty-five, and the highest proportion over the age of fifty-five. While the growth of bus transport has opened up the villages, social life remains backward and barren; what there is is controlled by bourgeois agencies like the Women's Institutes or the Rural Community Councils (financed by the Carnegie Trust) or the British Legion.

Trade Union organisation ploughs a very uphill furrow in the countryside; though the National Union of Agricultural Workers reports a steady increase in membership in the past three years, reaching its highest point since 1921. In Wiltshire, for instance, the union has more than doubled the number of its branches and more than trebled its income between 1927 and 1931. The main concentration of the union is in the eastern counties and in the "middle west" (Wiltshire and Dorset). The union's "cadre" numbers some 30,000 and 180,000 have passed in and out in recent years.

The revolutionary movement in this country has so far hardly touched the fringe of the countryside; but it is clear that only a revolutionary solution has any meaning for the problems of agriculture and its toilers in England to-day. Rural unemployment is assuming serious dimensions and will grow still bigger. The number of workers employed in agriculture decreased by over 60,000 in the years 1930-1931; and the unemployed agricultural labourer receives no unemployment benefit (another long-standing demand, incidentally, which the Labour Government side-tracked). What is the plight of the growing army of workless in the villages? Let a Yorkshire farm worker's wife answer:

It is now five months since my husband finished work. We have several times sat down to plain bread and tea for dinner. That isn't how the farmers live. I have been on a farm, and I know. In our parish unemployment means parish relief, and you have to agree to pay it all back when you can. . . . "Bad times" don't stop farmers running their cars, but they stop us eating when work ceases. It seems that farm-workers are the worst looked-on of any workers living. The country is heading for revolution as fast as it can. The sooner it comes the better.[11]

That letter breathes something of the spirit which, made conscious and given leadership, can inspire the far-flung battalions of the countryside to play their part in fighting to overthrow capitalism and landlordism and to build the Socialism which alone can make of England's green and pleasant land a place worth living in.

As a postscript it should be added that the poverty of the countryside is equalled, if not exceeded, by the poverty of the coast. On the one hand monopoly dominates the deep-sea trawling industry. On the other hand the position of the small fishermen is absolutely desperate. Here is a casual news item from the *Daily Telegraph* of January 3, 1933:

> So terrible is the plight of inshore fishermen all along the coast of Cornwall that many of them are on the border line of starvation. In the fishing village of Portloe, in the Roseland area, old fishermen, some over eighty years of age, are forced to plod around the beaches in all weathers gathering winkles in order to get the bare necessities of life. They are lucky if they get three gallons of winkles a day, and after taking them a long journey to sell to the merchant they only receive tenpence per gallon.

CHAPTER VIII

THE MIDDLE CLASS AND THE BLACK-COATED WORKERS

It is not easy to compute exactly the specific gravity, so to speak, of the middle class in British capitalist society. But a fair approximation is conveyed in the figure of 15 per cent. of the total population; on the same basis of calculation the capitalist class accounts for 5 per cent. and the working class for 80 per cent. of the population. The middle class, with its families, therefore numbers something under 7,000,000 persons out of a population of 48,000,000.[1] A very rough computation, based on the occupational figures of the 1921 census, gives a figure of 5,000,000 persons; but this includes only certain categories of the "professions," commerce and finance and personal service (lodging-house, restaurant and public-house keepers, hairdressers, etc.). The 15 per cent. ratio seems therefore tolerably accurate for ordinary purposes of political estimation. It is on the whole an under-statement; for the ratio of 5 per cent. given for the capitalist class includes many who should perhaps be rather considered as middle class.

Mathematical expressions of this kind inevitably convey an impression of definition and clear-cutness; and what is very evident about the British middle class is that it is an amorphous mass, embracing many differing elements. There is the petty bourgeois properly so called—the small shopkeeper or trader, the small man in business on his own account, the handicrafts-man; there are the professional men; and there are the large number of managers, technicians, and general administrators and supervisors who, while salaried employees, also depend for a greater or less part of their incomes on investments. Within this mass there are naturally wide variations alike in standard of living and in cultural level. The substantial fact is that the ideology is the same; the hopes and fears, the ambitions and expectations, the subjective attitude of the middle class to its mode of life, are of one pattern.

It is vital to note that this ideology also characterises the mass of the black-coated workers—the clerks and many of the shop assistants, although their economic status is that of proletarians and not petty bourgeois. But the middle-class characteristics of clerks are not merely a question of ideology; for an analysis of the social composition of clerical labour in its greatest centre, London, shows that clerks are mainly recruited from the working class and the middle class in roughly equal proportions. The ratio is actually slightly in favour of the middle class; in the case of women and girl clerks predominantly so. The investigation on which this conclusion is based shows that 20 per cent. of the total number of clerks come from families whose head is working class, and 24 per cent. from families whose head is middle class.*

A survey of the condition of clerks to-day reveals that they have suffered even more than the industrial workers from the cuts and unemployment that have followed the crisis. Imbued with the individualism, the lack of cohesion and solidarity, of the middle class, clerks have been mercilessly attacked by the capitalist employers to whom they have been so painfully "loyal." Let us note, first of all, that there are nearly 1,300,000 clerks in England and Wales (according to the occupational figures of the 1921 census), and that over one-third of these live and are employed in the London area, where their ratio to the total number of occupied persons is twice what it is for the country as a whole. And now here is a true story of the fate of a London clerk in 1932.

A. B. is a shipping clerk. He worked in an important shipping office in the City of London. His salary was £3 a week. Like many of his fellows, he lived on a new estate on the fringe of London, and he was buying his house. The house, the usual jerry-built "little palace," cost £650, or 19s. 2d. a week, plus rates. The season ticket on the railway cost 7s. a week. To help make ends meet a bedroom was sub-let for 10s. a week. Thus to feed, clothe, warm and light himself, his wife and a toddler, A. B. had a maximum of £2 a week, out of which also had to come any of the small amenities of life over and above bare subsistence. By dint of scraping and paring to the last shred, by weighing every farthing of the family's outgoings, A. B. was able, just able, to keep his head above water. A second child came last year; and at the same time the firm called its staff together and announced, with sobs and tears, like Lewis Carroll's walrus,

* For this information, and much that follows, I am greatly indebted to the kindness of Mr. F. D. Klingender, of the London School of Economics, who has allowed me to examine in manuscript the main conclusions of his work *The Black-Coated Worker in London*. This elaborate study is the first of its kind; portions of it, I understand, are to appear in a forthcoming volume of the *New Survey of London Life and Labour*, and the whole work will shortly be published as a separate monograph.

that it was compelled by the bad times, and in order to avoid dismissing old members of the staff, to reduce salaries. Poor struggling A. B. found his pittance slashed to the extent of 20 per cent. or 12s. a week—and he had now two little mouths to feed, two little bodies to clothe, instead of one.

Sustained only by the reflection that half a loaf (and this is what it pretty literally meant for him) is better than no bread, A. B. accepted the cut without a murmur, catastrophic though it was. It had been a bitter fight with £2 for three people; what on earth would it be with 28s. for four? A. B.'s standard of life must have been like that of another clerk's family of which I have record; the *pièce de resistance* of this family's Saturday dinner was a half-pound of sausages, price fourpence. And three months later came the last blow of all. The pretext for the cut had been that it would obviate dismissals; it was a pretext and nothing more; the unfortunate A. B. was himself dismissed— flung on the street with his prospects of securing fresh employment so remote as to be virtually nonexistent.

The unrelieved tragedy of this story is one that can be paralleled countless times. Just before the onset of the crisis in 1929-30 the average salary of male clerks was £3 5s. to £3 10s. a week, and of female clerks £2 to £2 5s. These salaries are below the average wage, in London, of the most highly-paid skilled workers—for example, compositors. And these average figures do not reflect the large numbers of clerks who are receiving substantially less than these salaries. The £3 earned by A. B. before the cut would be a very typical figure. Typical also was the 20 per cent. cut inflicted on the unhappy A. B. An elaborate investigation has shown that the general cuts in clerical salaries enforced as part of the crisis attack (mostly in 1931) ranged round about 20-25 per cent. The manager of a big City employment agency said plainly that what was afoot was "a retrogression to the pre-war level of clerical remuneration." Supplementary cuts in the spring of 1932 brought the slice carved out of clerks' salaries up to an average of 30 per cent. with some cases of as much as 50 per cent.[2]

The story of A. B. serves to illuminate the meaning of these cuts in the lives of hundreds of thousands of clerks. And it is the biggest and wealthiest monopoly concerns which are thus bringing disaster to the homes of a multitude of humble, industrious, modest men and women who have toiled year after year in their low-paid routine jobs, who have eschewed the path of class struggle and have prided themselves on their "loyalty" to "the firm" or (to be more up-to-date) the "House of ——." The ball for the crisis cuts was set rolling by the Midland Bank, which in 1930 announced its new salary scale, to be operated in the case of all new entrants; this scale prescribed a maximum of £205 a year as against the previous maximum of £370, and the cuts it imposed averaged nearly 23 per cent. on the previous scale.

The clerk's standard of life is not only being brought low by salary cuts, but by unemployment following widespread dismissals. There are cases of half the members of a large staff being dismissed. An important element in these dismissals has been the development of mechanisation. The general introduction of elaborate calculating, accounting and ledger-posting machines in this country is a recent phenomenon. In 1931 Professor H. Levy estimated that in the previous five years some 200,000 machines of this type had been introduced, displacing at least an equal number of clerks.[3] This process of mechanical rationalisation brings the speed-up of the modern industrial establishment, the drive of the conveyor, into the office; the manager of a bank where these machines were introduced complained that they "made the bank like a factory." Nowadays the whole of the routine clerical work of a big organisation, formerly employing scores upon scores of clerks can be done by a unit of the largest and most complicated machines (the Hollerith). The only labour needed is a handful of girl machine operators and a few expert accountants to supervise the results.

The clerk's margin over the poverty line is such that he is especially affected by unemployment and by the presence of dependants, or alternatively of additional earners, in his family. Thus the margin is highest in the case of single clerks; for married clerks without children it is more than double the figure for married clerks with dependant children. And the margin is inflated by the fact that the allowances for food and clothing made in the poverty line datum, as estimated in the *New Survey of London Life and Labour,* are absolutely inadequate for clerical standards; they amount to 7s. 1d. a week for food, and 58s. 6d. a year for clothing, in the case of an adult male. The following cases show how unemployment brings clerks and their families to the verge of or below the poverty line; and these cases were investigated before the operation of the "economy" cuts in unemployment benefit and the Means Test:[4]

(a) Widowed mother, with clerk son and two dependent children. Mother has 10s. pension. Son unemployed: benefit 23s. Rent 20s. for furnished room. Family 18s. below poverty line. (b) Unemployed clerk with wife and young child. Benefit 26s. Rent 15s. Family 11s. 7d. below poverty line. (c) Married clerk unemployed. Daughter earns

20s. as milliner. Total income 44s. Rent 16s. Family margin 1s. 7d. above poverty line.

Unemployment falls with peculiar severity upon the older clerks, who after many years' service have been earning a salary which carried them above the level for unemployment insurance, and have regarded their position as secure. A middle-aged clerk has no chance of getting another job; and the lot of younger men is very little better. What are these men to do? Many try their hand at that most thankless and wretched of all jobs, house-to-house canvassing for somebody's vacuum cleaner or other household what-not. It is a gruelling task to make a few shillings a week on the knocker; and the percentage of sales that any canvasser is likely to effect at houses where they may be having half-a-dozen similar calls a day will evidently be microscopic. The unwanted clerk is shortly driven to the alternative of becoming an unwilling pensioner on his family (if that is possible—if, say, his children are grown up and are working), or of dropping right down into pauperism.

The story of A. B. has indicated the heavy "overheads" that burden a clerk's budget; he has the mortgage-repayments on his house, he has his season ticket (for the majority of clerks in a city like London live in the suburban area, away from the centre)*— and he has usually instalments to pay on his furniture, and so forth. He is the serf of the speculative builder, the building society financiers and the monopoly distributor of cheap furniture at exorbitant prices: to these he constantly pays his regular tribute. When payment becomes impossible he is time and again driven to the serf's furtive refuge—flight. Anyone who has lately lived in the suburban regions of a big city will know that the "midnight flit" has become a commonplace.

A word needs to be said about the special case of the Civil Servants, who represent the most coherent and most politically conscious section of the black-coated workers. Civil Servants are notably affected by the heavy "overheads" that have just been noticed as a vital item in the clerk's budget. Mr. W. J. Brown, the general secretary of the Civil Service Clerical Associa-

---

* The percentage of clerks to the total occupied population in the different London areas indicates this. In the "inner ring" of boroughs the highest percentage is round about 12 (Deptford and St. Pancras), in the "middle ring" it rises to 17 (Stoke Newington), while in the "outer ring" it exceeds 22 (Lewisham), and 27 (Hornsey). In Greater London, outside the area of the *New London Survey*, the percentage averages 15.9, compared with 12.4 for the survey area. A conservative estimate of the average fares paid by clerks in travelling to and from work is 3s. 6d. a week (Klingender, op. cit.).

tion, has explained to me that many men in the Service assumed exacting obligations in respect of house mortgage, life insurance and so forth, in the years immediately after the war, when the bonus on basic salary was at its highest. The amount of bonus has now shrunk by two-thirds (there have been twenty-three drops in bonus during the past decade), but interest rates and insurance premiums have not. Civil Servants in this position are likewise hit by the rise in local rates; but none of these three items is taken into account in the official cost-of-living index whose movements govern the rate of bonus. The index makes no adequate allowance for rent increases (which often bring the rent to double the pre-war figure), nor for the middle-class standards of a great number of Civil Servants. Inquiries show that the expenditure of typical Civil Servants varies greatly from the index in the proportions allocated to food and miscellaneous items; the former is relatively less, the latter six to eight times more than the proportion assumed by the index—and it is precisely on these miscellaneous items that the increase in price is heaviest.[5]

Even with these serious qualifications the cost-of-living index is not fully applied to Civil Servants' salaries. The bonus, only applies in full to the first 35s. a week (or £91 5s. a year) of salary, and after that level is scaled down to one-half, one-third and nothing at all in the higher salary ranges. In the last ten years the drop in salaries amounts to some 30 per cent. in the higher ranges and 40 per cent. in the middle and lower ranges. If a comparison is made between Civil Servants and other persons in official service (for instance, army and navy officers, teachers and police) the salary drop of the former is two to eight times as great as that of the latter.[6] A present estimate shows that over two-thirds of the total number of non-industrial Civil Servants receive less than £4 a week, and considerably over one-half receive less than £3 a week. In the Post Office there are 25,500 members of the full-time staff who earn less than 40s. a week; and one-half of the 180,000 employees who compose the full-time staff are below the Rowntree Human Needs Standard, which is a low standard.* At the same time Post Office labour has been intensi-

---

* A full discussion of this subject is contained in the Statement submitted by the Civil Service National Whitley Council (Staff Side), Section 1, to the Royal Commission on the Civil Service, 1929-30 (*Appendix VI to Minutes of Evidence*, paras. 185-196, 197-204, 210). Mr. Seebohm Rowntree says of his standard: "I am here seeking to provide not for a standard of life which I consider desirable, but for one below which no class of workers should ever be forced to live" (*Human Needs of Labour*, p. 91).

fied; the volume of work increased 26 per cent. between 1922-23 and 1929-30, but the staff only increased by 10 per cent. And Post Office remuneration varies according to a complicated and excessively inequitable system of local differentiation, full of gross anomalies and inflicting hardship upon large numbers of employees.[7]

The Government has done nothing to meet the reiterated demands of the Civil Service for the rectification of this position. It has rejected the recommendation of the Royal Commission on the Civil Service to consolidate bonus with salary at a bonus level of 55, with a slight redistribution in the interests of the lower-paid grades. While it has agreed to stabilise the bonus at 50 per cent. of the basic salary until 1934, the "effect is to consolidate an inequitable bonus with salary at the bottom of the wage curve," as the Civil Service staff representatives put it.

We have now seen a little of what capitalist decline and crisis has meant in the worsening of the living standards of clerks and their families. What is the position of the general mass of the middle class? Boxed up in his little suburban house with his family, of which he still tries to play the patriarch, the middle-class man presents in caricature the traditional "national" characteristics of capitalist Britain; he sums up in himself the narrow, pettifogging outlook, the "respectability," the cant, humbug and hypocrisy, the insularity and chauvinism, the combination of practical energy with disgraceful intellectual indolence. He flatters himself still that "an Englishman's home is his castle" (when really it is the landlord's or the building society's) and believes that this England is in very truth a "land of hope and glory."

However, the glory nowadays is very elusive; and the hope so long deferred is making the heart of the middle class very sick. For the development of declining capitalism into giant monopoly, the chronic post-war depression and the three years of crisis, have been teaching the English middle class some cruel lessons.

Monopoly naturally crushes out the small man. The process can be seen typically in the distributive trades. These trades undergo a parasitic expansion during a period of acute depression in the basic industries; and this has been most marked in post-war Britain. But the countervailing factor, which the crisis has greatly intensified, is that the small shop-keepers and traders in the industrial areas see their business dwindling down and down as the impoverishment of the working class increases. At the same time the multiple shop, with its cheap mass-produced goods, gains ground daily. The small shop stands little chance against Woolworth's or the multiple shop concerns.*

What happens, then, to the shopkeeper? When he has come to the end, he may make a despairing effort to sell his business for some derisory sum; or he will go bankrupt. He is declassed. He becomes a propertyless man, a proletarian. Maybe he secures employment in a multiple shop; and this has been adduced as one of the causes of the increase in the number of insured workers in the distributive trades up to 1930.[8] Otherwise he will have little hope other than to struggle for whatever job he can. I doubt whether a case I recently noted in South Wales was unusual; it was that of an enterprising middle-aged man who had been an ironmonger in a mining township; ruined, he had had long spells down and out, and had latterly landed a temporary job as potman and general factotum in a village pub.

The lot of the "professional" people (including the technicians) the small business men and managers, has likewise been gravely worsened. The crisis has dealt severe blows to their small investments; if they wish to realise in order to augment their diminished incomes they can only do so at a heavy loss. The professions are overstocked as it is; and monopoly needs fewer professional men, fewer technicians, than before. Here is a police-court report, from the *Daily Telegraph* of January 24th, 1933, which throws a sidelight on the position of the technicians in a particularly hard-hit industry:

> Arthur Curtis Wilson, 52, described as a master mariner, of Wandsworth-road, S.W., was charged at Ealing yesterday with begging and wearing the uniform of the British Mercantile Marine in such circumstances as to be likely to bring contempt on the uniform. He pleaded not guilty. A police-constable stated that Wilson displayed a number of boxes of matches with the words, "Mercantile Marine officer. One thousand ships idle." In his possession was a master's certificate issued by the Board of Trade in 1914. Wilson told the court: "There are captains and chief officers of ships half starving in the City. Some of them are sleeping in the crypt of St. Martin's and some have committed suicide."

The middle class man finds that he is coming to a dead end; and so are his children. The old cycle of higher education—"good" school and university—is being painstakingly kept up,

---

* It is estimated that there are 500,000 retail outlets in the country; of these 90 per cent. are small shops, but these small shops only account for half the total trade. The remaining half passes through the hands of large concerns in the following estimated proportion: department stores 7½ per cent., multiple shops 15-20 per cent., fixed price chains (Woolworths, Marks and Spencers, etc.) 7½ per cent., Co-Operative Stores 12-15 per cent. (L. E. Neal: *Retailing and the Public*).

is indeed being fed with more and more raw material, as the matriculation figures show; but the old avenues for the absorption of the product are closed. The heavy decline in the export of capital, which expresses the acute and specific crisis of British imperialism, has its counterpart in the heavy decline in the export of the sons of the middle class to well-paid jobs in the apparatus of imperialist exploitation in the colonial countries. Technical and scientific posts at home are very few and far between; monopoly capitalism is a brake on the development of technique and science. Teaching—the traditional last resort of the university man or woman who can find nothing else to do—is hopelessly overcrowded. The middle class, unable to conceive that a qualification does not mean an open sesame to a "position," is breeding more intellectuals than ever; but its progeny are facing a future that, under capitalism, is of a gloom that grows daily deeper.

The middle class is being stirred to its depths, as a natural result of this whole process. Its intellectuals in particular are in the throes of a profound political ferment: the revolutionary movement in the universities has reached the highest level yet recorded. Old values are being revalued. Traditional answers are now unreal, and new answers have to be found. There is a general groping for some way out of the present slough of despond. And beyond question the biggest factor influencing the slow transformation of outlook that is in progress is the existence and achievements of the Soviet Union and its Five-Year Plan. The evidence of this is clear for all to see. Middle class intellectuals have been flooding to the Soviet Union in their thousands during the past two years, taking advantage of the many cheap tours in order to "see for themselves." The spate of books on the Russian Revolution, the Soviet Union and everything connected with it, rises higher and higher. Russia, object of unreasoning hatred and suspicion to the middle class man, has become fashionable. Of course there is much that is superficial in this change in view; but the unanswerable contrast between the capitalist world of anarchy and decay and the Socialist world of planning and growth is a thing that goes to the root of all preconceived ideas.

The deepening of the crisis is making many of the middle class sceptical of the policy and promises of the "National" Government and its leading party, the Conservatives. Whither, then, are they turning if not to the revolutionary path? They are turning, many of them (and this process has been developing for a number of years), to the Labour Party. That Party's schemes of public utility corporations (which open up vistas of secure bureaucratic jobs), its denunciation of the banks (a good old cry to appeal to the small man), the whole trend of its new programme, are eminently calculated, and designedly calculated, to propitiate and attract the middle class. Others, very few so far, are turning to the Fascism *pur sang* popularised by Sir Oswald Mosley, with its hollow demagogy and its blatant jingoism.

It is not possible to obtain any exact quantitative evaluation of these various trends among the middle class. It is significant enough to note that they exist. Here is one random example from the quintessentially middle class London suburb of Crouch End, a part of Hornsey. Almost simultaneously last autumn the Crouch End Young Liberal Association decided to join the Mosley Fascists;[9] and the Crouch End Literary and Debating Society, a most sober and respectable body which holds its meetings in a local church hall, invited a Communist speaker to address it (to the great perturbation of many of its members) on the Five-Year Plan. This incident is not of great moment in itself; but as a pointer to a tendency, and as showing in this singular coincidence in space and time the contradictory tencencies at work, it is interesting.

It is among the unorganised mass of the middle class and the black-coated workers that the Labour Party has made headway. The organised black-coats, among whom the Civil Service and the Post Office employees are pre-eminent, are widely disillusioned with the Labour Party as a result of their practical experience that a Labour Government was as hostile to their demands as was a Tory Government. The same process, to a lesser degree, is observable among the teachers, who are likewise strongly organised. It was the Civil Servants and Post Office workers, too, who showed in their tremendous and unprecedented Hyde Park demonstrations in the autumn of 1931 that the black-coated toiler is not content to remain a passive victim of the system which oppresses him, and that he can display a solidarity and an organised strength equal to that of his brethren of factory, mine, and mill.

CHAPTER IX

THE ATTITUDE OF THE BOURGEOISIE TOWARDS THE PROLETARIAT

THE working class are condemned to exist under the intolerable conditions that previous chapters have exposed in detail in order that a numerically tiny class of very rich people, the big capitalists, may live in idleness and luxury. Twelve million workers toil for an average income of 45s. a week to maintain a hundred thousand parasites with incomes of over £40 a week. Actually one-quarter of this number of workers have no work, and even if they receive full unemployment benefit they are below the harshest poverty line. In the past decade the wages of the working class have fallen by hundreds of millions of pounds a year; even the totally unsatisfactory official figures show a steady decline in real wages; but in the same period, a period of falling prices, the valuation of the capital of the hundred thousand super-tax payers increased from over $6\frac{1}{2}$ thousand millions to over $10\frac{1}{4}$ thousand millions sterling. The enormous slice of the national income that is appropriated by the exploiters is indicated by comparing the present average income of the working class with the fact that, excluding entirely the tribute drawn from imperialist exploitation of the colonies and the sums devoted to home investment, the equal distribution of the present national income would give an annual average of £270, or over £5 a week, to every family, including the unemployed.[1]

In a great coalfield, like South Wales, the miners are driven and sweated worse than within the memory of man, and they earn a couple of pounds if they are lucky enough to get a full six shifts in a week; whole areas are derelict; fresh milk is unknown on the unemployed worker's table; tiny children are horribly deformed by rickets, and a medical officer thinks that "the prolonged industrial depression in these parts is having its effect in some way on the mothers, and the possibility is that the disease has started in the child before birth." In Lancashire, the birthplace of British capitalist industry, the cotton textile workers have been driven to their lowest level; every possible device, from the use of bad material to every form of speeding-up, is being used to increase the intensity of labour to the utmost; in every Lancashire industry there is a real "trembling system" in operation on the job to-day; the unemployed have been brought to unheard-of poverty and wretchedness by the operation of the Means Test and the Anomalies Act. The story is the same for every industrial area. The devouring canker of mass unemployment; harder and faster work with less wages, and under worse conditions, for those who are still employed; this is the picture in the moribund shipyards of the Clyde and the Tyne, in every coalfield, in the heavy industry centres of the Midlands and the North, on the docks and in the factory areas of London. Everywhere we have seen that housing is as abominable as ever it was; overcrowding is in fact increasing; the general health conditions are sliding rapidly downhill.

That is one picture—the picture of the overwhelming majority, at the bottom. Here is the picture of the clique at the top. Among them are individuals of fabulous wealth. The *Sunday Express* on January 8th, 1933, gave a list of these people. Income tax amounting to some £1,000 a week is paid by Sir Hugo Hirst, head of that giant monopoly the General Electric Company, by Sir H. Cunliffe-Owen and Sir Louis Baron (both tobacco magnates), and by Viscount Borodale. Sir Edmund Davis, African copper king, pays in tax nearly £2,000 a week. The tax bill of Baroness Burton (beer) is £60,000 a year, and of Lord Devonport (tea) £30,000 a year. Incomes of over £100,000 a year pass into the pockets of Sir Robert Hadfield (steel) and Lords Bearsted and Wakefield (oil). Lord Melchett, the chemicals and anthracite monopolist, has an income of £150,000 a year. The heiress of Sir David Yule, Calcutta merchant, has in trust an annual income in the neighbourhood of £1,000,000. And what do this clique do with their lives?

Last year's "little season," according to the Society columns, was the most "brilliant" since the war. The biggest Hunt Balls have been far more largely attended than ever. Every day the gossip writers chronicle the gay parties, the weddings, the dances, sports and junketings of Mayfair and Belgravia. Every day, on the third page of *The Times*, the reader will find columns of advertisements for servants—"one lady, four staff," "three boys eight, six, four; six servants and governess," "two in family, four maids," "three family, six servants," "family three; servants seven," "small family; four servants; no children," and so *ad infinitum*. The idle rentiers, the useless social drones, have plenty of slaves to save their doing anything for themselves. It is the Government of these people that has "economised" out of existence the already grossly inadequate schemes for housing the workers; but all over the West End of London blocks of luxury flats have been built, at rentals up to £800 and far more a year; a Kensington block, advertised as "cheap" (!), but "for those who want only the best," with "polished plate glass in every window . . . soft water . . . refrigerators," let at from £300 to £525 a year.   When the Surrey mansion of Captain Woolf Barnato, South African diamond millionaire, was burnt down last January, he revealed that he had just spent £25,000 on re-decorating it; while workers in, say, Glasgow are living in conditions of unspeakable dirt and dilapidation.

Workers are too poor to afford bus and tram fares, as the decline in receipts of passenger road transport undertakings shows.   Yet of last year's motor show the *Daily Express* wrote on October 20th, 1932, that "the biggest surprise of all is the money that is being expended on the larger expensive cars.   One distributor of a car selling at just under £1,000 told me yesterday that he had already sold twenty-eight of these models. . . . Last year his total sales at the show amounted to six cars.   A firm selling cars costing above £2,000 had by yesterday completed business amounting to nearly £80,000."   The output of the supreme luxury car, the Rolls-Royce, is booked up for months ahead.

To own a large cruising or racing yacht has always been the sign of extreme wealth.   During the past year Mr. W. L. Stephenson, the head of Woolworth's (whose dividends are 70 per cent.), ordered one of the largest and most expensive racing yachts, the first of the kind to be built in this country for years. Thornycrofts, the shipbuilders, have received orders for four seagoing motor yachts, totalling well over £100,000 in value; it is stated that many years have passed since four luxury craft of this kind were under construction by one firm at the same time.[2]

The clothing of the workers is at its poorest.*   Children are unable to attend school because they have no boots to wear. But a glance at the advertisements of Revillon Frères and the other exclusive West End shops shows that fur coats of mink are

---

* Two clothing traders, one in London and one in the Midlands, recently told me quite independently that their turnover for 1932 was just one-half the 1931 figure. The man in the Midlands, a market trader on a fairly substantial scale, remarked that at the same time his bill for wrapping paper and string was up 25 per cent.; some sign that the cheap markets are attracting more purchasers, but for cheaper goods in smaller quantities per purchaser; thus, men's socks now cannot be sold at more than 1s. a pair, whereas a year ago the 1s. 11d. quality was a good seller. The London man, a tailor, said that he had had as many coats in for renovation in the first two weeks of the autumn season as he usually had in the whole season.

being offered at the "specially attractive price" of 200 guineas, with superior models ranging up to 800 guineas. And "Park-lane's first Lingerie Exhibition" is held in the blue and silver ballroom at Sir Philip Sassoon's luxurious mansion, showing "exquisitely worked" garments in silks of every hue, rich lace for bridal gifts, and all the seductive trappings of feminine parasitism.

Working-class families are jammed into the foul back-to-back hovels of the industrial North, overcrowded in the sunless slums of the big cities, where light and air are alike foreign. But the bourgeoisie find a comfortable escape on ocean cruises, which are more patronised now than ever. They may go for a trip round the world in the *Empress of Britain* ("spaciousness is her keynote. Seventy per cent. of the staterooms have private baths. There are wide sports and sun decks") at a minimum fare of 466 guineas. They may cruise to the West Indies for six weeks, at a fare whose minimum is the trifle of 86 guineas, on "a first class ship, a first class cruise for first class passengers. An airy ship for a sunny voyage."

The contradiction between the crushing regime of "economy" for the poor, and extending luxury for the rich, is even elevated into a doctrine of political economy. *The Times*, which considers the unemployment benefit allowance of 2s. a week for a child "very generous," has featured a correspondence from the leading bourgeois economists on the theme "Should the rich economise in their private spending?" Back comes the answer *ex cathedra* in a collective statement by Keynes, Stamp, Layton, Salter, Macgregor and old uncle Pigou and all, that "the public interest in present conditions does not point towards private economy; to spend less money than we should like to do is not patriotic." The surfeited rich, the capitalists, are to increase their surfeit; the desperately needy poor, the workers, must draw their belts in still more. This is the celebrated slogan of "equality of sacrifice" in real life.

Impoverishment, bitter and cruel impoverishment, has the working class in a grip that is growing daily tighter. For the bond-holders, the finance oligarchs, there is money in millions. On December 1st last the largest financial transaction ever recorded on any one day took place. Nearly £700,000,000 changed hands on Government account. Of this total the vast sum of £370,000,000 consisted of interest and repayments on the converted 5 per cent. and the 4½ per cent. War Loan, and the repayment of Treasury bonds. Interest and repayments on the 5 per cent. War Loan alone absorbed £215,000,000. Five per cent.

R

each year for fifteen years, and then the whole of your capital back into the bargain!

Well may we re-echo the words of Engels: "I have never seen a class so deeply demoralised, so incurably debased by selfishness, so corroded within, so incapable of progress, as the English bourgeoisie." And the attitude of this rotten ruling class towards the class by whose exploitation it exists may be summed up in this way; while the workers appear to be more or less quiescent, confuse, divide, distract and demoralise them by the whole elaborate technique of charity, "welfare" schemes and the infinite varieties of propaganda that the bourgeoisie monopolise; when the workers begin to take action, bring the enormous engine of the State to bear against them in a limitless and savage campaign of truly Tsarist repression. These two policies are complementary, not mutually exclusive. They are used alternatively, or in combination, as occasion demands.

The outstanding current example of the policy of charity is the "social service" drive to keep the unemployed safe for capitalism. The vile hypocrisy of this whole policy cannot be better described than in the scorching passage in which Engels apostrophised the philanthropic charitymongers of his day:

> Philanthropic institutions forsooth! As though you rendered the proletarians a service in first sucking out their very life-blood and then practising your self-complacent, Pharisaic philanthropy upon them, placing yourselves before the world as mighty benefactors of humanity when you give back to the plundered victims the hundredth part of what belongs to them. Charity which degrades him who gives more than him who takes; charity which treads the downtrodden still deeper in the dust, which demands that the degraded, the pariah cast out by society, shall first surrender the last that remains to him, his very claim to manhood, shall first beg for mercy before your mercy deigns to press, in the shape of an alms, the brand of degradation upon his brow. [3]

The housing question is another very pertinent example of the real meaning of capitalism's insolent charity and philanthropy. A section of the bourgeoisie are much agitated over housing. They have developed local housing associations and Public Utility Housing Societies at a considerable pace during the past decade. Constructively their efforts are absolutely infinitesimal. But the spirit that moves them is significant. They fear, and rightly, that bad housing conditions are a forcing-ground for revolutionary ideas and revolutionary movements. Sir Austen Chamberlain, in an unusually candid outburst of the paternal demagogy, asked the House of Commons on December 15th last year: "Why should anybody who lives in the conditions which I see there vote for me, or the causes for which I stand and which I commend to them? If I lived in such conditions. . . . I should feel that the circumstances to which I was condemned were intolerable, that there was something rotten in a State which had permitted them to exist so long and which permitted them to continue, and I might go on to—well, I do not know what I might go on to. . . . You cannot see those conditions and not feel your blood boil." The aristocratic Kensington Housing Association, in an appeal for funds, put the same point when it said that "bad housing is at the root of many of our present day troubles. Bad housing makes bad citizens." In other words, improve housing so that the capitalist system may be assured of its future.

It is not such considerations alone that move the slummers of to-day. "The solid tangible value of property investment in a world of passing dividends" (as a prominent Tory M.P. recently said) means that slumming, in its up-to-date Public Utility Society form, is most definitely good business. These societies pay a small, but fixed and certain, dividend and loan interest. An "appeal to investors" issued by Mr. E. G. Fairholme, the treasurer of the Fulham Housing Improvement Society Limited lets the "charity" cat out of the bag with naïve candour. This gentleman was at pains to stress that he was not appealing on "sentimental grounds"; he remarked that the society since its formation had regularly paid a 4 per cent. dividend and added:

> It has, therefore, clearly demonstrated that though its primary object is to do work which may justly be regarded as a charity, this object can be carried out on sound business lines, so that those who have already invested money have obtained a good financial return and possess the safe security of freehold properties in land and houses. The present trade depression and resultant decrease in Stock Exchange security values has created a position when those who, in better times, would have subscribed generously, without hoping for any financial return, must now decrease their charitable contributions and seek instead investments with a safe and certain financial return. It is to these people that this opportunity should appeal, and business men and women will recognise the fact that an investment concerned with London housing cannot depreciate or be adversely affected by any changing conditions of trade. [4]

Be charitable, and get a "safe and certain financial return"; that is a slogan really calculated to evoke a response from the English bourgeois!

What of the schemes of "industrial welfare" and their accompanying paraphernalia of fake works councils, sports clubs, "educational" societies and so forth? The aim of all these is transparent. Factory or shop sports clubs mean that those workers "who had a chance to play games came back to work with added energy, whereas the others were 'as dead as doornails' "; sport, in fact, is very useful in helping to increase the intensity of labour, in enabling more surplus-value to be extracted from the workers. A House of Commons Committee said straight out that employers who undertook welfare work did so because they realised that "*a healthy, intelligent and contented worker is a valuable asset.*"* Another authority says that welfare work aims at 'the promotion of loyalty [to the capitalist undertaking, of course] and a corporate spirit."[5]

Similarly with sport the bourgeoisie cynically avow that its purpose is to turn the attention of the masses from the class struggle and from harbouring revolutionary thoughts. Lord Askwith, giving evidence before the Royal Commission on Lotteries and Betting on behalf of the National Greyhound Racing Society, justified greyhound racing by stating that it "had provided a means of interest or distraction *as an antidote to discontentment of mind and social unrest.*"* That that antidote is of no mean order is indicated by the fact that attendances at "the dogs" are larger than those at any other sport, with the single exception of football.[6]

When the law and the constitution happen not to suit the needs and interests of the ruling class they are promptly flung on one side. It was in connection with the American debt payment that Major Astor's *Observer* wrote on December 4th, 1932: "Not again shall we comply with a legality that blindly holds every human interest in despite." That is the line of the bourgeoisie in conflict with its greatest imperialist rival. But let the working class adopt the same attitude to capitalist society, whose whole system of legality most devilishly "holds every human interest in despite"; then every cog and ratchet of a ruthless repressive machine will be instantly set in motion against the criminals who dare to defy law and order. The capitalist State in England to-day is a police-State on the most approved continental model. The classic land of bourgeois democracy, while retaining the "democratic" trappings and traditions as an essential camouflage, has developed during the epoch of imperialism, and particularly during the war and the post-war period, into a country as much under the heel of the police as Tsarist Russia was under the heel of the gendarmerie.

I have no space to enter in detail on this important theme; but a brief notice of the outstanding features of the situation is

* My italics.

necessary. The "state of siege" is commonly regarded as a very foreign device. But it exists in its fullest form in the Emergency Powers Act which, as the general strike showed, grants all power to the police (and the military). The hard-won rights of trade unionism and strike activity were abrogated by the "Blacklegs' Charter," the Trade Disputes and Trade Unions Act of 1927; in last year's Lancashire weavers' strike workers were arrested and charged under this Act because, standing peaceably at the side of the road (as the police admitted) they had shouted at some blacklegs.

The police themselves have undergone a process of militarisation. The high command of the police is predominantly in the hands of former officers of superior rank in the fighting forces. Lord Trenchard, appointed by the Labour Government, succeeds Lord Byng in the key post of Metropolitan Police Commissioner. A sensational new departure is made by the training of selected policemen in pistol shooting. Auxiliary forces are widely enrolled. A crack corps of mounted special constabulary is formed of ex-cavalry officers and similar gentry, who are providing their own horses. Business men, clerks and shop assistants—the latter under various inducements and forms of moral compulsion from their employers—flock into the ranks of the "specials," to be received with universal popular contempt when they were called out in London to relieve the regular police during the Hunger March demonstrations.*

Other supposed traditional rights have been violently suppressed. Even the pretence of free speech and free assembly is now openly abandoned. It was Lord Trenchard who arbitrarily banned all meetings of the unemployed at the Labour Exchanges in London; and it was for reasons like this, no doubt, that Captain Balfour, a former military colleague of Trenchard, told the House of Commons how "very happy" he was when Trenchard was appointed Commissioner, because of the "disturbed time, when none of us quite knew who were our friends and who were our enemies." Incomplete figures show that from the formation of the "National" Government up to last December over one hundred baton charges on mass demonstrations have taken place. Over 1,300 working men and women have been arrested for alleged

* The view of the Labour Party on the enrolment of special constables needs recording. It was expressed in the House of Commons on May 2nd, 1932, by Dr. Salter. His objection to the employment of specials under normal circumstances was merely that they were "amateurs." He was careful to add that "they may be all right under orders in squad formation at times of grave public emergency or disturbance. *No one has a word to say against their employment under such conditions*" (my italics).

offences in connection with their political activities, and 421 of these have been sentenced to a total of 923 months' imprisonment.[7] Sentences of a ferocity without modern precedent—two years' hard labour or three years' penal servitude—have been handed down in "incitement to mutiny" cases.

Descriptions of baton charges by observers who cannot be accused of bias against the police read, with a change here and there in local colour, like a twenty- or thirty-year old account of the smashing up of a demonstration of Russian workers by Cossacks. This is a report from the *Bristol Evening Post* of June 10th, 1932:

> The demonstrators assembled at night on the Welsh Back, and, following a meeting, singing the "Red Flag" and "International," moved in procession, banners flying, up Bridge Street into Castle Street. They were escorted by three or four policemen, but there was no hint of trouble till the crowd was half way down Castle Street. Just what precipitated the trouble is not clear, but suddenly there emerged from side-streets and shop doorways a strong body of police reinforcements with batons drawn. They set about clearing the streets. Men fell right and left under their charge, and women who had got mixed up in the crowd were knocked down by the demonstrators in the wild rush to escape. The cries of men and the terrified shrieking of women added to the tumult. Then came a troop of mounted police charging through Castle Street from the Old Market Street end, scattering the last of the demonstrators. In a few minutes the streets were clear, save for the men who lay with cracked heads, groaning on the pavements and in shop doorways, where they had staggered for refuge.

Following the Hunger March demonstration in Hyde Park, there was widespread public indignation over the furious police charges made there. Many letters of protest from outraged eyewitnesses appeared in the correspondence columns of the Liberal Press. For example, in the *New Statesman and Nation* of November 5th, 1932, Mr. James L. Grant, of Storrington, described how:

> Suddenly, for no apparent reason, the mounted police, accompanied by foot police, began to charge the crowd right and left . . . both unemployed and innocent spectators and passers-by. . . . The next performance of these riders was to charge into the peaceful groups standing around the meetings. People were forced to run for their lives in order to escape being trampled upon by the police horses or beaten by staves. There was no kind of disorder at any of these meetings, and no reason at all for the police to charge into them in the wanton way they did.

Even such elementary working-class action as the resisting of an eviction or distraint has now become a major crime. It was for committing this crime at Mardy that Arthur Horner and thirty-three other workers were indicted for "unlawful assembly" at the Glamorgan assizes in February last year. The case was outstanding for its revelation of naked and unashamed class justice. Mr. Justice Branson, in his summing up, had declared that "in these courts, we have nothing to do with politics." Then came the police report on those convicted. It was an incredible farrago. Arthur Horner was described as responsible for the collapse of the coal industry in the Rhondda (!), and it was suggested that "he is being well paid by Russia for his efforts to destroy the peace of this country." The others were similarly labelled: "a menace to law and order," "holds extreme views," "flouts the police," "sly, and would support any movement against the law." The *Manchester Guardian*, in an editorial comment on February 26th, 1932, said: "It would be absurd to suggest that the judge could be influenced by unsupported and crudely prejudiced tittle-tattle of this sort. The fact remains that it was seriously brought forward by the police with the object of assisting him to a judgment." The further fact remains that twenty-nine of the accused were found guilty, that Arthur Horner received a sentence of fifteen months' hard labour, and four others nine months' hard labour.

The Mardy scandal is cited as a leading example of police domination of the courts in a remarkable book entitled *English Justice*, written by a necessarily anonymous Conservative solicitor. This experienced lawyer seeks to arouse the governing class to an understanding of the "grave peril to the State" involved in the realisation by the workers that "the theory of the perfection of English justice is humbug." He points out that it is essential to avoid miscarriages of justice "from a purely selfish point of view," since workers who are victims of injustice "have the persistence that a grievance nearly always gives, and lack of confidence in the administration of justice provides them with fertile ground for revolutionary agitation."[8]

The courts of summary jurisdiction, this authority observes, sentence eight times as many people as all other courts put together. Yet, owing to the costly and complicated procedure, the number of appeals from these courts is negligible, though injustice continually occurs. Police courts habitually presume guilt. With the majority of benches it has become a principle to "support the police," and the issue of a prosecution by the police amounts virtually to conviction; magistrates "appear to act almost literally under the orders of the police." The Poor Prisoners' Defence Act is a dead letter.[9]

There is one law for the rich and another for the poor; the old saw was never more damnably true than it is to-day. "In the vital matter of housing, as in the case of matrimonial relations, a court which would not be tolerated by the rich is considered good enough for the poor." The myth that imprisonment for debt no longer exists in England dies hard. But in 1929 there were 12,860 persons imprisoned for debt and 11,579 in default of payment of fines. On maintenance orders, for example, "many men are ordered to pay amounts which are impossible even when they are in full work." Impoverished workers, saddled with arrears of rates, are ordered to pay sums which are utterly beyond their means;* "neighbours and relatives help to pay, and children go short of food and clothes, and even then 2,002 go to gaol." But the rich men who swindle on their income tax know how to manage things. Two thousand working people are imprisoned for rates arrears, but only eighty-four people for income tax default; "in April 1932 a High Court Judge expressed his astonishment that the Inland Revenue authorities should be willing to accept a composition of 10s. in the £ on a sum of about £70,000 owing by a man usually in receipt of a large income."[10]

One other instance of the class differentiation in English justice may be quoted from the London evening newspapers of January 3rd, 1933. Adelaide Mary Hill, a wealthy woman, living in a West End hotel, was fined £10 and £10 costs for shoplifting in a West End store; she had stolen a bottle of a rare perfume worth £5 15s. At the same court, on the same day, Rosey Russell, of Camberwell, was sentenced to six months' hard labour for being concerned in stealing three children's frocks from the same store; there were previous convictions against her.

The law relating to contempt of court precludes appropriate comment on one peculiarly repellent feature of the administration of "justice" by the English bourgeoisie. That is the general habit adopted by judges of all grades, of making workers in the dock the targets of every kind of insolence and contemptible displays of so-called wit, of sneers and unctuous homilies. In one case "a magistrate sneered at a man that he was an old soldier, 'and a pretty poor soldier I expect you were too.' The man replied: 'Most likely I was, but I got the Military Medal and the D.C.M., and was promoted sergeant, so I expect I was as good a b—— soldier as you ever were.' There was no apology

---

* "A man who had served in the navy in three wars and was, as he stated on oath, getting 25s. a week on which to keep a wife and one wholly and one partly dependent child, owed £9 6s. for rates. The partly dependent child earned 10s. a week. He was committed for 28 days, suspended for 28 days to give him time to find the money!" (*English Justice*, p. 203).

from the magistrate." The East Ham coroner held an inquest on the eleven-weeks old child of an unemployed man. The child had died from bronchial pneumonia, due to under-nourishment. There were three children in the family. The father drew 29s. 3d. in unemployment benefit, and the rent was 15s. No wonder the child died! And what was the reaction of the coroner to this heartrending tragedy of working-class life, to this slaughter of an innocent by the capitalist social order? He delivered himself of an outburst in which he told the unhappy father that it was a "scandal" for unemployed parents to have three children, and added that they should "restrain themselves."[11] When the Birmingham Recorder sentenced a revolutionary worker to fifteen months' hard labour, he said: "You are one of those under-witted people who, having access to sources of knowledge, are quite incapable of putting it to proper use. . . . As a speaker you are dangerous, for you are encouraging people who are more stupid than yourself." That is the authentic attitude, compound of hatred, fear and rage, of the bourgeoisie towards the workers.

When six workers were charged at Castleford, Yorkshire, last August, the court, contrary to all precedent, refused to adjourn the case, though the accused had been seriously injured in a police charge the previous night, when they were arrested, and were not in a fit state to plead. According to the report in the *Pontefract and Castleford Express* of August 12th, 1932, the chairman said to one of the accused, "they were not going to adjourn the case, but go on with it, so he had better pull himself together."

One final touch is needed to complete the picture of the perfect police-State as it exists in Britain to-day; that touch is provided by the existence, in its most finished form, of a secret political police, the Special Branch of the Criminal Investigation Department. This body, it is significant to recall, dates its birth from the eighties, when it was formed under the title of the Special Irish Branch to fight against the Irish national revolutionary movement. Its scope was later widened, until now it has long been a complete *Okhrana*, a genuine Tsarist secret police, using all the methods of Tsardom. The watching and besetting of meetings, of the offices of working-class organisations, of the houses of members of such organisations, the regular opening of correspondence and the tapping of telephone conversations, the introduction of spies and agents provocateurs into the ranks of revolutionary bodies, attempts by cajolery or threats to extract information from the dependants of militants—all this is but a part of the regular, and quite extra-legal, technique of this body. Anyone who has been a victim of the activities of this organisation will know how searches are invariably carried out without a search warrant, how personal belongings are illegally searched, how, in brief, the Special Branch contemptuously spurns all the supposed constitutional "rights."* The most remarkable example of this was the absolutely unprecedented and illegal use by the Special Branch of the true Tsarist device of preliminary censorship of the Press in the case of the notorious raid on the *Daily Worker* at the end of September 1931.

Of the use of spies there are enough examples. Last year one Croxall, a police spy who had been introduced into the Communist Party organisation in Birmingham, was exposed; upon which Croxall's masters arrested the district organiser of the party on a charge of "incitement to maim" the innocent lamb, and a sentence of six weeks' hard labour was handed down. The latest use of the provocateur was in the case of George Allison and William Shepherd, sentenced to three years' penal servitude and twenty months' hard labour on charges of incitement to mutiny. These two revolutionary workers had been put in touch with two sailors shortly after Invergordon. The two sailors, by name Bousfield and Bateman, were admitted in court to be provocateurs, acting under the orders of unnamed officers, who naturally did not appear.

Much was made by the defence of the admission that these two sailors were provocateurs. As a result this point was dealt with by Mr. Justice Acton in his summing-up. He said: "It is, of course, always for a jury, even in a case where the witness for the prosecution is in the strictest sense a provocateur, to come to the conclusion whether they believe him or not; and, if they believe him, there is no reason why they should not convict." Thus the blessing of the law is given to the most loathsome of all tools of an oppressing class. And exactly a century ago, in 1833, a Select Committee of the House of Commons declared that the use of agents provocateurs "was most abhorrent to the feeling of the people and most alien to the spirit of the Constitution." The significance of the radical difference in attitude revealed here requires no underlining.

To conclude, the Tom Mann case has shown the lengths to which the British governing class will go. With this as a precedent it is possible to arrest and imprison any revolutionary, any opponent of the regime, without having to make any charge against them. In other words, the bourgeoisie is operating that

* An authoritative exposure of the gross illegality of searches of this kind was made by Professor H. J. Laski in the *Manchester Guardian*, January 7th, 1933.

supreme dictatorial discovery of its French class-brethren, the system of "preventive arrest." To try and cloak this piece of blatant dictatorship, which is being extended to militant workers in other parts of the country, appeal is made to a six hundred year old statute of Edward III* (directed against impoverished mercenary soldiers returned from the Hundred Years' War) and the Seditious Meetings Act of 1817. This latter Act was passed by the oligarchic House of Commons of that day in a wild panic, exclusively on the "evidence" supplied in Secret Committee by police spies and agents provocateurs. It was the first of that body of violently repressive legislation of the revolutionary period following the Napoleonic Wars, which culminated in the notorious Six Acts of 1819, held up to scorn even in the bourgeois histories. The bourgeoisie in its prime could afford to be contemptuous of the methods, unrestrained in their violence and savagery, of its fevered infancy. In its dotage it is compelled to return to those very methods, in a frenzied effort to avert the execution of the doom that history has long since pronounced upon it.

* It is interesting to note that the operative clause of this statute embodies a forgery. The clause reads: "To take of all them that be [not] of good fame sufficient surety." The bracketed "not" does not appear in the original Norman-French, but was inserted when the statutes were first printed, in the eighteenth century. See the *Manchester Guardian*, January 7th, 1933, and Colonel J. C. Wedgwood's letter to the same journal, January 11th, 1933.

CHAPTER X

THE FIGHT FOR SOCIALISM

THIS book has framed the indictment of a whole social order. It has shown what the development of capitalism to its final phase means in the lives of working men, women and children. It has depicted the first stage of the governing class's frenzied efforts to find a capitalist solution to the problems of society. Those efforts have meant a further increase in large-scale unemployment. Their aim is to keep capitalism going by a series of blood-transfusions from its victims, the workers.

Things have reached such a pass that in February 1933 the Deptford Public Health Committee report, in words that apply to the whole country: "It is impossible to escape the conclusion that there are to-day many homes in which, after the rent is paid, and allowance made for heating and clothing, there is an insufficient sum available for food of the character and quantity necessary to maintain physiological health." Families have 4s. per head per week for food, when a normal medical estimate of the sum needed to purchase the necessary food, "quite plain," is 11s. 6d. per head.

Capitalism, in its moments of candour, does not even hold out any prospect of amelioration. MacDonald has spoken of the two millions of unemployed, the "superfluous scrap," that would remain even with "prosperity." Chamberlain has forecast a period of ten years with mass unemployment, pointing to the displacement of labour by new technique. Here, in the open, is that supreme contradiction of capitalist society—between the development of the productive forces and the existing property relationships, between social production and private appropriation of the product—before which its rulers stand helpless.

"People can't go on like this!" The words are on the lips of millions. Already we can see the first stirrings of the process that must lead to the maturing of the pre-requisites for a revolutionary crisis; namely, that the governing class can no longer continue governing in the old way, that the governed class is no longer willing to go on being governed in the old way, and that a first-class national crisis develops. The elements of instability and uncertainty in the capitalist camp, replacing the unquestioning unity of eighteen months ago, testify to the first point. The increasingly sharp and bitter clash between the classes, the stormy wave of struggles during 1932, which have been described in the course of this book, testify to the second.

What this upsurge, this forward movement, of the working class now needs is conscious direction by its revolutionary vanguard, its leading revolutionary party, towards the aim of the struggle for power and the establishment of a Socialist Britain. Socialism without revolution, without the smashing of capitalist dictatorship and the inauguration of the workers' dictatorship, is a contradiction in terms. That is why the Communists, for whom alone this is a fundamental principle, are the only leaders of the fight for Socialism.

The leaders of the Labour Party and the Trades Union Congress General Council do not fight for Socialism. They find it essential to employ "Socialist" phraseology. But their policy, as they have now clearly defined it, is based on the fallacy that it is possible to achieve an "organised capitalism"; they propose the organisation of industry under a series of Public Corporations, with the participation of the Trade Union bureaucracy, in a fashion redolent of the Corporations of Fascist Italy; they aim at assisting monopoly capitalism to develop to its logical end in State Capitalism. This standpoint is typified by Mr. Herbert Morrison, author of the London Transport Bill, who refers in the *Labour Magazine* for January 1933 to the times when "Conservative Governments nationalised the telephones, municipalised London water, set up the British Broadcasting Corporation and passed the Electricity Supply Act, 1926," and describes all these examples of State capitalism as "measures of socialisation."

This line has nothing whatever to do with Socialism: for it does nothing to solve the fundamental contradiction of capitalism, since it leaves the property relationships of capitalism untouched. It even strengthens those relationships and develops them to a further stage of parasitism, by completing the divorce of the capitalist from industry, and turning the capitalist class without exception into bondholders and rentiers.

The issue of capitalism or Socialism in Britain is not one that has been put suddenly on the agenda by the crisis. For the present general crisis of capitalism, so far as concerns Britain alone among all countries of the world, has been super-imposed upon a decade of stagnation and decline, when the unemployment figure never fell below one million. That decline has been the result of the final undermining of the British imperialist system, of that colonial monopoly, of that position of creditor

State instead of industrial State, which has for forty years been the linch-pin of the social system of this country.

During the past generation the British governing class have only been able to maintain power because of the fabulous parasitic tribute they have drawn from abroad as the usurers of the world and as colonial oppressors on the largest scale. That is now a situation of the past. The tribute, which was the one thing that enabled them to bridge the growing gap between imports and exports and still leave a net credit balance, has dwindled until the balance, from 1931 onwards, has for the first time in history gone to the debit side. The reasons for this are to be found in the nature of imperialism which led inevitably to the world war of 1914-18. The war ended with Britain ceding its position as the world's creditor to the United States, the power that had become its greatest imperialist rival after the crushing of Germany. And tribute could only be drawn from the colonial countries, from India, from Africa, through a regime of oppression and increasing impoverishment which caused the stormy rise of national-revolutionary movements and the falling off of the tribute. This impoverishment has reached its greatest height with the world agrarian crisis.

It is precisely because of the pivotal part that the colonial monopoly, with all its implications, has played; precisely because British imperialism, desperate, is using every effort to regain position by the most violent and repressive policy (the Meerut verdicts; the Kenya land robbery; oppression in South Africa, etc.); it is precisely because of all this that it is impossible to conceive of the overthrow of capitalism in Britain, impossible to look ahead to the new, utterly changed Britain of the workers' dictatorship, without placing the struggle for colonial liberation in the forefront. Here is the compelling reason for the forging of a common front between the working class of Britain and the workers and peasants of the colonies in their everyday struggles.

The revolutionary process for Britain is therefore a two-sided one. It must of necessity embrace both revolution in Britain itself, and the liberation of the colonies.

Only revolution, the seizure of power by the working class in Britain, can sweep away the whole parasitic burden of monopoly finance-capital, the exactions of the idle rentiers and the loan-mongering bankers, the vast tribute absorbed by the bondholders, which now strangle the forces of production. Only so can the natural resources of the country be developed, can derelict industry be reconstructed, can agriculture be born again. Only so can production be so vastly expanded that, with the general shortening of hours, unemployment, the greatest curse of capitalism, be abolished for ever—as it has been abolished in the Soviet Union. Only so can living conditions be transformed from top to bottom, and the standard of life of the mass of the people be rapidly and progressively raised, thus creating a vast home outlet for the increased industrial output.

Only the liberation of the colonies, the overthrow of the imperialist yoke by the countless millions of the exploited peasantry led by the working class of the towns, can free the "last reserves of mankind" from the barbarous backwardness and brutish poverty in which imperialism has held them. Once given the possibility of free development, the demands of these vast masses of the human race will be insatiable. They will need alike consumption goods (especially textile products) and machinery of all kinds to carry through the industrialisation of their countries, which imperialism has barred. At the same time they will be able to supply the need of Socialist Britain for agricultural products and raw materials that home resources cannot satisfy.

The task of elaborating a more detailed programme and plan for the Britain of the workers' dictatorship must be left to a later occasion. But from what has already been said some idea can be gained of the immense possibilities that will lie immediately to our hand. It is not difficult to realise, for instance, what the wiping out of the burden of loan capital, coupled with the soaring demand from the free colonial countries, would mean to the Lancashire cotton industry. We can see what the reconstruction of home industry, and assistance in industrialising the former colonies, with the consequent development of international exchange of products, would bring to the heavy industries, to engineering, shipbuilding, iron and steel.

All this great work of building a new social order, which would also involve such tasks as the complete electrification of the country, would bring an enormously increased demand for coal. The mining industry, freed from the grip of the monopolists, liberated from the feudal exaction of royalties, carrying through a rapid and complete survey of its resources (a job at which capitalism has only tinkered), with a six-hour day for all underground workers, would steadily expand. In South Wales to-day coal capitalism is abandoning its richest seams, because they are no longer profitable. Those seams would more than come into their own again with the development of coal treatment and by-product industries, or with the use of the smokeless steam coal of the Rhondda directly as a smokeless fuel—thus helping to abolish the atmospheric pollution in the big cities which is one of capital-ism's most objectionable accompaniments.

Consider, again, the colossal work waiting to be done in the sphere of housing and town-planning. This means not only the eradication of the slums, but the complete re-building of every working-class quarter in town and country, the complete chang-ing of the face of Britain. It means the reduction of rent to not more than one-tenth of income. All this can be achieved only by severing the tentacles of landlordism, by ending the extortions of loan capital in the financing of building, by providing accomo-dation for whole populations during the re-housing process through the confiscation of the mansions of the rich.

In 1885 Engels asked what would be the condition of the working class "when the present dreary stagnation shall not only become intensified, but this, its intensified condition, shall become the permanent and normal state of English trade?" That is the position to-day. "What will it be," he went on to demand, "when the increase of yearly production is brought to a complete stop?" Production has not only reached this stage, but is now decreasing year by year. And, Engels concluded in preg-nant words, "Here is the vulnerable place, the heel of Achilles, for capitalist production. Its very basis is the necessity of constant expansion, and this constant expansion nowbecomes impossible. It ends in a deadlock. Every year England is brought nearer face to face with the question either the country must go to pieces, or capitalist production must. Which is it to be?"

REFERENCES

[NOTE.—*For the sake of convenience in the extensive reference which will be found below to the Annual Reports of County and Borough Medical Officers of Health and School Medical Officers, these reports are throughout cited as* Health Reports *and* S.M.O. Reports *respectively, though in fact they are very variously titled.*]

CHAPTER I

[1] Facts from the Coal Commission (1919), ch. II.
[2] An Industrial Survey of South Wales, pp. 154–155.
[3] From local medical officers' reports quoted in the Welsh Housing and Development Year Book, 1930, pp. 132–135.
[4] *South Wales Argus*, September 1, 1932.
[5] Special Report upon the State of Nutrition of the School Children in Monmouthshire (Appendix II of Monmouthshire S.M.O. Report, 1931), p. 89.
[6] Welsh Housing, etc., Year Book, ibid.
[7] Merthyr Tydfil Health Report, 1929, p. 20.
[8] Rhondda Health Report, 1928, pp. 88–89.
[9] Abertillery Health Report, 1931, pp. 92–93.
[10] Welsh Housing, etc., Year Book, ibid.
[11] *South Wales Argus*, September 9, 1932.
[12] Ibid., September 14, 1932.
[13] Ibid., September 29, 1932.
[14] Census of England and Wales, 1931: Preliminary Report, pp. 44–46.
[15] An Industrial Survey of South Wales, pp. 20–21.
[16] Ibid., p. 18.
[17] *South Wales Argus*, September 25, 1932.
[18] An Industrial Survey, etc., p. 40.
[19] Communicated to the Labour Research Department.
[20] Annual Report, Chief Inspector of Mines, 1931, p. 62.
[21] Ibid., p. 67. Mines Inspectors' Reports: Cardiff and Forest of Dean division, 1931, pp. 21–23.
[22] Annual Report, Chief Inspector of Mines, 1931, p. 71. Cardiff division, 1931, pp. 28–29, 37–38. Swansea division, 1931, pp. 39–40.
[23] *South Wales Argus*, August 31, 1932.
[24] Mines Inspectors' Reports: Cardiff division, 1931, pp. 39–40. Swansea division, 1931, p. 37.
[25] Swansea Health Report, 1930, p. 91.
[26] Ibid., p. 93.
[27] Ibid., p. 9.
[28] *South Wales Argus*, September 28, 1932.
[29] An Industrial Survey, etc., pp. 98–99.
[30] *South Wales Argus*, ibid.

[31] *Daily Worker*, August 12, 1932.
[32] *South Wales Argus*, September 17, 1932.
[33] Ibid., November 15, 1932.
[34] Welsh Housing, etc., Year Book, 1930, p. 131; 1932, p. 30.
[35] Monmouthshire Health Report, 1931, p. 44.
[36] Glamorgan Health Report, 1931, p. 40. Newport Health Report, 1931, p. 5.
[37] *South Wales Argus*, September 13, 1932.
[38] Newport Health Report, 1931, p. 10.
[39] Ibid., pp. 7–8.
[40] Cardiff Health Report, 1930, p. 7; 1931, p. 117.
[41] Glamorgan S.M.O. Report, 1931, pp. 8, 9, 15, 17, 19, 21. Monmouthshire S.M.O. Report, 1931, p. 55.
[42] Newport S.M.O. Report, 1931, Appendix C.
[43] Newport Health Report, 1931, pp. 16–17.
[44] Monmouthshire Report upon Maternity and Child Welfare, 1931, p. 29.
[45] *South Wales Argus*, September 28, 1932.
[46] Welsh Housing, etc., Year Book, 1930, pp. 143–144.
[47] *South Wales Argus*, September 17, 1932.
[48] *Daily Herald*, October 31, 1932.
[49] *South Wales Argus*, September 29, 1932.
[50] Ibid., November 1, 1932.

CHAPTER II

[1] Engels: Condition of the Working-Class in England in 1844, pp. 41–42.
[2] Memorandum on the Cotton Industry (prepared by the Labour Research Department for the United Textile Factory Workers' Association, 1928), p. 66.
[3] *Evening Chronicle* (Manchester), November 29, 1932.
[4] Memorandum on the Cotton Industry, pp. 28–29.
[5] *Economist*, August 6, 1932, p. 262.
[6] *Ministry of Labour Gazette*, November 1932, p. 418.
[7] Accrington Health Report, 1931, p. 44.
[8] An Industrial Survey of Lancashire, pp. 106–108, 109.
[9] Quoted in Lancashire Health Report, 1931, p. 11.
[10] *Cotton Factory Times*, December 2, 1932. *Sunday Times*, December 25, 1932.
[11] 64th Annual Trades Union Congress, Newcastle, 1932: Report, p. 245.
[12] An Industrial Survey of Lancashire, pp. 17, 18, 145.
[13] Oldham Health Report, 1930, p. 9.
[14] *Northern Daily Telegraph* (Blackburn), December 1, 1932.
[15] Ibid.
[16] Oldham Health Report, 1930, p. 54; 1931, p. 35.
[17] Stockport Health Report, 1930, pp. 10, 50, 54.
[18] Bolton Health Report, 1930, pp. 47–51. Housing Conditions in East Ward: a report by the Bolton Housing Survey Committee, 1931, *passim*.

[19] Health Reports: Burnley, 1931, pp. 69, 168–174; Blackburn, 1931, pp. 35, 38; Bury, 1930, pp. 35–36; Lancashire, 1931, pp. 101–102; Rochdale, 1930, p. 36.

[20] Health Reports: Lancashire, 1931, pp. 76, 82; Rochdale, 1930, p. 19; Accrington, 1931, p. 36.

[21] Nelson Health Report, 1931, p. 51. Burnley Health Report, 1931, p. 66.

[22] St. Helens Health Report, 1930, pp. 101–107. Wigan Health Report, 1931, pp. 35, 37.

[23] *Manchester Guardian*, July 28, 1932. Manchester Health Report, 1931, pp. 219–220.

[24] Bootle Health Report, 1930, p. 64.

[25] University of Liverpool: the Social Survey of Merseyside: No. 1, Housing Conditions in Liverpool, pp. 7, 15–16.

[26] Liverpool Health Report, 1930, pp. 244–260; and 1931, pp. 268–274.

[27] Lancashire Health Report, 1931, p. 11.

[28] Health Reports: Liverpool, 1931, pp. xiv–xv; Bootle, 1930, p. 33; Bolton, 1930, p. 87; Preston, 1931, p. 8.

[29] Health Reports: St. Helens, 1931, p. 39; Salford, 1931, p. 62; Stockport, 1931, p. 73.

[30] *The Phoenix*, a Journal of Housing, No. 1 (January 1932), p. 5. Wigan Health Report, 1931, p. 68. Salford Health Report, 1931, p. 63.

[31] Manchester Health Report, 1930, p. 250; 1931, p. 58. Preston Health Report, 1930, p. 57; 1931, p. 49.

[32] Quoted in Lancashire Health Report, 1931, p. 105.

[33] Preston Health Report, 1930, pp. 60–61, 70; 1931, p. 51. Blackburn Health Report, 1931, pp. 61–62.

[34] Lancashire Health Report, 1931, p. 166.

[35] *Manchester Guardian*, August 4, 1932.

[36] Blackburn Health Report, 1931, pp. 11, 151. Preston Health Report, 1930, p. 114.

[37] Nelson Health Report, 1931, p. 77.

[38] Ibid., p. 7.

[39] Quoted in Lancashire Health Report, 1931, p. 34. Wigan Health Report, 1931, pp. 85–86.

[40] Preston Health Report, 1931, pp. 81, 85. Warrington Health Report, 1931, pp. 19–20.

[41] The Health of the School Child (Annual Report of the Chief Medical Officer of the Board of Education) 1931, pp. 107–108.

[42] Ibid., p. 124. School Medical Officers' Reports: Blackburn, 1931, p. 19; St. Helens, 1931, p. 13; Rochdale, 1930, p. 76; Nelson, 1931, p. 113.

[43] Burnley S.M.O. Report, 1931, p. 58.

[44] Preston Health Report, 1930, p. 105. Liverpool Health Report, 1930, p. 99.

[45] Blackburn S.M.O. Report, 1931, pp. 17–18. St. Helens S.M.O. Report, 1931, p. 14.

[46] Accrington S.M.O. Report, 1931, p. 10. Burnley S.M.O. Report, 1931, pp. 51–52.

[47] S.M.O. Reports: Burnley, 1931, pp. 10–13; Rochdale, 1930, p. 70; St. Helens, 1931, pp. 8–9; Nelson, 1931, p. 104.

[48] An Industrial Survey of Lancashire, p. 177.

[49] Ibid., pp. 159–160.

[50] Ibid., pp. 24, 27, 226, 229–231.
[51] Engels, op. cit., preface, pp. xiv, xvii–xviii.
[52] S. and B. Webb: Industrial Democracy, Vol. I, p. 196.
[53] S. and B. Webb: History of Trade Unionism (1920 ed.), p. 480.
[54] *Northern Daily Telegraph*, December 1, 1932.

CHAPTER III

[1] *Glasgow Herald* Trade Review, 1932, pp. 67 ff.
[2] Ibid., pp. 39, 63.
[3] J. T. W. Newbold and others: Steel, pp. 19–21, 29, 38–43.
[4] *Glasgow Herald* Trade Review, p. 63.
[5] An Industrial Survey of the South-West of Scotland, p. 39.
[6] Ibid., p. 161.
[7] Sir Archibald Hurd in *Observer*, January 22, 1933. An Industrial Survey of the South-West of Scotland, pp. 188, 191.
[8] *Glasgow Herald* Trade Review, p. 45.
[9] Ministry of Labour Gazette, January 1933, pp. 4, 8.
[10] *Daily Herald*, October 1, 1932.
[11] *Glasgow Herald* Trade Review, p. 29.
[12] An Industrial Survey of the South-West of Scotland, p. 179.
[13] An Industrial Survey of the North-East Coast Area, p. 46.
[14] An Industrial Survey of the South-West of Scotland, pp. 151–156, 210.
[15] *Daily Herald*, October 21, 1932.
[16] Glasgow Health Report, 1931, pp. 198–199.
[17] Engels, op. cit., pp. 37–38.
[18] Annual Report of Scottish Board of Health, 1926, pp. 49–50.
[19] Glasgow Health Report, 1931, p. 216.
[20] Ibid., pp. 219–220.
[21] Glasgow Education Health Service Report, 1931, p. 58.
[22] Ibid., p. 18.
[23] Constructed from Glasgow Health Report, 1931, pp. 24, 104, 107, 247, 254.
[24] An Industrial Survey of the South-West of Scotland, pp. 42–50. *Glasgow Herald* Trade Review, p. 63.

CHAPTER IV

[1] Engels, op. cit., pp. 23–24.
[2] Census of England and Wales, 1931: Preliminary Report, pp. xiii, xviii.
[3] An Industrial Survey of Lancashire, p. 376.
[4] *Observer*, February 5, 1933.
[5] New Survey of London Life and Labour, Vol. III, p. 57.
[6] Quoted in *Daily Herald*, November 11, 1932.
[7] Paddington Health Report, 1930, p. 33.
[8] Health Reports: Bermondsey, 1931, p. 50; St. Pancras, 1931, p. 62; Westminster, 1930, pp. 101–103.

⁹ Health Reports: Lambeth, 1930, pp. 104–105; Housing in Shoreditch [reprint from Shoreditch Health Report, 1930], p. 9; Greenwich, 1930, pp. 61–66; Battersea, 1931, p. 104.

¹⁰ Irene Barclay and E. E. Perry: Report on Housing Conditions in the Isle of Dogs (1930), pp. 13–14.

¹¹ Daily Telegraph, September 8 and 9, 1932.

¹² Finsbury Health Report, 1930, p. 108.

¹³ Health Reports: Bermondsey, 1931, p. 58; St. Pancras, 1931, p. 62. Stepney Housing Trust leaflet (December 1931).

¹⁴ Bermondsey Health Report, 1931, p. 57. New Survey, Vol. III, pp. 225, 233–235, 251–252.

¹⁵ New Survey, Vol. III, pp. 232, 249.

¹⁶ New Survey, Vol. I, pp. 153–154. Health Reports: Hammersmith, 1930, p. 57; Deptford, 1931, pp. 9, 44. The Times, January 30, 1933.

¹⁷ Evening Standard, January 27, 1933. Westminster Housing Association Annual Report (1930–31), p. 12. Islington Health Report, 1931, p. 64.

¹⁸ Housing: Still Westminster's Most Urgent Problem (1931), p. 4. Health Reports: St. Marylebone, 1930, p. 22 and 1931, p. 21; Wandsworth, 1931, p. 82. The Times, March 22, 1932.

¹⁹ Poplar Health Report, 1931, p. 57.

²⁰ Shoreditch Housing Association appeal (November 1931), pp. 3–5. Housing in Shoreditch, pp. 7, 8, 14.

²¹ Engels, op. cit., pp. 28–29.

²² Bethnal Green Health Report, 1931, pp. 100, 105; Stepney Housing Trust leaflet (December 1931).

²³ The Listener, February 1, 1933, pp. 156–157.

²⁴ Barclay and Perry, op. cit., pp. 11, 15.

²⁵ Hackney Health Report, 1930, pp. 122, 126–127.

²⁶ Ibid., pp. 131–147.

²⁷ Islington Health Report, 1931, p. 61.

²⁸ Health Reports: Greenwich, 1930, p. 61; Bermondsey, 1931, pp. 55, 62, 50.

²⁹ Bishop of Southwark: In the Heart of South London, p. 8.

³⁰ Health Reports: Hampstead, 1930, pp. 15, 125–126; St. Marylebone, 1930, pp. 66–67, and 1931, p. 62.

³¹ St. Marylebone Housing Messenger, January 1932, p. 19.

³² Housing: Still Westminster's Most Urgent Problem, p. 3.

³³ Kensington Health Report, 1930, pp. 50–51. The Listener, February 1, 1933, p. 158. Kensington Housing Association Report (1930–31).

³⁴ Holborn Health Report, 1930, pp. 34–44.

³⁵ Fourth Annual Report of Bishop of London's Housing Committee (1932), p. 2. House of Commons Official Report, May 4, 1931, cols. 49, 50, 68. Eighty-third Report from the Ecclesiastical Commissioners, p. 25.

³⁶ Daily Telegraph, January 28, 1933.

³⁷ Shoreditch Housing Association appeal, p. 6.

³⁸ Health Reports: Stepney, 1931, p. 12; Southwark, 1931, pp. 3, 10, 50; Hackney, 1930, pp. 123, 126.

³⁹ Chelsea Health Report, 1931, pp. 58–64.

⁴⁰ West Ham Health Report, 1931, p. 59. New Survey, Vol. I, pp. 154–158.

⁴¹ Health Reports: Paddington, 1930, p. 34; Wandsworth, 1931, pp. 71–72.

[42] Fifth Annual Report of the St. Marylebone Housing Association (1930–31). *St. Marylebone Housing Messenger*, January 1932, p. 16. Kensington Housing Trust Annual Report (1931). Lambeth Housing Movement leaflet. St. Pancras House Improvement Society Annual Report (1930–31).

[43] Shoreditch Housing Association appeal, p. 8.

[44] *The Phoenix*, a Journal of Housing, No. 2, pp. 21–24.

[45] *Daily Worker*, January 30, 1933.

[46] Engels, op. cit., pp. 30–31.

[47] *St. Marylebone Housing Messenger*, January 1932, p. 10.

[48] New Survey, Vol. III, pp. 170–171.

[49] *Daily Herald*, November 18, 1932. *The Listener*, February 1, 1933, p. 157.

[50] New Survey, Vol. III, pp. 26, 146, 12, 130–131, 81, 124.

[51] Health Reports: Deptford, 1931, p. 10; Bethnal Green, 1930, p. 11, and 1931, p. 50.

[52] New Survey, Vol. III, ch. x, *passim*, p. 283. Annual Report of the London County Council for 1930, Vol. II, p. 22.

[53] New Survey, Vol. III, ch. xii. *New Statesman and Nation*, September 3, 1932.

[54] New Survey, Vol. III, ch. xiii, *passim*; Vol. II, p. 217. *The Times*, January 26, 1933. *World's Press News*, February 2, 1933.

[55] *Daily Herald*, February 3, 1933.

[56] Bethnal Green Health Report, 1931, pp. 9, 35.

[57] Health Reports: Stepney, 1931, p. 100; London County Council, 1931 (Vol. III, Part I, of Annual Report of the Council), pp. 12–15.

[58] Health Reports: Battersea, 1931, pp. 118–119; West Ham, 1930, p. 118; Holborn, 1931, p. 65; Greenwich, 1931, p. 73; Finsbury, 1930, pp. 76–79, 89.

[59] Health Reports: Paddington, 1931, pp. 58–60; Kensington, 1930, Appendix I; Holborn, 1931, p. 53. The Health of the School Child, 1931, pp. 65–67.

[60] Health Reports: Bethnal Green, 1930, pp. 39, 31; Battersea, 1931, pp. 38–39; Finsbury, 1930, p. 57.

[61] Health Reports: Holborn, 1930, pp. 111–112; Lambeth, 1930, p. 46; Bethnal Green, 1930, p. 66.

[62] Health Reports: Kensington, 1930, pp. 93–101; Paddington, 1930, p. 3; West Ham, 1930, p. 157, and 1931, p. 171.

[63] Bethnal Green Health Report, 1931, pp. 42, 51, 63–64.

[64] *Housing Happenings*, No. 12 (Spring 1932), pp. 22–23. Bethnal Green Health Report, 1931, p. 99.

[65] Stepney Health Report, 1931, pp. 68, 77–81.

[66] Greenwich Health Report, 1930, p. 67.

[67] Health Reports: Bethnal Green, 1931, pp. 96, 87; Poplar, 1931, pp. 77–78, 79; St. Marylebone, 1931, p. 27.

[68] New Survey, Vol. II, Introduction, *passim*, pp. 472–475.

[69] Ibid., Vol. III, p. 64.

[70] Ibid., Vol. II, ch. iii, *passim*, pp. 19, 125, 205, 21.

[71] Ibid., Vol. II, p. 139. *Daily Worker*, July 7, 1932.

[72] New Survey, Vol. II, p. 20. Letter addressed by the General Secretary of the United Clothing Workers' Trade Union to Messrs. Lockwood and Bradleys, February 19, 1932.

[73] P. Glading: How Bedaux Works, pp. 7–8. *Daily Worker*, March 2, 1932.

[74] New Survey, Vol. II, pp. 39, 392, 393–399, 408, 403–404, 424, 419–420. *Daily Worker*, July 8, 1932.

[75] Memorandum by W. N. Hayter, secretary of the London District Council, National Union of Railwaymen, to the Labour Research Department (August 1932).

[76] *Daily Worker*, November 23, 1932. St. Pancras Health Report, 1931, p. 62.

[77] *Daily Worker*, August 12, 1932. *Daily Herald*, September 14 and 24, 1932. *The Times*, September 12, 1932.

[78] New Survey, Vol. II, ch. II, *passim*.

[79] Ibid., Vol. II, pp. 232, 377, 275–277. *The Listener*, February 1, 1933, p. 157.

[80] New Survey, Vol. I, pp. 272–277, 280–282. Finsbury Health Report, 1930, p. 45.

[81] New Survey, Vol. I, pp. 301–303.

[82] Ibid., Vol. I, ch. IX, *passim*. *Observer*, September 4, 1932.

[83] New Survey, Vol. III, p. 180.

CHAPTER V

[1] *South Wales Argus*, October 31, 1932.

[2] *New Stateesman and Nation*, November 26, 1932.

[3] Press reports, quoted in Brockway: Hungry England, ch. VI.

[4] *Daily Herald*, September 29, 1932.

[5] The references to the Final Report of the Royal Commission on Unemployment Insurance, contained in this and the succeeding paragraphs, are as follows (in order): Pp. 106–107, 376–377, 354, 225, 239–240, 243, 258–261, 352, ch. V, *passim*, pp. 150 ff., 133–134, 287 ff., 147, 425, Appendix to Minutes of Evidence part VIII para. 4, pp. 149, 282, 340–343.

[6] Report of the Committee on Local Expenditure (England and Wales) [the Ray Report], pp. 115 ff., 111–112.

[7] Ray Report, pp. 100, 108–109, 96, 87, 33, 36–37, 42–43. Private Members of the House of Commons Economy Committee Report, p. 17.

[8] *Daily Telegraph*, January 5, 1933.

[9] House of Commons *Official Report*, May 11, 1932, cols. 1943, 1978.

[10] Wigan Health Report, 1931, p. 22. Monmouthshire Health Report, 1931, p. 27.

[11] Ray Report, pp. 97, 94, 87, 91, 93.

[12] Norwich S.M.O. Report, 1931, p. 44. Shipley S.M.O. Report, 1931, p. 10. Ray Report, p. 44.

[13] Ray Report, p. 29.

[14] Report of National Federation of Class Teachers' conference, in *Observer*, September 25, 1932.

[15] *Daily Telegraph*, January 9, 1933 (letter from E. C. Bond).

[16] Report of an Inquiry into the Social Factor in Secondary Education, quoted in *The Times*, September 22, 1932.

[17] *Daily Worker*, April 19, 1932.

[18] *Manchester Guardian*, October 18, 1932. Home Office: Criminal Statistics (England and Wales), 1929 and 1930 volumes, Introductory Note, *passim*.

CHAPTER VI

[1] Engels, op. cit., pp. 145–146.
[2] A. F. Brockway: Hungry England, pp. 43, 58, 68.
[3] An Industrial Survey of South Wales, p. 18.
[4] An Industrial Survey of the South-West of Scotland, p. 186.
[5] New Survey of London Life and Labour, Vol. II, pp. 21, 477.
[6] An Industrial Survey of the North-East Coast, p. 45:
[7] An Industrial Survey of South Wales, p. 22.
[8] In a private memorandum written for the Labour Research Department.
[9] An Industrial Survey of the North-East Coast, p. 415.
[10] Report from the Select Committee on Shop Assistants, Vol. I (1931), p. 35.
[11] Ibid., p. 39.
[12] Ibid., p. 4.
[13] Ibid., p. 44.
[14] Ibid., p. 99.
[15] Ibid., p. 62.
[16] Ministry of Labour: Report on the Catering Trade (1929), pp. xxix–xxxi.
[17] Report from the Select Committee, etc., pp. 40–41.
[18] Ibid., p. 43.
[19] Ministry of Labour Gazette, February 1932, p. 47.
[20] Bishop of Southwark: In the Heart of South London, p. 27.
[21] Report from the Select Committee, etc., p. 63.
[22] Daily Telegraph, September 24, 1932.
[23] The Times, September 20, 1932.

CHAPTER VII

[1] Land Worker, April 1932, p. 9. Rowntree: How the Labourer Lives, p. 28.
[2] and [3] Land Worker, November 1930, p. 16.
[4] Land Worker, August 1932, p. 10.
[5] Ibid., July, 1932, p. 11.
[6] Quoted in Land Worker, February 1932, p. 4.
[7] This unpublished evidence has been kindly placed at the disposal of the Labour Research Department by the National Union of Agricultural Workers.
[8] Land Worker, September 1932, p. 9.
[9] Ibid., October 1932, p. 9; and see also, for instance, September, 1932, p. 15.
[10] New Statesman and Nation, October 8, 1932, p. 398.
[11] Land Worker, August 1932, p. 4.

CHAPTER VIII

[1] Emile Burns: The Two Classes in 1931, p. 6.
[2] F. D. Klingender: The Black-Coated Worker in London (MS.).
[3] *The Plebs*, August 1931, p. 182.
[4] Klingender, op. cit.
[5] Royal Commission on the Civil Service (1929–30): Appendix VI to Minutes of Evidence: Statement submitted by the Civil Service National Whitley Council (Staff Side), Section 1, paras., 53–63.
[6] Civil Service National Whitley Council (Staff Side): Civil Service Remuneration (leaflet date April 11, 1932).
[7] Statement made to the Postmaster-General on behalf of the Union of Post Office Workers, August 6, 1931. Royal Commission on the Civil Service (1929–30): Appendix XIV to Minutes of Evidence; Statement submitted by the Union of Post Office Workers and the Federation of Post Office Supervising Officers, paras. 73–87.
[8] An Industrial Survey of the North-East Coast, p. 413.
[9] *Islington Gazette*, September 21, 1932.

CHAPTER IX

[1] Emile Burns: The Two Classes in 1931, p. 10. Colin Clark: The National Income, 1924–1931, pp. 77–78.
[2] *Daily Telegraph*, December 31, 1932.
[3] Engels, op. cit., p. 278.
[4] *The Phoenix*, a Journal of Housing, No. 1, January 1932, p. 21.
[5] Report of the Select Committee of the House of Commons on Shop Assistants, 1931, p. 63. New Survey of London Life and Labour, Vol. II, p. 152.
[6] *Manchester Guardian*, September 16, 1932.
[7] *Daily Worker*, November 29, 1932.
[8] "Solicitor": English Justice, pp. 115, 117, x–xii, 189.
[9] Ibid., pp. 133, 47, 51, 55 ff., 248.
[10] Ibid., pp. 228, 200, 205.
[11] Ibid., p. 237. *Daily Herald*, October 11, 1932.

INDEX

This book was prepared with the co-operation
of the
LABOUR RESEARCH DEPARTMENT
60 DOUGHTY STREET, LONDON, W.C.1

An independent body, to which individuals
and working-class bodies are affiliated, it
conducts inquiries, publishes books and
pamphlets and a monthly Journal
Labour Research
(3d.)